LEARNING ITALIAN
WITH OR WITHOUT
A TEACHER

11-5-2018

There is joy in learning

Guido Farina

BY

GUIDO FARINA

LEARNING ITALIAN
WITH OR WITHOUT
A TEACHER

A COMPLETE TEXT
BY GUIDO FARINA

EDITED BY ANDREA GRAF

PICTURES SELECTED BY ELFRIEDE FARINA FROM *ENTI PROVINCIALI PER IL TURISMO GUIDES:* TOURISM OFFICE OF *PONTE MELFA, FROSINONE.*

PICTURES SET UP
BY ALEXANDER GRAF

FARINA PUBLISHING
YARMOUTH, MASSACHUSETTS

LEARNING ITALIAN
WITH OR WITHOUT A TEACHER

@ Copyright 2007
By GUIDO FARINA

Printed in the United States of America

0-9728898-3-3

Guido Farina is the author of **Montecassino / The People's Real Battle:** his autobiography, written both in Italian and in English in a floral and vivid style, as reviewed by the *Register* newspaper.

"Guido Farina has written an extraordinary and fascinating document." Says the **Post-Gazette.** "his writing is marvelous and spirited. It expresses pure integrity.

He has also written *Fire Over The Desert,* a romantic and fanciful Novel, where love flourishes and burns on the Sahara and blooms again on the North Sea.

His third novel is *Faith and Passion.* In Faith and Passion, inspired by the grandeur of those words, he evokes the power of his writing to heighten the deep feeling of the sweeping fervor of the Novel.

People who have read his books, are astonished by the command he expresses with the English Language, being his second language.

"His English flows smoothly." They say. "His English is exciting, harmonious, romantic. You are right on the scene of what you read."

His books are published both in English and in Italian. They are available through Barns and Noble. Com; and Amazon. Com on the Internet and at Book Stores.

CONTENTS

ITALIAN

Learning Italian with or without a teacher.

PREFACE

Well... If I were born in Italy, I would be speaking Italian.
And...If I were born in Austria, I would be speaking German...

I was born in a country where the mother language is English; therefore I learned how to speak English. Of course it is called the mother language because your mother and your father helped you patiently to acquire a rich vocabulary and to pronounce each word correctly.

Now, if you really wish to learn Italian, you have to start from scratch again. I will help you and guide you. If you follow my instructions and be patient, you will learn my first language and be proud of yourself.

I have learned five languages with and without teachers, as a result I will pass on to you, the learner, my experiences and my tricks to make the study of Italian pleasant, easy and successful.

Italian derives from Latin. It is a romantic Language. It has a delicious tone. It is gentle, smooth and floral. You probably know already why. It was born out of poetry. The greatest Italian poet: *Dante Alighieri,* used the Florentine Latin dialect to write his immortal *Divine Comedy.* In the 13th century the Florentine Language became the Italian Language.

Since that time, Tuscany has been the mother of the Italian language. There, it is spoken perfectly. It is delightful to hear it pronounced so beautifully.

I want you to reach the same efficiency. Why not? If you can spare at least half hour a day and you have a strong will to achieve that perfect result, no difficulty will stand in your way. You will reach perfection without much effort.

If you follow my teaching, without rushing, you will be able to learn how to understand, how to speak and how to write my beautiful Italian language.

The most difficult thing to learn in any language is how to separate one word from another. In the beginning every word seems to be tied together. It will take time until you can hear the difference. Once we have defeated such difficulty, we will have gone over the hurdle. The language is open to our ears. Of course when we study the syntax, we have to learn how to construct the sentence by joining words together.

The learner will enrich his vocabulary slowly and easily. Remember, you are at the beginning stage. You have to learn each word by memory. There is no other way. You have to retain the words you learn. Repetition does the trick; and, of course, by using many different methods.

Before I fell asleep each night, I used to stress my mind, trying to store those words I had learned that day. Another good learning process is to relate words that help you to remember; for example "more" for *morale.*

English comes from *the West Germanic* Family of Languages. However many, many words derive from the *Latin* Family of Languages. We'll expose these words and make good use of them; for instance "salute" *saluto;* "to salute" *salut*-are.

Come on: don't get nervous. We will have fun as we move along. You will be proud of yourself. There is no obstacle insurmountable.

We will proceed slowly. Within a short time you'll begin reading Italian fluently. Trust me: Italian is very easy to read. Dante made it very challenging for himself: The way you write it, is the same way you read it.

You will acquire the correct pronunciation by the accent indicated on the word. It tells you clearly where the stress of your voice must fall.

All right; then we'll begin slowly, using only a few words at a time, few rules and a lot of practice: **póco, fácile *e* béne.** *"Little, easy and well."*

FIRST LESSON

Lezione Prima

Buon giorno... *Good day.* I am so happy to have you here with me. I see joy on your face. You must be very interested. Of course it is wise to acquire wisdom and knowledge.

Well... Let's start to work. As I promised, there is nothing to it. There are only 21 letters in the alphabet: 5 vowels and 16 consonants.

To begin, you'll have to learn the sound of each letter.

Aa, Bb, Cc, Dd, Ee, Ff, Gg, Hh, Ii, Ll, Mm, Nn, Oo, Pp, Qq, Rr, Ss, Tt, Uu, Vv, Zz.

A is always pronounced like the *"a"* in *Father*.
I is always pronounced like the *" i "* in *Little*
O is pronounced like the *"o"* in *Dog*.
U is always pronounced like the *"u"* in *Pool*.
E is pronounced like the *"e "* in *Bed*

The sound of the vowels never changes. Only *O* and *E* are pronounced open or close. Not to worry: the accent will tell you. When Ó is loaded with the *acute* accent, it is pronounced *tight: short or closed;* when **Ò** is loaded with the *grave* accent, it is pronounced *large or open*.

Example: Pòco, (*little*) Ò grave. Pólizia, *(police)* Ó acute.
Example: Pècora, (sheep) È grave. Pésce, *(fish)* É acute.

When you read Italian, however, you'll find only È grave carrying the accent. It is marked to distinguish "è " *(is)*, verb, from "e " (and), conjunction.

1

Most of the consonants sound the same as in English. Few have double sound. Let's take a look.

C, sounds like K in front of **A**, **O**, and **U**. To make it sound like a **K** in front of *I* and *E*, we must add an ***H***: *chi, (Who); ché, (What)* Read *key, ké-g.*

    C, without an H in front of **I** and **E**, sounds like *ch* in English. Example: ***Chi-ck- peas,*** (English). **Ce-ci**, (Italian).

G, makes its hard guttural sound in front of **A**, **O**, and U, like in English: **Go**-lfo, *(Gulf);* **Gu**-ardia, *(Guard).* *To* let it keep the guttural sound in front of **I** and **E**, we have to compensate by adding an **H**: *Spaghe-tti,* **Ghi**-rlanda *(Garland).*

    G, without an **H** in front of **I** and **E** sounds like " *J* " in English: **Gi**-oia, *(Joy).* Pronounce every vowel separate: G-i-o-i-a.

    Avio-***ge***-tto, *(Jet-plane).*

Gl, in front of **A**, **O**, and **U**, sounds the same as in English: **Gl**oria, *(Glory).* In front of **I** and **E**, it has a difficult sound: almost like double **L** very stressed: fi-**gli**-o, *(Son)*

    Gn, is pronounced (ny) like in *Gnocchi,* in front of every vowel. You must have eaten some **gno**-cchi before. It is a delicious potato-pasta dish, enjoyed especially in Rome.

Sc, in front of **A**, **O** and **U**, sounds the same as in English: **Sca**-rso, *(Scarce);* **Sco**-zia, *(Scottland).* In front of **I** and **E**, it sounds like *"Sh"* in English. **Sci**-mmia, like if written *Shimmia (Monkey);* **Sce**-riffo, *(Sheriff).*

H, has no sound. Its role is to help out.

R, is very stressed and rolled: Rrr...oma, *(Rome).* So are the double consonants: Tutt...i, *(Everybody).* Double consonants require the full stress of your voice.

Keep smiling. I'll continue to help you out with all these sounds.

However, don't go on any further. Make sure that you learn this lesson well: especially if you are learning without a teacher. Take your time and continue to practice this lesson.

PRÀTICA: PRACTICE

I am going to list every Italian word contained in this lesson.
You are going to read them aloud over and over. Then I want you to translate them into English.

ITALIANO	ENGLISH
Buón buono	Good
Giórno	....
Pòco	....
Pólizia	....
Pècora	....
Pésce	....
È	....
É	....
Chi	....
Ché	....
Céci	....
Gólfo	....
Gùardia	....
Spaghétti	....
Ghirlanda	....
Giòia	....
Aviógetto	....
Glòria	....
Fìglio	....
Gnòcchi	....
Scarso	....
Scòzia	....
Scimmìa	....

ITALIANO	ENGLISH
Scériffo	....
Róma	....
Rómano	....
Tùtti	....

Now I would like you to pick ten words that you like best and memorize them.

SECOND LESSON

Lezione Seconda

Buon giorno... *Good morning.* Oggi è una bella giornata. *To-day is a beautiful day.*

If you have some difficulty reading these words, do not get discouraged. Listen carefully to how I pronounce them.

In this lesson we are going to deal with Grammar a bit. There is no way out. We cannot do without grammar's help, when studying a romantic language. We must get a taste of it. It is like eating spaghetti while visiting Naples. You must relish the flavor.

What is grammar? It is the basic principles of any area of knowledge. It is the system of rules involved in a language.

Oggi è – *una bella giornata.–* As you can see, each word rimes with the next word. You have already learned that Italian was first written in a poetic style. Therefore the whole language is a poem. It is the language of songs and of music.

Keep smiling... You'll see. It wont be so difficult. You will enjoy learning this language as we go along.

We'll begin with the parts of speech.

In Italian there are nine parts of speech. Five are variable: they change character. Four are invariable. They are always written the same.

The five variable parts are: **articolo:** *articles;* **nome:** *nouns;* **aggettivo:** *adjectives;* **pronome:** *pronouns; and* **verbo:** *verb.*

The four invariable parts are: **Avverbio:** *adverbs;* **preposizione:** *prepositions;* **congiunzione:** *conjunctions; and* **esclamazione:** *exclamation.*

5

The Italian language has only two genders: *masculine* and *feminine*. Most of the words end with a **vowel**. Therefore it is easy to recognize to which gender and which number they belong.

Let's begin with **The Article**. In English there is only one article: *"The"*, which is placed before the noun, regardless of gender and number.

In Italian we have to think seriously of the exact article to place before a noun. The Italian language has six definite articles: ***Il, Lo. La, I, Gli, Le.***

Il and **lo** are masculine singular. **I** and **Gli** are masculine plural. **La** is feminine singular. **Le** is feminine plural.

The Italian language also has three indefinite articles: **Un, Uno, Una:** *A and An* in English.

Un and **Uno** are placed before masculine nouns.

Una is placed before feminine nouns.

The indefinite article does not have a plural. Of course you already know that. Just a reminder...

It sounds a little confusing. However if you, the student, learn this by heart, the road ahead will be quite smooth.

I would like to give you some examples of the usage of these different articles; however I think we have had enough for to-day. Let's wait until the next lesson.

PRATICA *(Practice)*

You are going to read these words aloud over and over; then translate them into English. You must <u>memorize</u> them.

ITALIANO	ENGLISH
Il, lo, la, i, gli, le.	The........................
Un, uno, una.	....

6

ITALIANO	ENGLISH
Óggi	....
È	....
Bèlla	....
Giórnata	....
Articólo	....
Nóme	....
Aggéttivo	....
Prònòme	....
Vèrbo	....
Avvèrbio	....
Prépósizióne	....
Cóngiunzióne	....
Ésclamazióne	....
Pratica	....

Do not forget: practice these words. It will help you. However, do not waste any sleep over them... Everything will come together, in time.

THIRD LESSON

Terza Lezione

Buon Giorno... Come stai oggi? *How are you to-day?*

Before we go any further, I want to hear you repeat aloud each of the articles you have learned. I know you have memorized them So, come on... Say them aloud.

A bit of advice: when you read Italian, read it aloud. It doesn't matter where you are. Don't be afraid of whoever is around you. Just do it.

Now that you are comfortable with the articles, you, the student, are going to learn about the ***Noun or Substantive.***

What is a *Noun*? A noun is that part of speech which serves to name people, animals, things, places, ideas.

We distinguish them as ***common nouns***: ragazzo *(boy)*, barca *(boat)*, pittore *(painter)*, virtú *(virtue)*. They are written with lower case letter.

And we distinguish them as ***proper nouns***: Giorgio *(George)*, America *(America)*, Po *(Po)*. Po is the longest river in Italy. Proper nouns are written with a capital letter.

Each noun belongs to a ***masculine*** or a ***feminine*** gender. The masculine gender usually ends with the vowel *"O"*: ragazzo, libro *(book)*, pino *(pine)*.

The feminine gender usually ends with the vowel *"A"*: donna *(woman)*, casa *(house)*.

Usually each noun has two gender: ***singular*** *(singolare)* and ***plural*** *(plurale)*. A masculine noun ending with **"o"** in the singular, changes to an

8

"i" in the plural: libro, *libri*.

A feminine noun ending with – **a** – in the singular, changes a into – **e** – in the plural: casa, *case*.

Most of the nouns ending in "o" or "a" follow the above rules. However there are few nouns which end with a different vowel: padre (*father*), madre (*mother*).

Do not panic. We'll deal with them easily, as we go along.

Now let's put the definite article before the nouns we have learned. **Il, lo, la, i, gli, le** are called *articoli determinativi* in Italian.

Are you ready? Here we go. **Il libro, i libri.**

La casa, le case.

We are also going to learn how to use the indefinite article. **Un, uno, una** are called *articoli indeterminativi* in Italian: *un libro*, *una casa*.

We will learn about *lo* and *uno* in a separate lesson, because they require a little more attention.

As you can see, the article rimes with the noun. Together they sound smooth. It is like marveling at a picture painted by a famous artist. Each color matches perfectly.

You might ask, "Why do we have to learn so many rules?"
This reminds me of a conversation I had with a boat owner. He was telling me that during a crossing from Orleans (Cape Cod) to Nantucket Island, he ran into trouble. When he left, it was a nice day; however half way across, the ocean became rough. A thick fog obscured his vision. "Thank God I learned all the safety rules well, when I took a navigation course," he said, "otherwise I would have gotten lost."

You do <u>not</u> want to get lost... You have to learn the rules well. You need a good foundation to build upon.

Let's review all the words we have used in this lesson. Remember: you'll have to learn them by memory.

I'll write them in Italian, using the proper definite article before

9

each one. You translate them into English. I'll write these words only in the singular. If you wish to change some of them into the plural, it will be good exercise. Please, keep reading them aloud.

As you may realize, some of the nouns do not end with *"o"* *masculine* (maschile): or *"a" feminine* (femminile).

Don't worry. We'll tackle them later.

I am going to place the accent on top of the vowel over which you have to pose your pronunciation.

PRATICA

ITÀLIANO	ENGLISH
Il nòme	....
Il nòme cómune	....
Il ragàzzo	....
La bàrca	....
Il pittóre	....
La virtú	....
Il nòme pròprio	....
Giòrgio	....
Amèrica	....
Il Pò	....
Il libro	....
Il pino	....
La dònna	....
La càsa	....
Il pàdre	....
La màdre	....
L'artìcolo determìnativo	....
L'artìcolo indetermìnativo	....
Il maschìle	....
Il femmìnile	....

10

There are words which are similar in both language. If you have a little extra time, you may write them down as part of your exercise.

Don't forget to read and practice all these words aloud. "Practice makes wise": *póco é bène*.

FOURTH LESSON

Quarta Lezione

Buon giorno... Oggi non è una bella giornata. *To-day is not a beautiful day.* Piove. *It is raining.*

Let's take advantage of this bad weather by utilizing our time at home toward enriching the learning of the Italian language.

As I have told you, a second language is learned by repetition.
Our brain is a huge recipient in which to store intelligence; however it can be a lazy object in absorbing and retaining it. If you do not exercise daily, it refuses to accept and store anything.

Before you learn about the third part of speech, I would like to return to the second part of speech: the name: *il nome.*

Many names referring to people and some referring to a few animals form the feminine by changing the *last vowel* of the masculine to an *"A"* : **Giuli-o** *Julius,* **Giuli-a** *Julia;* **il maéstr-o** *male teacher;* **la maéstr-a** *female teacher;* **il ragazz-o** *boy;* **la ragazz-a** *girl;* **il signór-e** *gentleman;* **la signór-a** *lady;* **il cavàll-o** *horse;* **la cavàll-a** *mare.*

Some masculine names form the feminine by removing the last vowel and adding – *essa–* . Most of these names indicate profession; **il professóre** professor; **la professór-essa** *female professor;* **il dottóre** *doctor;* **la dottór-essa** *female doctor;* **il póeta** *poet;* **la póet-essa** *poetess;* **il princípe** *prince;* **la princíp-essa** *princess.*

Now that you are into it, let's attack one more case. A few masculine names ending in **tore,** form the feminine by adding –**trice**–: **at-tore** actor; **at-trice** *actress.*

12

There are other irregular ways to distinguish feminine nouns from the masculine. We'll save those for later.

A huge help is a good Italian–English dictionary. One that provides the gender and the accent.

As I mentioned earlier, in this lesson you are going to learn the function of the *Adjective (aggettivo)*.

What is an adjective? It is a class of words used to modify, to qualify or to specify a noun. The adjective harmonizes the word it serves and brings full color to it. It describes the word perfectly.

In English the adjective is placed before the noun. It does not change its gender or its number. It is invariable. In Italian it may be put before or after the noun, depending on the harmony of the sound. Article, adjective and noun have to rime perfectly.

In this lesson we'll learn about the **qualifying adjective** (*aggettivo qualificativo*).

Most of the qualifying adjectives ending in **"O"** masculine singular, change to **"A"** in the feminine singular, to **"I"** in the masculine plural and to **"E"** in the feminine plural: alt-**o**; alt-**a**; alt-**i**; alt-**e** (*tall*) *Il ragazzo **alto**; i ragazzi **alti**; la ragazza **alta**; le ragazze **alte***. You can feel the harmony of sound...

Adjectives ending in "E" in the singular, change "E" to "I" in the plural for both genders. Grand-**e** (*big*) singular; grand-**i** plural. Il ragazzo **grand-e;** i ragazzi **grand-i;** la ragazza **grand-e;** le ragazze **grand-i**.

Some of the adjectives form the gender and the number irregularly. We'll save them for another lesson.

Do not forget to memorize these basic rules. You will be happy you did... later.

Read and repeat these words aloud. Don't worry if you make a mistake. What you learn by making mistakes, will stay with you forever. I know this well... especially when I tried to pretend to know the German language. I was showing off all right!... I was with the well spoken people

13

at the time. They could not stop laughing. Well... I learned a valuable lesson. I made sure I knew the meaning of the words well, before I put another sentence together.

PRATICA

This time I am going to let you work a little harder. I will write the above words in English; and you will write them in Italian, putting the right article before the nouns that you have learned.

INGLESE	ITALIANO
Not	....
It rains	....
Julius	....
Julia	....
The teacher	....
The lady-teacher	....
The girl	....
The gentleman	....
The lady	....
The horse	....
The mare	....
The professor	....
The lady-professor	....
The doctor	....
The lady-doctor	....
The poet	....
The poetess	....
The prince	....
The princess	....
The actor	....
The actress	....
The qualifying adjective	....
Tall (four ways)	....

Big ....

The big boys ....

The big girls ....

These words are for exercise purposes. Read them aloud. Pick ten words that most interest you and memorize them.

FIFTH LESSON

Lezione Quinta

Buona sera signore. È già buio. *Good evening gentleman. It is already dark.*

As you have learned in lesson four, we have dealt with some qualifying adjectives that end in –e– in the singular, which changes into –i– in the plural. You have also learned about some nouns which end in –e–. Those nouns ending in e in the singular, change the final vowel into –i– in the plural.

Now... how are we going to recognize if they are masculine or feminine? Well... if there is an article before those nouns, the problem is solved: **il padre** *the father;* **la madre** *the mother.* If there is no article before them, you will have to get help from the dictionary (*dizionario*)

However, if you pay considerate attention to what I am going to say here, you can enrich your vocabulary immensely. All the nouns ending in **tion** in English: end in **zione** in Italian. They are feminine: la **na-zìone** *the nation;* la **rivolu-zìone** *the revolution;* la **sta-zìone** *the station;* la **se-zìone** *the section.* In the plural the final E changes to I: le **na-zìoni:** le **rivolu-zìoni...**

These nouns ending in **sion** in English, end in **sione** in Italian. They are feminine. In the plural the final *"E"* changes to *"I"*, same as above: la **divi-sìone** *the division; la* **disillu-sìone** *the disillution. la* **televi-sìone** *the television:* le **divi-sìoni;** le **televi-sìoni.**

It is easy to recognize that such nouns have the same meaning in both languages.

Later on we'll come back to these nouns and use them as part of

16

speech. So, please, <u>learn them well</u>.

I don't want to confuse you, however while we are learning about the nouns, I would like to go over another class of them.

Feminine nouns ending in **"ca"** or **"ga"** in order to keep the guttural sound, they change to **"che"** and **"ghe"** in the plural: **amì-ca amì-che:** *girl friends; la pà-ga, le pàghe: pay.*

Masculine nouns ending in **"co"** or **"go"** change to **"chi"** and **"ghi"** in the plural for the same reason: **il par-co, i par-chi;** *the parks;* **il la-go, i la-ghi:** *the lakes.*

There are a few more classes of nouns with different rules on how to form the plural; however we'll learn about them later. Nothing to worry about: you'll see. We'll keep it fun as we move along. It would be great if one could learn a language in only a short time! Do not forget that you begin studying your first language from the time you were born; and you'll keep studying it all the way through College... in order to reach excellence.

While studying the previous lesson, we learned about the **aggettivo qualificativo.** You learned that a qualifying adjective ending in **"O"** changes the **"O"** into **"I"** and the **"A"** into **"E"** in order to rime with the nouns it beautifies. If it ends in **" E"** in the singular, it changes only into **"I"** in the plural.

In this lesson we are going to learn about another class of adjectives: **the possessive adjective:** *aggettivo possessivo.*

In Italian possessive adjectives follow the same rules as the qualifying adjective. They are:

Mio, mia, miei, mie: *my, mine.* **Il mio, la mia, i miei, le mie.**

Tuo, tua, tuoi, tue: *your, yours. (thy, thine: used mostly in poetry in English.)*

Suo, sua, suoi, sue: *His, her, hers.*

Nostro, nostra, nostri, nostre: *our, ours.*

Vostro, vostra, vostri, vostre: *your, yours.*

Loro is invariable: **il loro, la loro, i loro, le loro:** *their, theirs.*

17

Now let's find out how we may indicate the possession. In English there are two way to form the possession: the *Saxon way: adding an apostrophy followed by an "s"* to the possessor; and *the normal way.*

Mary's *son: il figlio* **di** *Maria.* **The son of Mary:** *il figlio* **di** *Maria.* **My mother's horse and my brother's house:** *Il cavallo di mia madre e la casa di mio fratello.*

As you may have noticed, in Italian the possession is always expressed with the preposition **di** *in the singular.*

You can see that *mia madre and mio fratello* have no *article* before the *possessive adjective.*

Therefore the rule is that nouns belonging to members of the family **do not take the article** in the **singular:** *mio padre, yes; il mio padre, absolutely not; mio fratello, yes; il mio fratello, wrong.*

In the **plural**, however, those nouns must be written with the article before them: *i miei fratelli.*

These rules must be learned well.

People who speak rich Italian, recognize quickly who has studied Italian attentively.

Another simple rule you have to keep in mind is that in Italian the possessive adjective takes the gender and number of the noun it accompanies: *In English it refers to the owner of something.*

Mary is beautiful; her father is tall. **Her** refers to **Mary** (feminine). **Maria è bella; suo padre è alto.** *Suo* refers to **padre** (masculine): the noun it accompanies.

Remember: article, adjective and noun have to rime. If you can master this, you will have no difficulty in writing and speaking well.

I am going to write down all the nouns and adjectives in English contained in this lesson. Those which are omitted are included in the previous lessons. You are going to write them in Italian the correct way, including the article and the adjective.

I was going to write down the correct translation; however I think I will do the student a disservice.

18

It is better to listen to the recording, so you can correct your home work yourself.

PRATICA

ENGLISH	ITALIANO
The evening	....
Already	....
Dark	....
The dictionary	....
The nation	....
The revolution	....
The station	....
The section	....
The division	....
The disillusion	....
The television	....
The girl friend	....
The pay	....
The park	....
The lake	....
The possessive adjective	....
My, mine	....
Thy, thine, your, yours	....
His, her, hers	....
Our, ours	....
Your, yours	....
Their, theirs	....
The brother	....
Beautiful	....

Please, read these words aloud repeatedly. Take ten words that interests you and learn them by heart. Do the exercises. This is the best way to learn. Take your time. *Poco* e *bene*.

SIXTH LESSON

Lezione Sesta

Buon pomeriggio signora. Che ora è? *Good afternoon mam. What time is it?*

We begin this lesson with a special reminder. You might have asked yourself, "Why have we not dealt with the definite masculine articles –lo– –l'– singular; and –gli– plural yet ?"

If you remember, this article needs special attention. **Lo** is used before **masculine singular** nouns beginning with a **vowel, with "S" impure: S followed by another consonant**; and masculine nouns beginning with **"Z"**. If a masculine singular noun begins with a vowel **lo** loses the **"o"** and takes the **apostrophe: l'amico** *the friend.* If we would read **lo amico,** it would not sound as good as *l'amico.* **L'organo** *the organ.*

In the plural **gli** does **not** lose the vowel: **gli amici** *the friends;* **gli organi** *the organs.*

Masculine nouns beginning with **"S"** followed by another consonant also take **lo** in the singular and **gli** in the plural:example **lo sc-ienziato** *the scientist;* **lo st-udente** *the student;* plural **gli scienziati; gli studenti.**

The article **lo** and **gli** are also used before masculine nouns beginning with **"Z": lo zaino** *knapsack,* **gli zaini; lo zoologo** *the zoologist,* **gli zoologhi; lo zero** *the zero,* **gli zeri.**

The student must learn these rules very well. You will be tested often by people who are listening to you, when you speak.

The indefinite article **"uno"** follows the same rules which make **lo** interesting. However *uno loses the vowel, but does not take the apostrophe;* it never takes the apostrophe before a masculine noun that begins with a vowel: **l'amico yes, un'amico <u>wrong</u>**. It has to be written: **un amico**, *no apostrophe;* **un angelo** *an angel*, **un uomo** *a man*.

Before **"S"** followed by another consonant we use *uno:* **uno studente.** The same applies before a masculine noun beginning with **"Z"**: **uno zero.**

The student must be very careful when presented with *l'articolo determinativo* **lo;** and *l'articolo indeterminativo* **uno.**

Sometime I have to stress my memory to make sure that I too apply these rules correctly.

While we are working with these articles, let's complete the last rule. You already know that the article **la** is used before feminine singular nouns. However, if a feminine singular noun begins with a vowel, **la loses the vowel** (vocale) and takes the **apostrophe** (apostrofo) in its place: **la casa** *the house;* **la scùola** *the school. yes;* **l'àrte,** *yes: the art;* **la arte** *<u>wrong</u>.* It does not sound good at all.

In the plural, **le** does not lose the final **e.** It does **not** take the apostrophe: **le arti,** *yes;* **l'arti,** *<u>very wrong</u>;* **l'educàzione, le educazioni,** *<u>yes</u>: education.*

In the previous lesson the student learned about the *possessive adjective:* **l'aggettivo possessivo.**

In this lesson the student will learn how to use the *demonstrative adjective:* **l'aggettivo dimostrativo.**

What is a demonstrative adjective? It specifies or singles out the person or thing it refers to.

In Italian they follow the same rule applied to the qualifying adjective.

They are: **questo, quest', questa, quest':** *this;* **questi, queste:** *these;* **quel, quello, quell', quella, quell':** *that;* **quelli, quei, quegli, quelle:** *those.*

They follow the same rule as those required by the articles in the singular. Before nouns beginning with a vowel they lose the final vowel and take the apostrophe.

21

Questo ragazzo è alto. *This boy is tall.*
Questa ragazza è bella. *This girl is beautiful.*
Questi ragazzi sono alti. *These boys are tall.*
Queste ragazze sono belle. *These girls are beautiful.*
Quest'arte è bella. *This art is beautiful.*
Quest'uomo è alto. *This man is tall.*
Quelle arti sono belle. *Those arts pieces are beautiful.*
Quel signore è **il** mio amico. *That gentleman is my friend.*
Quei signori sono **i** miei amici. *Those gentlemen* are my friends.
Quello stùdente è intellìgente. *That student is intelligent.*
Quegli stùdenti sono intellìgenti. *Those students are intelligent.*
Quell'amico è buono. *That friend is good.*
Quegli amici sono buoni. *Those friends are good.*
Quella casa è grande. *That house is big.*
Quelle case sono grandi. *Those houses are big.*
Quell'amica è alta. *That girl friend is tall.*
Quelle amiche sono alte. *Those girl friends are tall.*

There is still a lot more to learn about the adjectives. For now try to learn as much as you can from this lesson. If the student learns the functions applied to the articles, you will have less to memorize.

I would like you to read all the words you have in front of you aloud. Get your ears ready to recognize each word.

I will list all the new words contained in this lesson. I'll write them in English; and you'll write them in Italian.

PRATICA

ENGLISH	ITALIANO
The organ	....
The scientist	....
The student	....
The knapsack	....

ENGLISH	ITALIANO
The zoologist	....
The zero	....
The angel	....
The man	....
The apostrophe	....
The vowel	....
The school	....
The art	....
The education	....
The demonstrative adjective	....
This	....
These	....
That	....
Those	....
Intelligent	....
Good	....

You have already learned many words and many rules. After few more lessons, you'll begin to excel in the Italian language.

If you can spare some free time, it would be a good idea to compare the above sentences and write down some of your own.

Remember: Italian is the easiest language to read and to write. If you have mastered the proper sound of the vowels and of the consonants, in addition to a few rules, you wont have any problem reading and writing it. Don't be afraid to try.

SEVENTH LESSON

Lezione Settima

Buona notte, signore. È tardi. Arrivederci. *Good night, Sir. It is late. Good bye.*

There are other classes of adjective which the student has to learn; however we'll go back to them later on.

I know that by now you have a clear sense of confidence to achieve success; therefore it is time to begin building sentences.

We are almost there. To build a sentence we need at least a noun, or a pronoun and a verb.

In this lesson the student will learn all about the pronoun.

What is a pronoun? A pro-noun takes the place of the noun it refers to. The prefix **pro** means: *in favor.*

There are many classes of pronouns; some of which follow the same rules the student has already memorize, learning about the adjectives.

They are: **Personal pronouns**
Possessive pronouns
Demonstrative pronouns
Relative and interrogative pronouns
Indefinite pronouns
Numeral pronouns

It is a long list. You may get a little discouraged. Not at all... Everything will easily fall into place as we go along.

They say that – *All things come to him who waits* –

Let's begin with **Personal pronouns.**

Singular

Soggètto *subject*		**Oggètto** *object*	
1st **Ió**	*I*	**Mi, mé**	*Me*
2nd **Tu**	*You (thou)*	**Ti**, **té**	*You (thee)*
3rd **Égli, lui, Lèi**	*He*	**Ló, lui, gli, si, sé**	*Him*
3rd **Élla, éssa, lèi**	*She*	**La, lé, si, sé**	*Her*
3rd **Éssó**	*It*	**Ló, la, si, sé**	*It*

Plurale

1st **Nói**	*We*	**Nói, ci, cé**	*Us*
2nd **Vói**	*You*	**Vói, vi, vé**	*You*
3rd **Éssi, éssé**	*They*	**Lóró, li, lé**	*Them*

Personal pronouns are a little more intriguing than their English counterpart. Do not panic: they will fall into place nicely.

There are so many vowels involved; therefore remember the right vowels' pronunciation in Italian. They never change. Do not get confused with the English pronunciation. I know it is very easy to do.

I am going to write down only a few examples; so you'll get the idea.

Io sono con mio padre. Egli è con me.
I am with my father.   *He is with me.*
Mia madre ama me e mia sorella.
My mother loves me and my sister.
Lei ci ama. *She loves us.*
Io ti prègo. *I beg you. (I beg thee).* Not used in conversation.
Io vi prego. *I beg you.*
Io la prego. *I beg her.*
Io lo prego. *I beg him.*

These few examples will help you to use these pronouns correctly. I am certain that it wont take you too much time to master them.

Possessive Pronouns

As I mentioned earlier, the possessive pronouns are the same as the possessive adjectives. They take the same gender and number of the nouns they are referred to. They are:

Mine or my own	*Il mio, la mia, i miei, le mie*
Thine or thine own	*Il tuo, la tua, i tuoi, le tue*
His or his own	*Il suo, la sua, i suoi, le sue*
Hers or her own	*Il suo, la sua, i suoi, le sue*
Its own	*Il tuo, la tua, i tuoi, le tue*
Ours or our own	*Il nostro, la nostra, i nostri, i nostre*
Yours or your own	*Il vostro, la vostra, i vostri. le vostre*
Yours or your own	*Il tuo, la tua, i tuoi, le tue*
Theirs or their own	*Il loro, la loro, i loro, le loro*
Own	*Proprio*

I wrote down **Yours** twice because it can be translated with **il tuo** or with **il vostro**. *Thine* is not used much in English; yet **il tuo** is used almost always in Italian, in the singular form.

Example: *This is mine.*   **Questo è mio.**
Yours is not good. **Il tuo non è buono.**
Yours is not good. **Il vostro non è buono.**

Now you may realize why it is very important to learn these basic rules. As we go along you'll find out how much a little bit of hard work pays off.

I know that we have already done too much in this lesson. However, it will help the student to refer to some of the rules within easy reach.

26

Therefore I would like to add a couple of more classes of pronouns.

Demonstrative Pronouns

They do not differ from the *Demonstrative adjectives.*
They are:

This	*Quéstó, quésta*	**That**	*Quélló, quélla*
These	*Quésti, quésté*	**Those**	*Quélli, quégli, quéllé*

Including a couple of examples, it is easy to distinguish which one is an adjective; and which one is a pronoun.

This division is easy;   *but that is difficult.*
Questa divisione è facìle;   **ma quella è difficile.**
This man is big;   *but that is tall.*
Quest'uomo è grande;   **ma quello è alto.**

As you can see, the first *this* is adjective, because it demonstrates the noun. *That* is a pronoun, because it takes the place of the noun *division.*

If you compare the formation of the above sentences, you can see clearly that there is no difference between English and Italian.

There are other classes of pronouns which are very important. I would like to go over them, so that they will be within reach.

Relative and Interrogative pronouns

Who	*Chi*
Whom	*Ché, cui, il qualé, la qualé, i quali, le quali*
Which	*Che, cui, il quale, la quale, i quali, le quali*
That	*Che, cui, il quale, la quale, i quali, le quali*
What	*Che. ciò che, quello che.* **Che is invariable.**
Whose	*All the above preceded by preposition*

Example: *Who are you?*
             ***Chi* sei tu? *Chi* siete voi?...**
             The lady whom I see often.
             La signora *che* io vedo spesso.
             Which one is it? This or that?
             ***Qual'è?* Questa o quella?**
             It is that one.
             È quella.
             Who is that gentleman?
             Chi è quel signore?
             Which one?
             Quale?
             What time is it?
             ***Che* ora è?**
             The house that (or which) is here.
             La casa *che* (o *la quale*) è qua.
             The woman whose husband is tall.
             La dònna il *cui* marìto è alto.

Those other classes of pronouns?... We'll learn them later.
For now these are the most important. You don't have to memorize them
all in one day.

PRATICA

ENGLISH   ITALIANO

Late   ....
Good bye   ....
The personal pronoun   ....
The subject   ....
The object   ....
The sister   ....
She loves   ....
I beg you   ....

28

ENGLISH	ITALIANO
Own	....
The demonstrative pronoun	....
Easy	....
Difficult	....
The man	....
You are	....
I see her	....
Now	....
The woman	....
The husband	....
Goes	....
Slow	....
Safe	....
Far	....

Take your time. Chi va piano, va sano e va lontano.
Who goes slow, goes safe and goes far.

EIGHTH LESSON

Lezione Ottava

Signora, è questa casa tua? Essa è grande e bella: piacere mio.
Lady, is this your house? It is big and beautiful: I am pleased for you.

As you may have realized, you have learned a lot already. Now we have reached that part of speech which is the back bone of any language: **the verb,** *il verbo.*

What is a verb? It is that part of speech that expresses existence, action or occurrence. It constitutes the nucleus of a sentence.

I have already mentioned that the Italian language comes from poetry. Dante Alighieri, one of the great Italian poets, desired to hear the Florentine language spoken in every region of Italy: from the Alps to Sicily.

During his time, in the thirteenth century, Giotto and Cimabue, two great painters, rose to fame by introducing a new style of painting. Dante says that their paintings were so perfect, so much to imitate the minutest details of Nature. They brought the art of painting again to light: to its highest perfection. He says that they made *"the dead look dead and the living look alive."*

He desired to summon light to the Italian language. During his time every kingdom, every province, almost every city, had its dialect, peculiar, separate, distinct, rude in construction, harsh, in different degree, in utterance.

Rev. H. H. Milman wrote: *"Dante ranged over the whole land. He discussed the Sicilian and the Apulian, the Neapolitan and the Roman, the Spoletan, the Tuscan and the Genoese, the Romagnole and the Lombard, the Trevisan and Venetian, the Istrian and the Friulian, the Piedmontese and the Bolognese. He found all those dialects coarse, harsh, mutilated, defective."*

*"Out of such a chaos Dante chose not to complete his great "**Devine Comedy**" in Latin. Following a profound meditation, he deliberately resolved on his appeal to the Italian mind and heart. To a certain extent he chose to form the pure, vigorous, picturesque, harmonious Italian, which was to be intelligible: which was to become native and popular to the universal ear of Italy. He had to create; out of a chaos he had to summon light. He desired a noble and pure language, common to all, peculiar to none: a language which he describes – Illustrious, Cardinal, Courtly, Parliamentary.–"*

"Thus in Italy, with the Italian language, of which, if he was not absolutely the creator, he was the first who gave it permanent and vital being, arose one of the great poet of the world."

"Those famous painters had the faculty of giving life to human emotion by natural images, by imparting to natural images human life and human sympathies with their brushes and with their colors. Dante did the same with his rare talent. He painted with words, with the fewest possible words; yet his picture lives and speaks forever."

Yet, not withstanding the peculiarities, out of these dialects came the most beautiful songs of the world.

While studying the **verb,** we have to deal with the **Conjugation,** which includes the many **forms** or **variations** of the **verb.** It may change according to its **gender**, its **mood**, its **tense**, its **person** and its **number**.

The moods of the verb

The **moods** of the verb that present a real and own conjugation, according to the **persons** and the **numbers**, are:
The indicative
The subjunctive
The conditional
The imperative
They are called; **finite moods.**

31

On the other hand **the verbs** which have no **persons** and no **numbers** are called **indefinite.** They are:

The infinite
The participle
The gerund

The indicative

The **indicative mood** is used to affirm or to negate a state or an action considerate as reality.

The **subjunctive mood** depends upon the indicative. It expresses doubts, uncertainty, feelings, will.

The **conditional mood** expresses that which happens or that which could happen as the action becomes true.

The **imperative mood** expresses command, giving orders and exhortation, appeal.

Let's look at them.

The indefinite

The **infinite** –present– expresses an action which is going on at the time it is called on.

The past infinite expresses a completed action.

The participle –present and past– is used like an adjective. It has two genders and two numbers: **masculine, feminine; singular, plural.**

The gerund –present– indicates a contemporary action.

The gerund –**past**– indicate a past action in respect to the principal verb.

I bet you are thinking: "What can be more confusing than this?" Don't worry. I'll try to make it as clear as possible and as easy as possible as we go along.

Every language uses the same forms and the same variation of the verb. However some are easier than others.

It takes a lot of hard work to get everything right. The verb is the back bone of the sentence. Its moods indicates *"the action that happened yesterday; the action that happens to-day; the action that will happen to-morrow; the action that could happen, if..."*

Gender of the verb
Transitive and Intransitive

A word of advise: The student must learn these two words really well.

The English language has only one auxiliary verb: a verb which helps the others to form compound tenses. It is the verb – **to have** – .

The Italian language has two auxiliary verbs which help forming compound tenses. They are *to have:* **"avere"** and *to be:* **"essere"**.

Many people who have not learned the proper grammar well, make a lot of mistakes when they speak Italian involving **transitive** and **intransitive** verbs. Many times they do not use the proper auxiliary verb. They use the helping verb **to have,** when they should use **to be.** Such a mistake has incomparable consequences.

Transitive Verbs

Transitive verbs take the auxiliary **avere** *to have.*   Transitive means that the action of the **subject** is transmitted to the **object.** *If you ask a question, the answer must immediately be*: **who, whom, what: chi, che cosa?** The answer is **trasmitted directly to the object.**

Mia madre ama *mia sorella.*

*My mother loves **my sister**. My sister is the object.*

Whom does my mother love? She loves my sister. The action is passed directly to the object.

Intransitive verbs

Intransitive verbs take the auxiliary **essere** *to be.*

Intransitives means that the action of the subject is not transmitted.
Usually the answer to the question is *where, when, why*: **dove, quando, perché.**

Most of the intransitive verbs indicate movement from one place to another. They are **to go** *andare*, **to come** *venire*, **to return** *ritornare...* When you are using these verbs, you must absoutely make sure that you use the auxiliary verb *to be* **"essere".**

Example: **I have gone to school.**　　**Io sono andato a scuola.**
　　　　I have returned for you.　　**Io sono tornato per te.**

Reflexive verbs

Reflexive verbs are another class of verbs that **must have** the auxiliary **"essere"** when forming compound tenses.
Reflexive means that the action is mirrored upon the person who is the subject of the action. The action reflects upon **"oneself".**

Every time there is a reflexive pronoun involved, we must use **the auxiliary verb** *to be* **"essere"**
.

Reflexive pronouns are:

English	Italian
Myself	Mi
Yourself	Ti
Himself	Si
Herself	Si
Itself	Si
Ourselves	Ci
Yourselves	Vi
Themselves	Si

Example: **I wash myself**　　　　　**Io mi lavo.**
　　　　I have washed myself　　**Io mi sono lavato.**

34

As you can see, in English the reflexive pronoun is after the verb. In Italian it is before the verb.

Atmospheric Verbs

All the verbs which indicate atmospheric phenomenons must also take the auxiliary "**essere**". They are called **impersonal verbs** in Italian. It means that they do not have a subject.

Example: **It rains.**   **Piove.**
        It has rained.   **È piovuto.**
        It snows.   **Fiocca.**
        It has snowed   **È fioccato.**

If the student can memorize these three major classes of verbs that require the auxiliary "**essere**," he will have accomplished a heavy task.

I know it is too much to absorb in one lesson. I have put these classes of verbs together, for quick references: yes, for convenience.

PRATICA

ITALIAN   ENGLISH

Il vèrbo   ....
La coniugazìone   ....
Le variazìoni   ....
Il mòdo   ....
Il tèmpo   ....
Il numèro   ....
L'indicatìvo   ....
Il congiuntìvo   ....
Il condizionàle   ....
L'imperatìvo   ....
Il modo finìto   ....

ITALIAN	ENGLISH
Il modo infinìto	....
Il mòdo indefinìto	....
Il particìpio	....
Il gerúndio	....
Il presènte	....
Il passàto	....
Ierì, oggì, domanì	....
Il transitìvo	....
L'intransitìvo	....
Avére	....
Essère	....
Dóve, quàndo, perché	....
Andàre	....
Venìre	....
Ritornàre	....
Riflessìvo	....
Atmosferìco	....
Impersónale	....

I have gone a little overboard. I have done this because many of the words have the same meaning in both languages.

As I already said: you do not have to rash anything.
A German proverb says that *"Patience is the best teacher"*.

NINTH LESSON

Lezione Nona

Io ho nove anni. Quanti anni hai tu? *I am nine years old. How old are you?*

As you can see in the above case, the Italian language uses the verb *"avere"* to have, regarding *age*. English, on the contrary, uses the verb *"essere"* to be, to ask the same thing.

This is another case when the student must know the proper use for each language.

Up to this lesson we have been using the verbs *essere* and *avere* sparingly. We have called them **auxiliaries** *ausilìari.*

Now it is time to begin working with them. We have learned all about the personal pronouns to prepare ourselves for this great adventure. You may call it what you may; but this is the toughest part of every language. This part of speech requires a bit more time for your brain to adjust; however do not despair. We'll explore the easiest way possible to make this happen.

In Italian we have **three conjugations: first, second, third.**

All the verbs ending in *are: am-are to love,* belong to the first conjugation. The greatest number of verbs belong to this conjugation.

All the verbs ending in *ere: av-ere to have,* belong to the second conjugation.

All the verbs ending in *ire: serv-ire to serv,* belong to the third conjugation.

As you can see, we can divide the verbs in two parts: *the root and the ending:* **am-are, av-ere, serv-ire.**

You may also notice that in many cases the English language drops the ending **are, ere, ire,** from Italian verbs; and uses only their roots to express the same meaning: **salút-are** *to salute;* **spènd-ere** *to spend;* **offr-ìre** *to offer.*

As in other languages, Italian has **regular and irregular verbs.** *Regular verbs* follow the model which we will learn in future lessons. They follow the model in every form of the conjugation.

Irregular verbs, most of them belonging to the second conjugation, like *avere and essere,* do not follow the verb models in some of their forms.

Before we get into the models of regular verbs, I would like to prepare the student by giving the conjugation of the verbs *to have* **"avere"** and *to be* **"essere" in the simple forms.**

The student will learn the **compound forms** in future lessons.

VERBO AUSILIARIO AVERE
Simple indicative mood

Present tense		**Imperfect tense**	
Presente		*Imperfetto*	
Io ho	*I have*	**Io avevo**	*I used to have*
Tu hai	*You have*	**Tu avevi**	*You used to have*
Egli, Ella ha	*He, She has*	**Egli aveva**	*He used to have*
Noi abbiamo	*We have*	**Noi avevamo**	*We used to have*
Voi avete	*You have*	**Voi avevate**	*You used to have*
Essi hanno	*They have*	**Essi avevano**	*They used to have*

Past tense		**Future tense**	
Passato remoto		*Futuro*	
Io ebbi	*I had*	**Io avrò**	*I will (shall) have*
Tu avesti	*You had*	**Tu avrai**	*You will have*
Egli, Ella ebbe	*He had*	**Egli avrà**	*He will have*
Noi avemmo	*We had*	**Noi avremo**	*We will have*
Voi aveste	*You had*	**Voi avrete**	*You will have*
Essi ebbero	*They had*	**Essi avranno**	*They will have*

38

Simple Subjunctive mood

Tempo Presente		Tempo imperfetto	
Che io abbia	*That I have*	**Se io avessi**	*If I had*
Che tu abbia	*That you have*	**Se tu avessi**	*If you had*
Che egli abbia	*That he have*	**Se egli avesse**	*If he had*
Che noi abbiamo	*That we have*	**Se noi avessimo**	*If we had*
Che voi abbiate	*That you have*	**Se voi aveste**	*If you had*
Che essi abbiano	*That they have*	**Se essi avessero**	*If they had*

Simple and past conditional mood

Tempo Presente		Tempo passato
Io avrei	*I should (would) have*	**Io avrei avuto**
Tu avresti	*You should have*	**Tu avresti avuto**
Egli avrebbe	*He should have*	**Egli avrebbe avuto**
Noi avremmo	*We should have*	**Noi avremmo avuto**
Voi avreste	*You should have*	**Voi avreste avuto**
Essi avrebbero	*They should have*	**Essi avrebbero avuto**

I have not indicated how to form the **past conditional mood** in English. I have written it down for another purpose.

Io avrei avuto is translate to be as follows in English: **I should or would have had etc.** We take the simple tenses and make all of them compound by adding the past participle to the simple tenses.

The past participle of **avere is "avuto"** *had*. **Therefore, if we add "avuto" to all the simple tenses, we will have the compound tenses completed.**

I am sure that you can form all of the compound tenses by yourself. As I have said, you just add the **past participle to the simple tenses.**

Please notice that **avere** uses its own **past participle** to form the compound tenses.

There is one other thing I want to make you aware of. I have used both **Egli** and **Ella** a couple of times. For the rest of the conjugation I have used only **Egli** for the third person singular.

In Italian when the gender is not specified, it is always referred to the masculine gender. Even if there are a great number of feminine words in a group and there is only one masculine word with it, the gender always takes the masculine form.

Esempio: **Quelle nove sorelle e il loro fratello sono belli.**
Those nine sisters and their brother are beautiful.

As you can see there are nine girls and one boy in the sentence. Yet the adjective **belli** is masculine plural, because the masculine noun takes over.

Now let's get back to the verb. I was planning to stop you here; however I think that it will be better to have everything laid out in front of you. Indeed I know when it is too much; yet I don't want you to have to look throughout the book to find something which is so important.

I am trying to make the difficult study of Italian verbs as easy as possible. This is the reason why I want you to have easy access to the complete form of the verbs..

My advise to you is to make copies of the entire conjugation and have them available for quick reference.

Imperative mood

Present tense

Che io abbia	*Let me have*
Abbi tu	*Have you*
Abbia egli, ella, esso	*Let him, her, it have*
Abbiamo noi	*Let us have*
Abbiate voi	*Have you*
Abbiano essi, esse	*Let them have*

40

Indefinite tenses

Present infinite:	**Avere**	*To have*
Past infinite:	**Avere avuto**	*To have had*
Present participle:	**Avente**	*Having*
Past participle:	**Avut-o-a-i-e**	*Had*
Gerund –present–	**Avendo**	*Having*
Gerund –past–	**Avendo avuto**	*Having had*

You have before you the whole form of the auxiliary verb *to have*. I wish you could learn all this within a short time. Indeed it is quite a task.

Look at the **past participle**. It has the same functions of an adjective. Note, though, that **"avuto"** does not change in the active form. When it is used with the auxiliary **to have,** it always remains **avuto.** Here are some examples using the compound tenses.

Egli, ella, **esso ha avuto.** Noi **abbiamo avuto.** Essi, esse **avranno avuto.** Io **ebbi avuto.** Voi **abbiate avuto.** Tu **avresti avuto.** Io **avevo avuto.**

I know, however, that you are anxious to begin building sentences. I know that you are anxious to talk with people. I do not blame you for showing off. You have learned a lot already. So I suggest you use just the infinite form of the verb, for now, with the help of **ieri, oggi, domani**: *yesterday, to-day, to-morrow,* to express what you have learned

Io avere dieci dollari ieri.	*I had ten dollars yesterday.*
Io venire a casa tua oggi.	*I come to your house to-day.*
Tu andare a scuola domani.	*You'll go to school to-morrow.*

This is not the correct way of speaking; indeed it will help you out a great deal. People understand what you are trying to say. It should be a lot of fun for you, trying to express yourself. People will be proud of you.

At the height of the Second World War, while the Allied Forces were fighting the German Forces in 1944-45, during the many battles fought around Montecassino, the Monastery which is situated half a way between Rome and Naples in Italy, soldiers from both sides used to speak Italian to us like the example I have given you. I was right there in that area at that time, in the middle of all that shelling and bombing.

We could understand very well what they were trying to say. In fact after the big battle moved to the Central part of Italy, we kids used that same language for fun. Of course I do not recommend it as habit forming.

TENTH LESSON

Lezione decima

Che tempo fa? Oggi piove. Fa cattivo tempo. *How is the weather? To-day it rains. The weather is bad.*

It is important to repeat that we have reached the height of the Italian language, or of any language by the same token. The verb means action. We couldn't do without it.

When I was going to elementary school in Italy, I had the same teacher each year in primary school. She came from Florence. She made absolutely certain that we learned the Italian language as well as it is spoken in Tuscany. She made sure that we learned the verbs like the *Ave Maria.* She gave us one tense at a time. After everybody had learned them by heart, she used to pick each one of us randomly and ask us to say that verb fluently. Those who hesitated, had to stay after school to learn how to say them smoothly and fluently.

She was all about grammar. She used to say that grammar is the basic principle of any area of knowledge.

Dante compared grammar to the Moon which has a dark side and a bright side. Its brightness shines more with each passing day during crescent, so much as to reach the greatest brightness at full Moon. Grammar has these two properties: dark and bright. Those who achieve the full brightness, reach the height of graceful eloquence.

When we were growing up, we used the dialect outside of the classroom. It was an easy way of speaking for us. Our dialect still has a lot of Latin in it. If we tried to speak the proper Italian, people used to make fun of us.

Now, though, the younger generation speaks the real Italian throughout Italy. It is hard to hear young people speak the dialect.

Well, let's continue on with the verbs.
In this lesson we will tackle the conjugation of the verb **"essere"** *to be.*

VERBO AUSILIARIO ESSERE

Simple indicative mood

Tempo presente

Io sono	*I am*
Tu sei	*You are*
Egli è	*He is*
Noi siamo	*We are*
Voi siete	*You are*
Essi sono	*They are*

Imperfetto

Io ero	*I used to be*
Tu eri	*You used to be*
Egli era	*He used to be*
Noi eravamo	*We used to be*
Voi eravate	*You used to be*
Essi erano	*They used to be*

Passato remoto

Io fui	*I was*
Tu fosti	*You were*
Egli fu	*He was*
Noi fummo	*We were*
Voi foste	*You were*
Essi furono	*They were*

Futuro semplice

Io sarò	*I will (Shall)be*
Tu sarai	*You will be*
Egli sarà	*He will be*
Noi saremo	*We will be*
Voi sarete	*You will be*
Essi saranno	*They will be*

Simple subjunctive mood

Tempo presente

Che io sia	*That I be*
Che tu sia	*That you be*
Che egli sia	*That he be*
Che noi siamo	*That we be*
Che voi siate	*That you be*
Che essi siano	*That they be*

Tempo imperfetto

Se io fossi	*If I were*
Se tu fossi	*If you were*
Se egli fosse	*If he were*
Se noi fossimo	*If we were*
Se voi foste	*If you were*
Se essi fossero	*If they were*

Simple and past conditional mood

Tempo presente		Tempo passato
Io sarei	*I should (would) be*	Io sarei stat-o-a-i-e
Tu saresti	*You should be*	Tu saresti stato
Egli sarebbe	*He Should be*	Egli sarebbe stato
Noi saremmo	*We should be*	Noi saremmo satat-i-e
Voi sareste	*You should be*	Voi sareste stati
Essi sarebbero	*They should be*	Essi sarebbero stati

To make the compound tenses we take the simple tenses and add the past participle to them, the same way we have learned for the verb *to have*. **Essere** uses its own past participle which is **stat-o-a-i-e**.

Notice that when we use the auxiliary verb "essere", the past participle becomes an adjective. It takes the same gender and number of the subject.

Maria è stat-a brava. *Mary has been brave.*
Giovanni è stat-o bravo. *John has been brave.*
Maria e Giovanni sono stat-i bravi. *Mary and John have been brave.*

You, the student have a lot of work to tackle. It takes a lot of time to absorb all this. I shall continue for the convenience of the learner.

Imperative mood
Present tense

Che io sia	*Let me be*
Sii tu	*Be*
Sia egli	*Let him be*
Siamo noi	*Let us be*
Siate voi	*Be*
Siano essi	*Let them be*

45

Indefinite tenses

Present infinite:	**Essere**	*To be*
Past infinite:	**Essere stato**	*To have been*
Present participle:	**There is none**	
Past participle:	**Stat-o-a-i-e**	*Been*
***Gerund* –present–**	**Essendo**	*Being*
Gerund–past–	**Essendo stato**	*Having* been

You have before your eyes the full spectrum of the functions of the verb <u>to</u> <u>be</u> **"essere"**.

The auxiliary **essere** helps to form all the compound forms of **intransitive verbs.** Remember, those verbs that indicate movement, which answer: when, where, why?

It is used with **reflexive verbs, with atmospheric verbs and also with the passive form of the verbs.**

> **Esempio: Mia madre ama mia sorella.** *Active form*
> *My mother loves my sister.*
> **Mia sorella è amata da mia madre.** *Passive form*
> *My sister is loved by my mother.*

As one can see, both languages form the *passive* the same way: by using the auxiliary *to be*. The *object* becomes the **subject**; and the subject takes the preposition "*by*" in English: "**da**" in Italian.

We'll learn all about the preposition in future lessons.
I do not want you to get overwhelmed. To-morrow it will be easier to accomplish what seemed very hard to-day.

ELEVENTH LESSON

Lezione undicesima

Signora, Le piace (di) parlare Italiano? Si, mi piace, grazie.
Mam, do you like to speak Italian? Yes, I do like to, thank you.

In this lesson we will continue to learn about the verbs. You have learned the whole conjugation of the auxiliary verbs **avere and essere.** Now you will learn all the moods of the regular verbs belonging to the first conjugation. It will be good to have the whole picture before our eyes.

The greatest number of verbs belong to the first conjugation.
Most of them are regular verbs. They follow the form of the verb model. In this case we'll use the verb **"parlare" as our model.**

If you go back to the first sentence, you'll notice that I have used *parlare* for exercise purpose.

From the first lesson on, I have tried to use words that have the same meaning in both languages. It is easier to refer to them.

Which word can we make out of parlare? We can make the word *Parliament.* Well done... if you had figured it out on your own.

Referring to words that have the same meaning, will help you to learn the language faster.

Another way to learn a language quickly is to talk with people who speak the language. Don't be afraid to make mistakes. You want your ear to get used to separating one word from another quickly.

Another good way to practice is to go to an Italian market where they keep imported goods. That's what it is called visual aid.
To-day we have the convenience of *radio* and *television* at our reach. It is helpful to spend a few minutes a day listening to programs transmitted in the language you are studying.

47

Of course the best way to learn a language fast, is to reside in the country where the language is spoken.

Indeed, let's get back to the verbs. The first thing we are going to do is to separate the root from the ending: **pàrl-are** *to speak.*

All through the declination the accent rests on the **a of pàrl.** I like to make the student aware of it, so I don't have to put the accent on each form of the verb.

Each person of each tense has a special ending. All regular verbs follow the same procedure. It is a must to memorize those endings by heart.

It is good practice to make copies of the model verbs and keep them handy for quick reference.

VERBO MODELLO PARL– ARE

Prima coniugazione

Modo Indicativo

Presente		Imperfetto	
Io parl–**o**	*I speak*	Io parl–**avo**	*I used* to speak
Tu parl–**i**	*You speak*	Tu parl–**avi**	*You used to speak*
Egli parl–**a**	*He speaks*	Egli parl–**ava**	*He used to speak*
Noi parl–**iamo**	*We speak*	Noi parl–**avamo**	*We used to speak*
Voi parl–**ate**	*You speak*	Voi parl–**avate**	*You used to speak*
Essi parl–**ano**	*They speak*	Essi parl–**avano**	*They used to speak*

Passato Remoto		Futuro	
Io parl–**ai**	*I spoke*	Io parl–**erò**	*I will (shall) speak*
Tu parl–**asti**	*You spoke*	Tu parl–**erai**	*You will speak*
Egli parl–**ò**	*He spoke*	Egli parl–**erà**	*He will speak*
Noi parl–**ammo**	*We spoke*	Noi parl–**eremo**	*We will speak*
Voi parl–**aste**	*You spoke*	Voi parl–**erete**	*You will speak*
Essi parl–**arono**	*They spoke*	Essi parl–**eranno**	*They will speak*

Modo Congiuntivo

Presente		Imperfetto	
Che io parl–**i**	*That I speak*	Se io parl–**assi**	*If I spoke*
Che tu parl–**i**	*That you speak*	Se tu parl–**assi**	*If you spoke*
Che egli parl–**i**	*That he speak*	Se egli parl–**asse**	*If he spoke*
Che noi parl–**iamo**	*That we speak*	Se noi parl–**assimo**	*If we spoke*
Che voi parl–**iate**	*That you speak*	Se voi parl–**aste**	*If you spoke*
Che essi parl-**ino**	*That they speak*	Se essi parl–**assero**	*If they spoke*

Modo Condizionale

Presente

Io parl–**erei**	*I would (should) speak*
Tu parl–**eresti**	*You would speak*
Egli parl–**erebbe**	*He would speak*
Noi parl–**eremmo**	*We would speak*
Voi parl–**ereste**	*You would speak*
Essi parl–**erebbero**	*They would speak*

Condizionale Passato

Io avrei parl–**ato**	*I would (should) have spoken*
Tu avresti parl–**ato**	*You would have spoken*
Egli avrebbe parl–**ato**	*He would have spoken*
Noi avremmo parl–**ato**	*We would have spoken*
Voi avreste parl–**ato**	*You would have spoken*
Essi avrebbero parl–**ato**	*They would have spoken*

The past participle of **parlare is parlato. Parlare takes the auxiliary avere to form the past tenses.**

As you can see, when we use the auxiliary **avere** the **past participle** remains unchanged for each **person** and for each **number.** It is formed by adding **"ato"** to the **root** of each **verb** belonging to the **first conjugation.**

Modo Imperativo

Presente

Che io parl–**i**	*Let me speak*
Parl–**a** tu	*Speak*
Parl–**i** egli	*Let him speak*
Parl–**iamo** noi	*Let us speak*
Parl–**ate** voi	*Speak*
Parl–**ino** essi	*Let them speak*

Tempi indefiniti

Infinito presente: parl–are   *To speak*
Infinito passato: aver parl–ato   *To have spoken*

Participio presente: parl–ante   *Speaking*
Participio passato: parl–ato   *Spoken*

Gerundio presente; parl–ando   *Speaking*
Gerundio passato: avendo parlato   *having spoken*

Now you have before your eyes the whole declination of a regular verb belonging to the first conjugation. We call this a **"model verb"**. All regular verbs belonging to the first declination, will be conjugated in the same way.

Remember: we form the past tenses (or compound tenses) by using all the forms of the auxiliary **avere** for all transitive verbs.

Example: Io ho parlato. Tu avevi parlato. Egli ebbe parlato. Lei avrà parlato. Essi avranno parlato. Che noi abbiamo parlato. Se io avessi parlato. Se voi aveste parlato. Essi avrebbero parlato.

There are some exceptions to this rule; however we'll learn about them in later lessons. Indeed this will keep you busy for quite a while.

There are times when even I have to go back to look at some of these exceptions, to make sure that I am not making a mistake. I tell you this so you do not get discouraged. I want you to keep your enthusiasm high; thus you will use your knowledge in your favor.

A good artist paints his picture based on his expert knowledge. Then he looks at it, checks its colors and shakes his head. Indeed one touch here, one touch there and he refines it, showing his satisfaction with a delightful smile.

Oh yes!... Another good way to practice is to go to an Italian market where they keep imported goods. That's what it is called "visual aid".

TWELFTH LESSON

Lezione dodicesima

Mamma mia! Tutto questo lavoro... Povero me! *Good gracious! So much work... Poor me!*

Well, you are right. Indeed an Italian motto says, "Chi lavora, mangia. " *Who works hard, will have plenty to eat.*

I was planning to get into the verbs belonging to the **second conjugation** right away. However I would like to go over a couple of exceptions regarding some very important rules which deal with verbs of the first conjugation. I cannot leave this behind. Please, open your mind to what I want you to learn; and try hard to retain it.

Dante wrote that, "*It is not knowledge the having heard, unless you retain what you have heard.*"

When I arrived to this Country, the manager of the factory where I started working told me that, "*What you earn does not matter; what matters is how much you save each day.*"

I have already mentioned that repetition is the basic rule for learning a second language.

You have certainly noticed while watching T.V. , you see the same ads over and over again. There is no doubt that you have probably learned some of them by heart. Equally, to learn a language fast, you must go over the same words until they are fixed in your mind.

You have already learned that the **"h"** has no value in Italian.
It is used only in special cases so one word is not confused with another. It is also used to keep the guttural sound in front of **"i" and "e"**. Unfortunately there are some verbs which must use the **"h"** in some of their

particularities to keep the sound of *"K" and "G" as in **ghost***.

The verbs ending in **"care" and "gare"** keep the guttural sound through the whole conjugation. In order to do this they have to change **"c" into "ch" and "g" into "gh"** every time the ending begins with **"e" or "i"**.

Let's take the verb **cari–care**: *to load*. It ends in **care.** It belongs to the first conjugation because it also ends in **are.** Let's conjugate it.

Indicativo

Presente		Futuro	
Io caric-o	*I load*	Io cari-**cherò**	*I'll (shall)load*
Tu cari-**chi**	*You load*	Tu cari-**cherai**	*You will load*
Egli caric-a	*He loads*	Egli cari-**cherà**	*He will load*
Noi cari-**chiamo**	*We load*	Noi cari-**cheremo**	*We will load*
Voi caric-ate	*You load*	Voi cari-**cherete**	*You will load*
Essi caric-ano	*They load*	Essi cari-**cheranno**	*They will load*

Congiuntivo Presente		Condizionale Presente		
Che io cari-**chi**	*That I load*	Io cari-**cherei** *I would (shd.) load*		
Che tu cari-**chi**	*That you load*	Tu cari-**cheresti**	*You*	*"*
Che egli cari-**chi**	*That he load*	Egli cari-**cherebbe**	*He*	*"*
Che noi cari-**chiamo**	*That we load*	Noi cari-**cheremmo**	*We*	*"*
Che voi cari-**chiate**	*That you load*	Voi **carichereste**	*You*	*"*
Che essi cari-**chino**	*That they load*	**Essi caricherebbero** *They*		*"*

Imperativo

Che io cari-**chi**	*Let me load*
Caric-a tu	*You load*
Cari-**chi** egli	*Let him load*
Cari-**chiamo noi**	*Let us load*
Caric-ate voi	*You load*
Cari-**chino essi**	*Let them load*

These are the only moods, tenses and numbers that have particularities. The rest of the tenses do not present any deviation from the model verb.

I would like to give you some of the verbs ending in **"care"**.

They are particular in the same mood, tenses and persons of the above **verb caricare.**

Example: Giudi-**care** *to judge.* Comuni-**care** *to communicate.*
Indi-**care** *to indicate.* Dedi-**care** *to dedicate.* Romanti-**care** *to romance.* Masti-**care** *to chew or masticate.* Medi-**care** *to treat or medicate.* Re-**care** *to bring...* Caval-**care** *to ride...* **Prati-care** *to practice, etc.*

If you have some free time, I would like you to practice with some of these verbs. It would help immensely. Most of the verbs have the same meaning in both language. Remembering them will help to build your vocabulary.

Now That we are on a roll, we may as well deal with those verbs which end in **"gare"**. Our **model** will be **pa-gare** *to pay.*

They follow the same particularities as the verbs ending in **"care"**, therefore I am going to list only the moods and the tenses which present those particularities.

Example: **Indicativo Presente** Io pag-o, tu pa-**ghi,** egli pag-a, noi pa-**ghiamo,** voi pag-ate, essi pag-ano.

Futuro Io pa-**gherò,** tu pa-**gherai, etc.**

Conguintivo Presente Che io pa-**ghi,** che tu pa-**ghi, etc.**

Condizionale Io pa-**gherei,** tu pa-**gheresti etc.**

Imperativo Che io pa-**ghi,** pag-a tu, pa-**ghi** egli, pa-**ghiamo** noi, pag-ate voi, pa-**ghino** essi.

These particularities will keep the guttural sound the same throughout the conjugation: **chi, che** sound like *ki, ke: kidney, kettle;* **ghi, ghe** sound like the **"g"** in **good:** *give, get.*

I know this is a lot of information. Please, don't get discouraged.

THIRTEENTH LESSON

Lezione Tredicesima

Andiamo al ristorante. È ora di mangiare. *Let's go to the restaurant. It is time to eat.*

We have learned that most of the irregular verbs belong to the second conjugation. Yet we have three important irregular verbs which belong to the first conjugation.

They are: **andare** *to go,* **dare** *to give,* **stare** *to stay. These verbs are also irregular in English.*

Before we deal with these verbs, I have other particularities to make you aware of.

If you look at the first sentence you meet both the verb **andare** and also the verb **mangiare.**

The verbs which end in **ciare** and **giare** lose the **"i"** if the ending begins with **"e"** and with **"i".**

Let's work with the particularities of the verb **cominciare** *to begin or to start* and of the verb **mangiare** *to eat.*

I'll give you only the particularities of the moods and the persons affected.

Example: **Cominci-are.**

Presente indicativo: Io cominci-**o,** tu cominci-**i** (wrong, we must take one **"i"** away) tu cominc-**i** (right), egli cominci-**a** etc.

Futuro: Io cominci-**erò** (wrong). Io cominc-**erò** (right) etc.

Congiuntivo presente Che io cominci-**i** (wrong). Che io cominc-**i** (right) etc.

Condizionale presente Io cominci-**erei** (wrong). Io cominc-**erei**

(right), tu cominc-**eresti,** egli cominc-**erebbe,** noi cominc-**eremmo,** voi cominc-**ereste,** essi cominc-**erebbero** (all right).

We remove the **"i"** for the sake of a pleasant and smooth sound.

The verbs ending in **"giare"** follow the same rules as those ending in **"ciare.**

Example: tu mang-**i** (not mang-**ii**). Io mang-**erò** (not mang-**ierò**). Che io **mang-i** (not mang-**ii)** Io mang-**erei** (not mang-**ierei**).

You should try to complete the rest of the above tenses on your own. I know you can do it.

Please notice, either **to begin or to start** are translated only with the verb *cominciare* in Italian.

Indeed there are verbs which have more than one meaning. For example take the verb **grattare.** It means *to scratch, to scrape, to grate and to steal.* We use them correctly according to their function or context

One day a farmer's boy went to the city. Passing before a store window, he saw a sign which said "formaggio da grattare*" Cheese to be grated.* For him, however, that sign meant *"Cheese to be stolen".*
Wise to the challenge, he broke the window and took the cheese. A few steps ahead he was caught by the Police and taken before a judge. His defense rested on the meaning of the word. The judge smiled, told him to pay for the window and let him free. Then he turned to the store owner and told him to change his ad.

Indeed the ad was changed to "formaggio duro per spaghetti".
Hard cheese for spaghetti.

Well, let's get back to the irregular verbs belonging to the first conjugation. Cominciamo con **and-are** *to go.*

Indicativo presente: Io **vado,** tu **vai,** egli **va,** noi and-iamo, voi and-ate, essi **vanno.**
Imperfetto: Io and-avo, tu and-avi, egli and-ava, noi and-avamo, voi and-avate, essi and-avano. **It follows the regular form.**

56

Passato remoto: Io and-ai, tu and-asti, egli and-ò, noi and-ammo, voi and-aste, essi and-arono. **It also follows the regular form.**

Futuro: Io and-rò, (not **and-erò**) **tu** and-**rai**, egli **and-rà**, noi and-**remo**, voi and-**rete**, essi and-**ranno**.

Congiuntivo presente: Che io **vada,** che tu **vada,** che egli **vada,** che noi and-iamo, che voi and-iate, che essi **vadano.**

Congiuntivo imperfetto: Se io and-assi, se tu and-assi, se egli and-asse, etc. **It also follows the regular form.**

Imperativo: Che io **vada, vai** tu, **vada** egli, and-iamo noi, and-ate voi, **vadano essi.**

Participio passato: and-ato (regular).

Remember, **andare is an intransitive verb.** The compound tenses take the auxiliary **essere.** Io sono andato... Io sarei andato, etc.

This rule is very important. Please, make sure you memorize it. Those who listen to you, will pay fierce attention to the use of the auxiliaries. You must use **l'ausiliario essere** with the verb **andare.**

Being a very common verb, it tends to test the people who use it.

Another common verb is **dare** *to give.* Most of its tenses are **regular** and are formed following the verb model.

I am going to give you only the irregular forms. You already know how to conjugate the regular forms.

Passato remoto: Io **diedi,** tu **desti,** egli **diede,** noi **demmo,** voi **deste,** essi **diedero.**

Cungiuntivo presente: Che io **dia,** che tu **dia,** che egli **dia,** che noi **diamo,** che voi **diate,** che essi **diano.**

Congiuntivo imperfetto: Se io **dessi,** se tu **dessi,** se egli **desse,** se noi **dessimo,** se voi **deste,** se essi **dessero.**

Participio passato: d-ato.

Dare is a transitive verb; as such it requires the auxiliary **avere.** Tu hai **dato.** Ella aveva **dato.** Noi avremmo **dato... etc.**

There is only one more type of verb to learn. Should we tackle it or let it rest? I think we should include it in this lesson.

Stare *to stay:* its irregularities are the same as **dare.** I will give you only the irregular forms.

Pass. remoto: Io **stetti,** tu **stesti,** egli **stette,** noi **stemmo,** voi **steste,** essi **stettero**

Cong. presente: Che io **stia,** che tu **stia,** che egli **stia,** che noi **stiamo,** che voi **stiate,** che essi **stiano.**

Cong. imperfetto: Se io **stessi,** se tu **stessi,** se egli **stesse,** se noi **stessimo,** se voi **steste,** se essi **stessero.**

Part. passato: st-ato.

This verb is intransitive; therefore it takes **essere** to form compound tenses.

At last we have gone over all the verbs belonging to the first declination.

Do not get discouraged if you cannot learn them all in one lesson. It takes a long time to memorize their complete forms.

When I was going to school in Italy, we began studying the verbs in the early elementary grades. We continued studying them through High School and beyond.

I would like to give you same regular verbs of the first declination for exercise purpose. They have the same meaning in both languages. It is an easy method to enrich your vocabulary quickly.

You don't have to stride to learn them. *"All things come to him who waits."* – Col tempo e con la paglia maturano le nespole.–

The following verbs have the same meaning in both languages. What you have to do is to put the English version next to the Italian.

ITALIAN	ENGLISH	ITALIAN	ENGLISH
Example: Onorare	*To honor*	Addizionare	....
Generare	....	Funzionare	....
Accettare	....	Controllare	....
Arrestare	....	Partecipare	....
Formare	....	Comunicare	....
Lavorare	....	Depositare	....
Passare	....	Sopportare	....
Mandare	....	Professare	....
Adornare	....	Annunciare	....
Negare	....	Determinare	....

You can add to this list. There are many more verbs belonging to the first conjugation which are almost written the same and have the same meaning in both languages. It is a challenge; yet it is an advantageous process for enriching our vocabulary.

"You *got* to work hard to see rewarding results." I heard this motto many times.

FOURTEENTH LESSON

Lezione Quattordicesima

Oggi sono contento. Ho dedicato il mio tempo a studiare.
To-day I am happy. I have dedicated my time to studying.

As you can see, in many cases Italian omits the personal pronoun before the verb. Now you know why each person of the moods of the verb has a unique ending. You know by each ending if it is the first person, the second, etc.; if it is the present tense, the future, and so on.

I hate to do this to you; however it must be done. In this lesson we are going to study the regular verbs belonging to the second conjugation.
For a **verb model** we are going to select the **verb "vend-ere"** *to sell.* You already know that all the verbs which end in **"ere"** belong to the **second conjugation**.

Indicativo

Presente		**Imperfetto**	
Io vend-**o**	*I sell*	Io vend-**evo**	*I used to sell*
Tu vend-**i**	*You sell*	Tu vend-**evi**	*You used to sell*
Egli vend-**e**	*He sells*	Egli vend-**eva**	*He used to sell*
Noi vend-**iamo**	*We sell*	Noi vend-**evamo**	*We used to sell*
Voi vend-**ete**	*You sell*	Voi vend-**evate**	*You used to sell*
essi vend-**ono**	*They sell*	Essi vend-**evano**	*They used to sell*

Pass. Rem.

Io vend-**ei**	*I sold*		
Tu vend-**esti**	*You sold*		
Egli vend-**é**	*He sold*		
Noi vend-**emmo**	*We sold*		
Voi vend-**este**	*You sold*		
Essi vend-**erono**	*They sold*		

Futuro

Io vend-**erò**	*I will (shall) sell*		
Tu vend-**erai**	*You*	"	
Egli **vend-erà**	*He*	"	
Noi vend-**eremo**	*We*	"	
Voi vend-**erete**	*You*	"	
Essi vend-**eranno**	*They*	"	

Congiuntivo

Presente

Che io vend-**a**	*That I sell*
Che tu vend-**a**	*That you sell*
Che egli vend-**a**	*That he sell*
Che noi vend-**iamo**	*That we sell*
Che voi vend-**iate**	*That you sell*
Che essi vend-**ano**	*That they sell*

Imperfetto

Se io vend-**essi**	*If I sold*
Se tu vend-**essi**	*If You sold*
Se egli vend-**esse**	*If He sold*
Se noi vend-**essimo**	*If We sold*
Se voi vend-**este**	If *You sold*
Se essi vend-**essero**	*If They sold*

Condizionale

Presente

Io vend-**erei**	*I would (should) sell*	
Tu vend-**eresti**	*You*	"
Egli vend-**erebbe**	*He*	"
Noi vend-**eremmo**	*We*	"
Voi vend-**ereste**	*You*	"
Essi vend-**erebbero**	*They*	"

Passato

Io avrei **vend-uto**
Tu avresti vend-**uto**
Egli avrebbe vend-**uto**
Noi avremmo vend-**uto**
Voi avreste vend-**uto**
Essi avrebbero vend-**uto**

You know how to form the compound tenses of verbs both in Italian and in English. We take the entire conjugation of the auxiliaries **to have** or **to be** in the simple form and add the **past participle** of the verb we are conjugating. **Io avrei venduto:** *I would (should) have sold, etc.*

Modi Indefiniti

Infinito presente: vend-ere	*To sell*
Infinito passato: aver vend-uto	*To have sold*
Participio presente: vendente	*Selling*
Paricipio passato: vend-uto	*Sold*
Gerundio presente: vend-endo	*Selling*
Gerundio passato: avendo vend-uto	*Having sold*

Vendere is a transitive verb. As you can see from the example of the past conditional mood, it takes the auxiliary **"avere"**.

Don't be surprised if you'll came across the first and third persons of the passato remoto ending in **etti, ette, ettero**: <u>io vendei</u> or **io vendetti**, <u>egli vendé</u> **or egli vendette**, <u>essi venderono</u> or **essi vendettero**. It depends on the speaker's preference.

Contrary to the first conjugation, verbs of the second conjugation ending in **"cere"** and **"gere"** do not have to keep the guttural sound. They do not add the "h" before **"e"** and **"i"**.

Let's take the verb **vinc-ere** *to win*. It ends in **"c-ere"**.

In order to exercise what we want to learn, let's also take the verb **string-ere** *to tighten*. It ends in **"g-ere"**. The **"e"** and **"i"** do not take the **"h"** for phonetic reason.

Indicative present

Example: Io vinc-**o** *I win etc.*   Io string-o *I tight etc.*
         Tu vinc-**i** (not **vin-chi**)   Tu string-**i** (not **strin ghi**)
         Egli vinc-**e** (not **vin-che**)   Egli string-**e** (not **strin ghe**)
         Noi vinc-**iamo**   Noi string-**iamo**
         Voi vinc-**ete**   Voi string-**ete**
         Essi vinc-**ono**   Essi string-**ono**

Vincere and stringere are irregular verbs. I'll give you only those tenses which deviate from the verb models.

Pass. rem. Io vinsi, tu vincesti, egli vinse, noi vincemmo, voi vinceste, essi vinsero.

Participo passato. Vinto.

Pass. rem. Io strinsi, tu stringesti, egli strinse, noi stringemmo, voi stringeste, essi strinsero.

Participio passato. Stretto.

Vincere and stringere are transitive verbs. They take the auxiliary **avere.**

You already know how to form the compound tenses; therefore I will give you only a couple of examples.

Io ho vinto. Se egli avesse vinto. Voi avreste vinto. Avendo vinto. Tu hai stretto. Noi avemmo stretto. Che io abbia stretto.

Few verbs ending in **"cere"** keep the sweet sound by adding an **"i"** before the ending of the past participle in **"uto"**

Giacere *to lie.* **Giac-iuto** *lain.*

Nuocere *to harm.* **Noc-iuto** *harmed*

Piacere *to please, to like.* **Piac-iuto** *pleased, liked.*

These are all irregular verbs. We'll learn all about their peculiarities in future lessons. We have enough to work on for now.

FIFTEENTH LESSON

Lezione Quindicesima

Mi piace comprare regali per i miei genitori. *I like to buy presents for my parents.*

Notice the difference. In this sentence **piacere** in Italian is used in the third person singular of the present indicative. In English, however, it is used in the first person.

Piacere is almost always used in the third person either singular or plural of every tense when it is preceded by mi, ti, gli, le, ci, vi, a loro. **Mi ha piaciuto.** *I have liked it.* **Gli piacevano.** *He used to like it.* **A loro pacerà etc.** *They will like it.*

When it is preceded by a pronoun subject, it is conjugated using each person of the verb. **Tu mi piaci.** *I like you.* **Essi ci piacevano molto.** *We liked them very much.*

In the previous lesson I chose this verb, trying to help clear only confusion created when comparing the construction of one language to the other. **Piacere** is a very common verb, so we have to respect it a lot. I'll give you the rest of its peculiarities just ahead.

As I mentioned before, the second conjugation has the most irregular verbs. I don't like to remember how many times I had to stay after school to deal with such an enormous task.

I mentioned earlier that my teacher used to call on a student at random and ask him or her to say a selected person of a particular mood of a verb. Then she would turn to another student and ask him to say the first person plural of a different mood and different tense. She required that you answered quickly. If you didn't, you had to stay after school until you learned the whole conjugation of that verb. Even if you knew it, she would make you stay after school to help the ones who needed to learn it.

Some of us got wise, trying to fool the teacher by answering incorrectly, even if we knew the answer, so we wouldn't have to stay too long after school. It did not work. One way or another we were punished.

Many times my mother came looking for me, when I was late getting home, thinking that I was up to no good. She used to fly into a rage listening to the teacher telling her that I had not done my home work well.

Indeed, if I didn't get punished by the teacher, I was punished by my mother.

I hate to say this, but we are really punished by the verbs belonging to the second conjugation. There are close to one hundred of them which are irregular.

Fortunately we seldom use some of them. Some of them are irregular in the **present**, in the **past**, in the **future**, in the **conditional** and in the **past participle** tenses. Some are irregular only in the **past tense** and in the **past participle**.

In this lesson we will learn the peculiarities of a few of the most common verbs. The rest of them will be listed in future lessons.

I will not list the compound tenses, because you have learned that, once you know the past participle, you conjugate them by using the auxiliary tenses of **avere or essere.**

Throughout most of the persons of each tense, the **accent** falls on the second vowel, if there are more than two. It falls on the first vowel if there are less than two.

I will list only the moods and the tenses of those irregular verbs which present peculiarities.

Accend-ere *to light (up).*
Ind.: Pass. rem. Io accesi,(not accend-**ei**) tu accend-esti, egli accese, noi
        accend-emmo, voi accend-este, essi accesero.
Part. pass. Acceso. **Gerund** Accendendo.

If you look closely, you notice that only the first, third person singular and the third person plural are irregular.

Append-ere *To hang (up).*
Ind. Pass. rem. Io appesi, tu appendesti, egli appese, noi appendemmo, voi appendeste, essi appesero.
Part. pass. Appeso. **Ger.** Appendendo.

Assum-ere *To assume.*
Ind. pass. rem. Io assunsi, tu assumesti, egli assunse, noi assumemmo, voi assumeste, essi assunsero.
Part. pass. Assunto. **Ger.** Assumendo.

Bere (rare bev-ere) *To drink*
Ind. pass. rem. Io bevvi (or bevetti), tu bevesti, egli bevve (or bevette), noi bevemmo, voi beveste, essi bevvero (or bevettero).
Part. pass. Bevuto, (regular). **Ger.** Bevendo.

Cad-ere *To fall.*
Ind. pass. rem. Io caddi, tu cadesti, egli cadde, noi cademmo, voi cadeste, essi caddero.
Par. pass. Caduto, (regular). **Ger.** Cadendo.

Chied-ere *To ask.*
Ind. pass. rem. Io chiesi, tu chiedesti, egli chiese, noi chiedemmo, voi chiedeste, essi chiesero.
Part. pass. Chiesto. **Ger.** Chiedendo.

Chiud-ere *To close (up).*
Ind. pass. rem. Io chiusi, tu chiudesti, egli chiuse, noi chiudemmo, voi chiudeste, essi chiusero.
Part. pass. Chiuso. **Ger.** Chiudendo.

Conosc-ere *To know.*
Ind. pres. Io conosco, tu conosci, egli conosce, noi conosciamo, voi conoscete, essi conoscono.

Pass. rem. Io conobbi, tu conoscesti, egli conobbe, noi conoscemmo, voi
conosceste, essi conobbero.
Part. pass. Conosciuto. **Ger.** Conoscendo.

Corr-ere *To run.*
Ind. pass. rem. Io corsi, tu corresti, egli corse, noi corremmo, voi correste,
essi corsero.
Part. pass. Corso. **Ger.** Correndo.

Cresc-ere *To grow (up).*
Ind. pres. Io cresco, tu cresci, egli cresce, noi cresciamo, voi crescete, essi
crescono.
Pass. rem. Io crebbi, tu crescesti, egli crebbe, noi crescemmo, voi cresceste
essi crebbero.
Part. pass. Cresciuto. **Ger.** Crescendo.

Cuoc-ere *To cook.*
Ind. pres. Io cuocio, tu cuoci, egli cuoce, noi cuociamo, voi cuocete, essi
cuociono.
Pass. rem. Io cossi, tu cocesti, egli cosse (or cocette), noi cocemmo, voi
coceste, essi cossero.
Futuro Io cocerò, tu cocerai, egli cocerà, noi coceremo, voi cocerete, essi
coceranno.
Cong. pres. Che io cuocia, che tu cuocia, che egli cuocia, etc.
Cong. imp. Se io cocessi, se tu cocessi, se egli cocesse, etc.
Cond. pres. Io cocerei, tu coceresti, egli cocerebbe, noi coceremmo, voi
cocereste, essi cocerebbero.
Imperativo Cuoci tu, cuocia lui, cociamo noi, cocete voi, cuociano essi.
Part. pass. Cotto. **Ger.** Cocendo.

Difend-ere *To defend.*
Ind. pass. rem. Io difesi, tu difendesti, egli difese, noi difendemmo, voi
difendeste, essi difesero.
Part. pass. Difeso. **Ger.** Difendendo.

Dire (or dic-ere) *To say, to tell.*

Ind. imper. Io dicevo, to dicevi, egli diceva, noi dicevamo, voi dicevate, essi dicevano.

Pass. rem. Io dissi, tu dicesti, egli disse, noi dicemmo, voi diceste, essi dissero.

Part. pass. Detto. **Ger.** Dicendo.

Divid-ere *To devide.*

Ind. pass. rem. Io divisi. tu dividesti, egli divise, noi dividemmo. voi divideste, essi divisero.

Part. pass. Diviso. **Ger.** Dividendo.

Dov-ere *Must, shall, to have to.* This verb serves other verbs.

Ind. presente Io devo (or debbo), tu devi, egli deve, noi dobbiamo, voi dovete, essi devono (or debbono).

Futuro pres. Io dovrò, tu dovrai, egli dovrà, noi dovremo, voi dovrete, essi dovranno.

Cong. pres. Che io deva (or debba), che tu deva, che egli deva, che noi doviamo, che voi doviate, che essi devano (or debbano).

Cond. pres. Io dovrei, tu dovresti, egli dovrebbe, etc.

Part. pass. Dovuto. **Ger.** Dovendo.

Fare (or fac-ere) *To make, to do.*

Ind. pres. Io faccio, tu fai, egli fa, noi facciamo, voi fate, essi fanno.

Pass. rem. Io feci, tu facesti, egli fece, noi facemmo, voi faceste, essi fecero.

Cong. pres. Che io faccia, che tu faccia, che egli faccia, che noi facciamo, che voi facciate, che essi facciano.

Cong. imp. Se io facessi, se tu facessi, se egli facesse, etc.

Part. pass. Fatto. **Ger.** Facendo.

Legg-ere *To read.*

Ind. pass. rem. Io lessi, tu leggesti, egli lesse, noi leggemmo, voi leggeste, essi lessero.

Part. pass. Letto. **Gerund.** Leggendo

Mett-ere *To put.*
Ind. pass. rem. Io misi, tu mettesti, egli mise, noi mettemo, voi metteste, essi misero.
Part. pass. Messo. **Ger.** Mettendo.

Nasc-ere *To be born.*
Ind. pass. rem. Io nacqui, tu nascesti, egli nacque, noi nascemmo, voi nasceste, essi nacquero.
Part. pass. Nato. **Ger.** Nascendo

Pia-cere *To like*
Ind. pres. Io piaccio, tu piaci, egli piace, noi piacciamo, voi piacete, essi piacciono.
Pass. rem. Io piacqui, tu piacesti, egli piacque, noi piacemmo, voi piaceste, essi piacquero.
Cong. pres. Che io piaccia, che tu piaccia, che egli piaccia, etc.
Part. pass. Piaciuto. **Ger.** Piacendo.

Piang-ere *To cry.*
Ind. pass. rem. Io piansi, tu piangesti, egli pianse, noi piangemmo, voi piangeste, essi piansero.
Part. pass. Pianto. **Ger.** Piangendo

Pot-ere *May. Can*
Ind. pres. Io posso, tu puoi, egli puó, noi possiamo, voi potete, essi possono.
Fut. pres. Io potrò, tu potrai, egli potrà, noi potremo, voi potrete, essi potranno.
Cong. pres. Che io possa, che tu possa, che egli possa, che noi possiamo, che voi possiate, che essi possano.
Cond. pres. Io potrei, tu potresti, egli potrebbe, noi potremmo, voi potreste essi potrebbero.
Part. pass. Potuto. **Ger.** Potendo.

Prend-ere *To take. To get.*
Ind. pass. rem. Io presi, tu prendesti, egli prese, noi prendemmo, voi prendeste, essi presero.
Part. pass. Preso. **Ger.** Prendendo

Rid-ere *To laugh.*
Ind. pass. rem. Io risi, tu ridesti, egli rise, noi ridemmo, voi rideste, essi risero.
Part. pass. Riso. **Ger.** Ridendo.

Riman-ere *To remain. To stay*
Ind. pres. Io rimango, tu rimani, egli rimane, noi rimaniamo, voi rimanete, essi rimangono.
Pass. rem. Io rimasi, tu rimanesti, egli rimase, noi rimanemmo, voi rimaneste, essi rimasero.
Fut. pres. Io rimarrò, tu rimarrai, egli rimarrà, noi rimarremo, voi rimarrete, essi rimarranno.
Cong. pres. Che io rimanga, che tu rimanga, che egli rimanga, che noi rimaniamo, che voi rimaniate, che essi rimangano.
Cond. pres. Io rimarrei, tu rimarresti, egli rimarrebbe, noi rimarremmo, voi rimarreste, essi rimarrebbero.
Imper. Rimani tu, rimanga lei, rimaniamo noi, rimanete voi, rimangano essi.
Part. pass. Rimasto. **Ger.** Rimanendo

Rispond-ere *To answer. To respond.*
Ind. pass. rem. Io risposi, tu rispondesti, egli rispose, noi rispondemmo, voi rispondesti, egli rispose.
Part. pass. Risposto.
Gerund Rispondendo

Sap-ere *To know.*
Ind. pres. Io so, tu sai, egli sa, noi sappiamo, voi sapete, essi sanno.
Pass. rem. Io seppi, tu sapesti, egli seppe, noi sapemmo, voi sapeste, essi seppero.

Fut. pres. Io saprò, tu saprai, egli saprà, noi sapremo, voi saprete, essi sapranno.

Cong. presente Che io sappia, che tu sappia, che egli sappia, che noi sappiamo, che voi sappiate, che essi sappiano.

Cond. presente Io saprei, tu sapresti, egli saprebbe, noi sapremmo, voi sapreste, essi saprebbero.

Part. pass. Saputo. **Ger.** Sapendo

Scend-ere *To go down. To come down.*

Ind. pass. remoto Io scesi, tu scendesti, egli scese, noi scendemmo, voi scendeste, essi scesero.

Part. pass. Sceso. **Ger.** Scendendo.

Scriv-ere *To write.*

Ind. pass. rem. Io scrissi, tu scrivesti, egli scrisse, noi scrivemmo, voi scriveste, essi scrissero.

Part. pass. Scritto. **Ger.** Scrivendo.

Sed-ere *Ti sit (down)*

Ind. pres. Io siedo or (seggo), tu siedi, egli siede, noi sediamo, voi sedete, essi siedono or (seggono).

Pass. rem. Io sedei or sedetti, etc. (Regular form)

Fut. pres. Io siederò, tu siederai, egli siederà, noi siederemo, voi siederete, essi siederanno.

Cong. pres. Che io sieda or (segga), che tu sieda, che egli sieda, che noi sediamo, che voi sediate, che essi siedano or (seggano)

Cond. pres. Io siederei, tu siederesti, egli siederebbe, noi siederemmo, voi siederesti, essi siederebbero.

Imperativo Siedi, sieda, sediamo, sedete, siedano.

Part. pass. Seduto. **Ger.** Sedendo

Spend-ere *To spend.*

Ind. pass. rem. Io spesi, tu spendesti, egli spese, noi spendemmo, voi spendeste, essi spesero.

Part. pass. Speso. **Ger.** Spendendo

Ten-ere *To keep. To hold.*

Ind. presente Io tengo, tu tieni, egli tiene, noi teniamo, voi tenete, essi tengono.

Pass. rem. Io tenni, tu tenesti, egli tenne, noi tenemmo, voi teneste, essi tennero.

Fut. presente Io terrò, tu terrai, egli terrà, noi terremo, voi terreste, essi terranno.

Cong. pres. Che io tenga, che tu tenga, che egli tenga, che noi teniamo, che voi teniate, che essi tengano.

Cond. pres. Io terrei, tu terresti, egli terrebbe, noi terremmo, voi terreste, essi terrebbero.

Imperativo Tieni, tenga, teniamo, tenete, tengano.

Part. pass. Tenuto. **Ger.** Tenendo.

Ved-ere *To see.*

Ind. pass. rem. Io vidi, tu vedesti, egli vide, noi vedemmo, voi vedeste, essi videro.

Fut. pres. Io vedrò, tu vedrai, egli vedrà, noi vedremo, voi vedrete, essi vedranno.

Cond. presente Io vedrei, tu vedresti, egli vedrebbe, noi vedremmo, voi vedreste, essi vedrebbero.

Part. pass. Visto or veduto. **Ger.** Vedendo.

Vinc-ere *To win.*

Ind. pass. remoto Io vinsi, tu vincesti, egli vinse, noi vincemmo, voi vinceste, essi vinsero.

Part. pass. Vinto. **Ger.** Vincendo.

Viv-ere To live.

Ind. pass. rem. Io vissi, to vivesti, egli visse, noi vivemmo, voi viveste, essi vissero.

Fut. Io vivrò, tu vivrai, egli vivrà, noi vivremo, voi vivrete, essi vivranno.

Cond. pres. Io vivrei, tu vivresti, egli vivrebbe, noi vivremmo, voi vivreste, essi vivrebbero.

Part. pass. Vissuto. **Ger.** Vivendo.

72

Vol-ere *To want. Will.*

Ind. pres. Io voglio, tu vuoi, egli vuole, noi vogliamo, voi volete, essi vogliono.

Pass. rem. Io volli, tu volesti, egli volle, noi volemmo, voi voleste, essi vollero.

Fut. pres. Io vorrò, tu vorrai, egli vorrà, noi vorremo, voi vorrete, essi vorranno.

Cong. pres. Che io voglia, che tu voglia, che egli voglia, che noi vogliamo, che voi vogliate, che essi vogliano.

Cond. pres. Io vorrei, tu vorresti, egli vorrebbe, noi vorremmo, voi vorreste, essi vorrebbero.

Imperativo Vogli tu, voglia lei, vogliamo noi, vogliate voi, vogliano essi.

Part. pass. Voluto. **Ger.** Volendo.

I have listed the most common irregular verbs. Indeed, it is a long list... By having them listed together, it will be convenient to refer to them quickly. We'll learn about the rest in future lessons.

I know it is impossible to learn all of them in one lesson. It takes a long time to memorize their peculiarities. You will soon get used to recognizing some of their irregularities. As such, you will challenge your knowledge.

I too find it surprising how to remember to conjugate all these irregular verbs the correct way. It is quite overwhelmed.

SIXTEENTH LESSON

Lezione Sedicesima

Antonio, per piacere chiudi la porta. Fuori fa molto freddo. *Anthony, please close the door. It is very cold outside.*

You have already learned a great deal. So much as to be able to form meaningful sentences for every day speaking.

We have gone over some of the verbs model of the first and second conjugation and some of the irregular verbs for each conjugation. I know it takes a lot of studying to master so much work.

Yet we cannot stop when we come across obstacles along the way. We can remove them with time and keep moving ahead.

Indeed there is no way out. We still have the third conjugation to deal with.

You already know that all the verbs ending in **"ire"** belong to the third conjugation.

Most of the Italian grammar books use the verb **"sérv-ire"** *to serve* as a **verb model.** It is a useful choice for us, because it has the same meaning in both languages.

The accent rests on the **"e"** of **sérv** all through the conjugation, except for the first and third person of the *future present* which have, like every other verb, the accent resting on the last vowel. If we forget to mark it down, we have committed a big mistake.

In few cases the third person singular of the **Passato remoto** must also be marked with the accent.

As I said at the end of the last lesson, I was overwhelmed to still remember correctly the conjugation of all these verbs. The teacher was right in making us learn all these particularities fluently.

74

Servire is a transitive verb. It takes the auxiliary **Avere** to form the compound tenses. I know you can do that on your own.

VERBO MODELLO SERV-IRE
Terza Coniugazione
Modo Indicativo

Presente		Imperfetto	
Io serv-**o**	*I serve*	Io serv-**ivo**	*I used to serve*
Tu serv-**i**	*You serve*	Tu serv-**ivi**	*You* "
Egli serv-**e**	*He serves*	Egli serv-**iva**	*He* "
Noi serv-**iamo**	*We serve*	Noi serv-**ivamo**	*We* "
Voi serv-**ite**	*You serve*	Voi serv-**ivate**	*You* "
Essi serv-**ono**	*They serve*	Essi serv-**ivano**	They "

Pass. Rem.		Futuro	
Io serv-**ii**	*I served*	Io serv-**irò**	*I will (shall) serve*
Tu serv-**isti**	*You* "	Tu serv-**irai**	*You will serve*
Egli serv-**ì**	*He* "	Egli serv-**irà**	*He will serve*
Noi serv-**immo**	*We* "	Noi serv-**iremo**	*We will serve*
Voi serv-**iste**	*You* "	Voi serv-**irete**	You will serve
Essi serv-**irono**	*They* "	Essi serv-**iranno**	*They will serve*

Modo Congiuntivo

Presente		Imperfetto	
Che io serv-**a**	*That I serve*	Se io serv-**issi**	*If I served*
Che tu serv-**a**	*That you serve*	Se tu **serv-issi**	*If you* "
Che egli serv-**a**	*That He serve*	Se egli serv-**isse**	*If he* "
Che noi serv-**iamo**	*That we serve*	Se noi serv-**issimo**	*If we* "
Che voi serv-**iate**	*That you serve*	Se voi serv-**iste**	*If you* "
Che essi ser-**ano**	*That they serve*	Se essi serv-**issero**	*If they* "

Modo Condizionale

Presente

Io serv-**irei**	*I would (shall) serve*
Tu serv-**iresti**	*You will serve*
Egli serv-**irebbe**	*He will serve*
Noi serv-**iremmo**	*We will serve*
Voi serv-**ireste**	*You will serve*
Essi serv-**irebbero**	*They will serve*

Modo Imperativo
Presente

Che io serv-**a**	*Let me serve*
Serv-**i** tu	*Serve*
Serv-**a** lui	*Let him serve*
Serv-**iamo** noi	*Let us serve*
Serv-**ite** voi	*Serve*
Serv-**ano** essi	*Let them serve*

Tempi Indefiniti

Infinito presente: serv-ire	*To serve*
Infinito passato: aver serv-ito	*To have served*
Participio presente: serv-ente	*Serving*
Participio passato: serv-ito	*Served*
Gerundio presente: serv-endo	*Serving*
Gerundio passato: avendo servito	*Having served*

For purposes of phonetic quality of words, some verbs of the third conjugation form the present indicative, the conjunctive present and the imperative by adding **"isc"** to the root.

Example: **Fin-ire.** *To finish; to end.*
Ind. Pres. Io fin-**isc-o,** tu fin-**isc-i,** egli fin-**isc-e,** noi fin-**iamo,** voi fin-**ite,** essi fin-**isc-ono.** *"Io fin-o"* etc. does not sound right.

Subj. Pres. Che io **fin-isca**, che tu **fin-isca**, che egli **fin-isca**, che noi finiamo, che voi finiate, che essi **fin-iscano**.

Imperative Fin-isci tu, **fin-isca** lei, finiamo noi, finite voi, **fin-iscano** essi.

Many more verbs belonging to the third conjugation follow the same form of **finire.** I will give you some of the most common.

Capire *to understand;* **ammon-ire** *to admonish;* **ubbid-ire** *to obey;* **custod-ire** *to keep, to guard, to take care;* **costru-ire** *to construct.*

Now you try to form **l'ind. present,** the **subj. present** and the **imperative** of the above verbs, using the same format as of **finire.**
It will be a very good exercise. I know you'll enjoy practicing and be proud learning how to do this without any difficulty.

SEVENTEENTH LESSON

Lezione Diciassettesima

È il ventuno Dicembre. Oggi finisce l'Autunno e comincia l'Inverno. In questo giorno accade il Solstizio d'Inverno.

It is December twenty first. To-day Autumn ends and Winter begins. On this day the Winter Solstice occurs.

Isn't it nice? We can express our thoughts fully. This is a beautiful time of the year; yet it is depressing. The days are short. The sun is low. There is so much to do to prepare for the holidays.

Buon Natale. *Merry Christmas.*

It is depressing as much, trying to learn all those verbs. Don't get discouraged. Nothing is invincible. Think about history. Napoleon was invincible; yet at the battle of Waterloo (1815) he was defeated by the Duke of Wellington.

When I got my second heart attack, my cardiologist told me to stay busy both physically and mentally. "Don't get depressed, thinking about your illness," he advised. "Keep your mind occupied on something else."

I took his advice; as a result I wrote three books both in English and in Italian.

My advice to you is to keep studying the verbs, even if it is depressing thinking about it. When you have mastered them, everything else will fall into place. Just think... if you had nothing to do, you would end up feeling depressed just the same.

We have only a few more verbs to learn. In this lesson we are going to deal with the most common irregular ones belonging to the third conjugation. Are you all set to move ahead?

As you have learned in the previous lessons, I'll give you only the

78

moods and the tenses which have peculiarities.

Third conjugation irregular

Apr-ire *To open.*
Ind. pass. rem. Io apr-**ii** (or apersi), tu **apr-isti**, egli **apr-ì**, noi apr-**immo**, voi apr-**iste**, essi apr-**irono**.
Part. pass. Aperto. **Gerund.** Aprendo.

Copr-ire *To cover.*
It is conjugated the same way as **aprire. Part. pass.:** Coperto.

Offr-ire *To offer.* **See aprire. Part. pass.:** Offerto.

Sal-ire *To rise; to climb; to go up.*
Ind. pres. Io sal-**go**, tu sali, egli sale, noi saliamo, voi salite, essi sal-**gono**.
Cong. pres. Che io sal-**ga**, che tu sal-**ga**, che egli sal-**ga**, che noi saliamo, che voi saliate, che essi sal-**gano**.
Imperat. Che io sal-**ga**, sali tu, sal-**ga** lei, saliamo noi, salite voi, sal-**gano** essi.
Part. pass. Salito. **Gerund.** Salendo.

Ud-ire *To hear.*
Ind. Pres. Io **odo**, tu **odi**, egli **ode**, noi udiamo, voi udite, essi **odono**.
Cong. Pres. Che io **oda**, che tu **oda**, che egli **oda**, che noi udiamo, che voi udiate, che essi **odano**.
Imperat. Che io oda, odi tu, oda lei, udiamo noi, udite voi, odano essi.
Part. pass. Udito. **Gerund.** Udendo.

Usc-ire *To go out; to come out; to get out.*
Ind. Pres. Io **esco**, tu **esci**, egli **esce**, noi usciamo, voi uscite, essi **escono**.
Cong. pres. Che io **esca**, che tu **esca**, che egli **esca**, che noi usciamo, che voi usciate, che essl **escano**.
Imperat. Che io **esca**, **esci** tu, **esca** lei, usciamo noi, uscite voi, **escano** essi.
Part. pass. Uscito. **Gerund.** Uscendo.

Ven-ire *To come.*

Ind. Pres. Io **vengo**, tu vieni, egli viene, noi veniamo, voi venite, essi **vengono**.

Pass. rem. Io **venni**, tu venisti, egli venne, noi venimmo, voi veniste essi vennero.

Fut. pres. Io **verrò**, tu **verrai**, egli **verrà**, noi **verremo**, voi **verrete**, essi **verranno**.

Cong. Pres. Che io **venga**, che tu **venga**, che egli **venga**, che noi veniamo, che voi veniate, che essi **vengano**.

Cond. Pres. Io **verrei**, tu **verresti**, egli **verrebbe**, noi **verremmo**, voi **verreste**, essi **verrebbero**.

Imperativo Che io **venga**, **vieni** tu, **venga** lei, veniamo noi, venite voi, **vengano** essi.

Part. pass. Venuto. **Gerund**. Venendo.

Venire is respected the same way as **andare.** They are intransitive verbs indicating motion; therefore you must use the forms of the auxiliary **essere** to make compound tenses. **Io sono venuto, etc.**

A great number of irregular verbs show their particularities in the past simple tense. My suggestion to you is that, until you master the **passato remoto,** you can use the **present perfect** in its place.

You can say: **io ti sono venuto a trovare ieri;** instead of: **io ti venni a trovare ieri.** *I have come looking for you yesterday;* instead of: *I came looking for you yesterday.* Yesterday specifies the time.

Many verbs are derived from other verbs. They are conjugated the same as the verbs they derive from.

Example **Fare: disfare** *to undo;* **rifare** *to do again; to remake;* **soddisfare** *to satisfy.*

Venire: divenire *to become;* **sfinire** *to exhaust;* **rifinire** *to finish off.*

If you are able to recognize some of the verbs which derive from those verbs that you already know, it will be a great help to make things easier and to build your vocabulary.

Dovere *must; shall; to have to;* **potere** *may; can;* **volere** *will; to want;* **solere** *ought,* are called **verbi servili:** *modal auxiliary verbs.* They are always followed by a verb at the infinite present. They serve another verb.

> Example: **Io devo andare a casa.** *I must go home.*
> **Puoi darmi un libro?** *May you give me a book?*
> **Vogliamo aiutarvi, ma non possiamo farlo.** *We want to help you, but we cannot do it.*

You have worked very hard so far. You should be proud of your accomplishment. You cannot learn the verbs in one lesson, in one week or in one month; however, once you have mastered them, people will reward your knowledge with a surprising gentle smile.

"Non devi mai disperare." *"Never say die!"*

EIGHTEENTH LESSON

Lezione Diciottesima

Elena, oggi è il tuo compleanno, i migliori auguri.
Helena, to-day is your birthday, my best wishes.

I anticipate you are as happy as I am. We have had it with verbs. We haven't had a dull moment learning about their peculiar actions. Indeed by choosing their proper function in a sentence, they will enlighten and exalt the expression of a brilliant thought.

There are a few more types of verbs that we have to go over. We'll deal with them as we continue along.

So far we have learned about the functions and the rules of the five **variable** parts of speech.

In this lesson we'll begin learning the functions of the four **invariable** parts of speech.

Adverbs

What is an adverb? It is an invariable part of speech which modifies a verb, an adjective or another adverb.

Invariable means they do not change. They are words always written or spoken always the same. You just have to memorize each one.

The adverbs are distinguished into specific classes, according to their functions and the nature of their modification. Indeed we may distinguish them as **Adverbs of mood, of place, of time, of quantity, of affirmation, of negation, of doubt, etc.**

Adverbs which indicate **mood** are formed from adjectives and nouns. In English they end in **"ly"**. In Italian they end in **"mente"**. They are the most numerous.

Example: **Lenta-mente** *slow-ly;* **fortemente** *strongly;* **virilmente** *manly;* **certamente** *certainly;* **recentemente** *recently;* **gentilmente** *gently;* **amabilmente** *aimably;* **pienamente** *fully;* **facilmente** *easily;* **felicemente** *happily.*

You recognize them by asking *come* **"how"?**

Per piacere, parlami (cóme)? chiaramente. *Please, speak to me (how)? clearly.* Do not confuse **come** (Italian adv.) with *to come (English verb).* Be also careful about their different pronunciation.

Special forms of these adverbs are: **Bene** *well;* **male** *badly.* **volentieri** *willingly;* **come** *how;* **così** *so.*

In future lessons we'll learn that they have the comparative and superlative corresponding to the adjectives.

Volentieri *willingly;* **come** *how;* **così** *so,* are used to form **exclamation expressons.**

Che bel regalo mi hai portato. Grazie, sei così generoso!
What a nice present you have brought me. You are so kind! Thank you.

Adverbs which indicate place respond to "where" *dove?*

They are: **Qui, qua** *here;* **quaggiù** *down here;* **lassù** *up here;* **costì, costà** *here;* **li, là** *there;* **laggiù,** *down there;* **lassù** *up there.*

Venite *qui;* *là* **non** *ci* **sta il sole.** *Come here; there is no sun there.*

Davanti *in front, before;* **dentro** *inside;* **presso** *near by;* **sopra** *above;* **sotto** *under;* **fuori** *outside,* are adverbs only when they modify the verb.

Example: **Io abito sopra.** *I live up stairs*
Esci fuori; stai sempre dentro. *Go outside; you are always inside.*

We must also pay attention to **ci, vi, ne** *here, there.*
Do not confuse them with **personal pronouns.** They are adverbs when they indicate **place.**

Example: **Non conosco Boston: non *ci* sono mai stato.** *I don't know Boston: I have never been there.*

Adverbs that indicate time respond to "when" *quando.*

The most common are: **Ora, adesso** *now;* **subito** *at once;* **allora** *then;* **ieri** *yesterday;* **oggi** *to-day;* **domani** *to-morrow;* **presto** *soon;* **già** *already;* **prima** *before;* **dopo** *after;* **poi** *afterwards;* **tardi** *late;* **spesso** *often;* **sempre** *always;* **mai** *never;* **ormai** *by now;* **giornalmente** *daily;* **mensilmente** *monthly;* **annualmente** *yearly.*

Allora, quando andrete a scuola oggi? *Ci* andiamo adesso.
Then, when will you go to school to-day? We are going there now.

The adverb **mai,** when it is used after a verb, requires the negation ***non*** *not.*
Non sono *mai* stato a Plymouth. *I have never been in Plymouth.*

Adverbs that indicate quantity respond to "how much" *quanto?*

A word of advise: many people who know Italian well, still make mistakes when they write **quando** or **quanto.** Quando with **"d" indicates time. Quanto** with "t" indicates *quantity.*

Quando verrai a visitarci? *When will you come to visit us?* (**Time**).
Quanto costa la frutta? *How much does the fruit cost?* (**Quantity**).

Please, try to recognize the difference.

Other adverbs that indicate quantity are: **Nulla, niente** *nothing;* **poco** *little, not much;* **troppo** *too much;* **molto** *much, very;* **assai** *a lot;* **alquanto** *some;* **tanto** *so much;* **quanto** *how much;* **più** *more;* **quasi** *almost;* **abbastanza** *enough.*

Quanto costano le tue scarpe? Costano troppo.
How much do your shoes cost? They cost too much.

Some of the adverbs that indicate affirmation are: **Sí** *yes;* **Certo, certamente** *certainly;* **sicuro** *sure;* **sicuramente** *surely;* **indubbiamente** *undoubtedly.*

Those that indicate negation are: **No** *no;* **non** *not;* **niente** *nothing;* **nemmeno** *not even;* **mai** *never etc.*

Some of those that indicate doubt are: **Forse** *perhaps;* **probabilmente** *probably;* **possibilmente** *possibly etc.*

Sometimes **sí** and **no** are used to answer entire questions which do not need to be repeated.

Sei andato a comprare le scarpe? Sí. (si = ci sono andato a comprare le scarpe).
Have you gone to buy the shoes? Yes...

The above adverbs constitute many words to memorize. As I said earlier, I do this for the convenience of the student. I also said that if you can memorize more than one word a day, within 100 days you will have memorized 100 words or more. It would be of great help to you. Imagine what you can do with 100 words?...

Some of the above adverbs serve double functions. They are adverbs when they modify the verb. They become prepositions when they are with a name.

You will learn their respective functions in the next lessons.

I am going to give you a few sentences, each containing an adverb. You are going to translate them into English and indicate what class they belong to: mood, place etc...

Io cammino lentamente   ....

Ci siamo visti ieri   ....

Il ragazzo è caduto qui   ....

Noi abbiamo comprato molto ....

Si, abbiamo visto il pittore ....

Forse potrò venire   ....

NINETEENTH LESSON

Lezione Diciannovesima

Oggi è il ventiquattro Dicembre. È la vigilia di Natale. Mia madre passa l'intero giorno in cucina, preparando le nove pietanze che servirà all'intera famiglia questa sera. A lei piace mantenere viva la tradizione.

To-day is December twenty fourth. It is Christmas Eve. My mother spends the entire day in the kitchen preparing the nine courses which she will serve to the entire family this evening. She likes to keep the tradition alive.

Such a tradition has been handed down from generation to generation. In addition to the family dinner, the churches hold the Novena: one vesper (evening prayer) for nine consecutive nights. The shepherds also go house to house for nine days spreading the Good News, singing carols and playing the *zampogne (bagpipes)*.

The nine courses consist of vegetable soup, home made egg noodles with tomato sauce made with eels or shrimps, baccalà (dried Cod fish) and other types of fish, fried dough filled with baccalà, with apples or with other vegetables, cookies made with honey and hazel nuts, roasted chestnuts, fennel and fruits, *panettone* and *torrone.*

In some parts of Italy the long supper consists of twelve courses which represent Jesus and His twelve disciples.

All this food is enjoyed slowly, while waiting for the birth of the Bambino at the midnight Mass, which is attended by the whole family. Christmas Eve is celebrated with firecrackers and with fireworks display.

Another tradition is to put a huge Yule-log on the fire place on Christmas Eve which should keep burning until the New Year. If it lasts the full nine days, it means that there will be happiness and prosperity during the coming year.

What we are going to learn next, is not so exiting; however we must continue on.

Preposition

What is a **preposition**? It is an invariable part of speech which sets words in relation with other words.

Simple prepositions are: **Di** *of;* **a** *at, to;* **da** *from, by;* **con** *with;* **in** *in;* **su** *on;* **per** *for;* **tra, fra** *between.*

When **di, a, da, in, su** are combined with the article, they are called: **articulated preposition.**

Their combination follows the same rule applied to the determinative article.

Singular: Di + il = del; di + lo = dello (dell'); **di + la = della.**
Plural: Di + i = dei; di + gli = degli; di + le = delle.

Singular: Al, allo, alla (all'). Plural: **ai, agli, alle.**
Singular: Dal, dallo, dalla (dall'). **Plural: dai, dagli, dalle.**
Singular: Nel, nello, nella (nell'). **Plural: nei, negli, nelle.**
Singular: Sul, sullo, sulla (sull'). **Plural: sui, sugli, sulle.**

Example: Quella casa è **del** padre **dello** zio. *That house belongs to the uncle's father.*

La madre **dell'**alunno ha comprato molti libri. *The student's mother has bought many books.*

While studying the articles, we learned that, if we place them before nouns beginning with vowels, we remove their vowels and use an apostrophe.
As seen on the above example, we have to do the same thing when the articles are combined with a preposition.

In the last lesson I mentioned that some invariable words may be either adverbs or prepositions, depending on their active functions.
They are prepositions if they set a word in relation. They are adverbs if they modify the verb they are with.

Contro *against;* **davanti** *before, in front;* **dietro** *behind;* **dopo** *after;* **insieme** *together;* **intorno** *around;* **oltre** *beside;* **presso** *nearby;* **prima** *before, first;* **sopra** *above;* **sotto** *under;* **dentro** *inside, etc.*

The above invariable words serve a double purpose. They can be either prepositions or adverbs.

Example: Mia sorella è **dentro** la casa. *My sister is inside the house.*
           Dentro is a preposition because it holds the noun **house**.

       Carlo, vieni **dentro.** *Charles, come inside.*
       Dentro is an adverb. It modifies the verb **vieni**.

       Some prepositions: **Contro** *against*; **dopo** *after*; **senza** *without*; **sopra** *above*; **sotto** *under*; **tra** *between;* **verso** *toward*, when they are with a personal pronoun, they require the preposition **di**.

       Egli parla spesso **contro di me.** Io leggerò **dopo di** Carlo.
       He often speaks against me.   *I will read after Charles.*

       Davanti *before;* **dentro** *inside;* **fino** *as far as, until* require the preposition **a.**

       Ti ho visto **davanti a** casa tua. *I saw you in front of your house.*

       Insieme requires to be together with **con.**

       Sono andato a scuola **insieme con** Carlo. *I went to school together with Charles.*

       Some prepositional expressions have the same functions as the preposition: **In mezzo a** *in the middle of;* **a cagione di** *because of;* **sul conto di** *in account of ;* **per mezzo di** *by means of etc.*

       Siamo ancora qui **a cagione del** cattivo tempo.
       We are still here because of bad weather.

It took me a long time to memorize and recognize the various functions of all the above words; therefore do not get discouraged if you are somewhat confused. There comes a time when you'll be proud of yourself.

I would like to remind you that *it is easy to forget things, if you do not learn them well.*

Please do the following exercises to recognize the functions of the above words. Write down which word is an adverb and which word is a preposition.

La penna è sopra il libro.   ....
The pen is on top of the book.

Sono andato insieme con Carlo.   ....
I have gone together with Charles.

Andate avanti. Non rimanete indietro ....
Go ahead. Do not stay behind.

Venite da me insieme. Voglio vedervi. ....
Come by me together. I want to see you both

TWENTIETH LESSON

Lezione Ventesima

Oggi è un bel giorno. C'è un sole chiaro fuori.
To-day is a beautiful day. There is a clear sun outside.

Indeed, I hope you have noticed that we are applying what we have learned so far. I also know that you are anxious to find out if you have given the right answers to the exercise posed to you in the two previous lessons. You'll find the answers at the end of this lesson. In the meantime you should review those lessons to make sure that you are clearly satisfied with what you have learned.

We will encounter those words again, because they serve different functions.

Conjunctions

What is a conjunction? It is an invariable part of speech that connects other words, phrases, clauses or sentences.

They are divided into two groups: **coordinative and subordinative.** These two groups are broken up into several functions. I will try to include all of their functions in this lesson.

Coordinative conjunctions connect similar terms within the limits of a sentence or the same type of sentences within a period.

Subordinative conjunctions connect one or more secondary sentences to the principal sentence through a connection by which the conjunction indicates their subordination.

91

Coordinative Conjunctions

Copulative: E (ed) *and;* **anche** *also;* **inoltre** *moreover;* **pure** *too;* **né** *neither. nor, either;* **neanche, neppure** *not even, etc.*

Carlo **e** suo fratello sono cattivi; non voglio **neppure** vederli.
Charles and his brother are bad; I do not even want to see them.

Disjunctive: O (od) *or;* **oppure** *otherwise;* **ovvero** *or;* **altrimenti** *otherwise, etc.*

Devi scegliere: il libro **o** la penna. Presto **altrimenti** chiuderò.
You must choose the book or the pen. Quickly otherwise I'll close up.

Adversative: Ma *but;* **anzi** *in the contrary;* **invece** *indeed;* **tuttavia** *yet, nevertheless, etc.*

Pietro non ha saputo la lezione **ma** non è stato punito.
Peter did not know his lesson but he has not been punished.
Pietro è buono, **tuttavia** si comporta male.
Peter is good, however he behaves badly.

Declarative: Infatti *in fact;* **difatti** *as a matter of fact;* **cioè** *that is.*

Mio padre lavora molto; infatti lavora 12 ore al giorno.
My father works very much; in fact he works 12 hours a day.

Conclusive: Dunque, perciò *then, therefore;* **quindi** *indeed;* **pertanto** *so, etc.*

Faceva troppo caldo, perciò non sono venuto.
It was too warm, therefore I did not come.
Non hai finito il tuo lavoro, quindi quando lo finirai?
You have not finished your job, indeed when will you finish it?

Correlative: they correlate two terms or two sentences.

    E...e *and...and;* **o...o** *or...or;* **sia...sia** *either...or;* **sia...che**
    either...that; **così...come** *so much...as;* **tanto...quanto** *as much...as;*
    non solo... ma anche *not only...but also, etc.*

    Dovete deciderevi: **o** con noi **o** contro di noi.
    You must decide: or (either) with us or against us.
    Io amo mia madre tanto quanto amo mio padre.
    I love my mother as much as I love my father.

Subordinative Conjunctions

There are many subordinative conjunctions. Their function is as important.
They get their name according to the explicit function they perform.

Causal: Perché *why...because;* **poiché, giacché** *since, as;* **affinché**
    so that; **acciocché** *in order that, etc.*

    Non vogliamo questa frutta **perché** non sembra fresca.
    We don't want this fruit because it does not seem fresh.
    Venite piú vicino **affinché** vi possa sentire meglio.
    Come closer so that I can hear you better.

Temporal: Quando *when;* **mentre** *while;* **prima che** *before that;*
    dopo che *after that;* **finché** *until, etc.*

    Quando piove rimarremo in casa finché **tornerà** il sole.
    When it rains, we'll stay home until the sun will come out.

Conditional: Se *if;* **purché** *provided, as long as;* **qualora** *in case etc.*
    Portati l'ombrello **qualora** pioverà.
    Take the umbrella with you in case it (should) rain(s).

Comparative: Più che *more than,* **meglio che** *better than;* **piuttosto che**
    rather than; **eccetto che** *except that, etc.*

Piuttosto che stare in casa, andrò al cinema.
Rather than stay home, I'll go to the movie.

Interrogative: Perché? *why?;* **se** *if;* **come** *how;* **quando** *when, etc.*

Dimmi **perché** non hai voluto mangiare.
Tell me why you did not want to eat.

As you can see through the definitions and the examples, the conjunctions are defined in relation to the sentences they introduce.

The conjunction **che:** *that,* may define many functions related to the different sentences it introduces.

It is easily recognized as a conjunction when it sets relations with verbs which indicate doubts, conditions, such as *to think:* pensare; *to believe:* credere; *to anticipate:* antecipare; *to assume:* assumere; *to infer:* dedurre; *to suppose:* supporre; *to presume:* presumere; etc.

The functions in both language are the same. The hard work is to learn all these words in Italian.

I want to remind you that I have listed most of the functions of the conjunctions together, for your convenience.

Do not get discouraged because we only have one more part of speech to finish up. And... it is fairly easy.

You may have noticed that **e** and **o** can be written **ed** and **od**. Before a vowel they may take the **"d"** for euphonic purpose.

Please, turn to page 86. Let's go over the exercises.

Io cammino **lentamente.**	*I walk **slowly**. mood*
Ci siamo visti **ieri.**	*We saw each other **yesterday**: time*
Il ragazzo è caduto **qui.**	*The boy did fall **here**: place*
Noi abbiamo comprato **molto.**	*We have bought very **much**: quantity*
Si, abbiamo visto il pittore.	*Yes, we have seen the painter: afferm.*
Forse potrò venire:	***Perhaps** I will come: doubt*

Now go to page 90. Let's see if your home work is done well.

1) **Sopra** il libro: *preposition*
2) **Insieme con** Carlo: *preposition*
3) **Avanti, indietro:**   *Adverbs*
4) **Insieme:**   *Adverb*

If you still have difficulties distinguishing which same word is an adverb and which one is a preposition, depending on their functions in a sentence, please go over those lessons carefully.

Notice: **qui, qua, sta, fa,** l'accento non ci va.
Here, (here), stays, does, don't take the accent.

TWENTY FIRST LESSON

Lezione Ventunesima

È il trentuno Dicembre. È mezzanotte. Bòtte, tric-trac, fuoco artificiale, suono di campane, pop di spumanti si spandono tutto intorno. È entrato l'Anno Nouvo fra gli abbracci e l'allegria.
La tradizionale minestra di lenticchie, servita in famiglia, è segno di prosperità e di salute.

It is December thirty first. It is midnight. Loud bangs, fire crackers, fire works, spumante pops, bells ringing are heard all over. A New Year has began amongst cheers and embraces.
The traditional lentil soup, served to the family, indicates prosperity and health.

It is also a delightful day for the student who is studying my beautiful language. Indeed you have come a long way. We can already write full sentences and read them fluently.

I am very proud of your great achievement. I am also proud of the way you pronounce the Italian vowels. You no longer let the English pronunciation interfere with the Italian pronunciation.

In the last lesson I mentioned that we have one more part of speech to learn. Should we go on with it? Oh!... bravo!

We cannot give up. You have learned so much already. You can be proud of yourself.

Exclamation

What is an exclamation? It is an invariable part of speech that expresses emotion, feeling, happiness, sorrow, admiration, fear, etc.
Some common exclamation are: **Ah!, eh!, oh!, uh!, ahi!, ehi!, ohi!,**

deh! **ohibó!** *now then!,* **olà!** *hey there!,* **urrà!** *hurrah!,* **magari!** *if only!*
che!? *What!?*

The meaning of some of them varies according to the circumstances and the sound of the voice.

Ah! **oh!..** could express joy, surprise, sorrow...

Oh! che meraviglia! *Oh, how wonderful!*
Magari venisse! *If only he would come!*
Ah! poteva succedere a me! *Ah! it could have happened to me!*
Che modi sono questi! *What is the matter with you!*

Ahi and **ohi,** united with *me, form* **ahimé** or **ohimé** *dear me!* which can be used indifferently for each person.

Ahimé, che peccato! *Dear me, what a sin!*

Many words and many sounds may become exclamations, whose value is given by the tune of the voice, even if they belong to other parts of speech.

Coraggio! *Courage!;* **diavolo!** *devil!;* **guai!** *troubles!;* **Peccato!** *what a sin!;* **bravo!** *darling!;* **zitto!** *quiet!;* **bene!** *well!;* **ecco!** *here it is!;* **presto!** *hurry up!;* **via!** *away!;* **Viva!** *long live!;* **evviva!** *hurrah!, long live!*

Vai al **diavolo!** *Go to hell!*
Su, che **bravo!** *Oh, what a darling!*
Stai **zitto!** *Keep quiet!*
Evviva la regina! *Long live the queen!*

Sometimes the expression of your voice may change a sentence to a complete reverse meaning. In Italian it happens quite often.

Uh... come sei bello! It really means: *You are very ugly.*
Che bella figura hai fatto! *What an ugly example you have made!*
Bravo, sei davvero intelligente! *You are really smart!*

97

This concludes the nine basic parts of speech. As we go on, we'll continue to refine and deepen our vocabulary and our learning by going over what we left behind.

I am going to write a few sentences using words that you have memorized already. Please, read them aloud.

Esercizio di lettura *Reading exercise*

Buon giorno signor maestro, mi piace molto l'Italiano, benché abbia poco tempo per studiarlo. La mia prima lezione è stata molto difficile. Ora ho più tempo per studiare.

Sono stato nella Scozia. Ho visto la Pólizia e ho domandato a un poliziotto quale fosse l'aviogetto per Roma. L'ho guardato e ho visto la gioia nei suoi occhi. C'era anche una guardia e uno sceriffo con lui.

Il golfo di Napoli è molto bello. Ci sono tante varietà di pesci nelle sue acque. Gli spaghetti di Napoli sono squisiti. Anche gli gnocchi con i ceci sono deliziosi.

La pecora è un animale domestico. La scimmia è un animale selvatico. Dal latte di pecora si ricava formaggio forte.

Il figlio di Antonio è scarso di volontà. Tutta la gloria va a sua sorella.

I have used most of the words contained in the first lesson. It is a good way to review what we have studied from the beginning.

TWENTY SECOND LESSON

Lezione ventiduesima

Felice Anno Nuovo, Signora Lombardi. Tanti Auguri di prosperità, di felicità e di buona salute a tutta la tua (la sua, la vostra) famiglia.

Happy New Year, Mrs Lombardi. Many wishes for prosperity, happiness and good health to your entire family.

My dear student, you have worked very hard. You should feel rewarded. You should feel happy and proud of yourself. I can see in you that inner beauty of great achievement. Indeed it has not come easy.

Many visitors who go to Italy, talk vividly about its beauties. They wish to go back again.

Yes, when Nature created the world, It intended that a small portion of land would gather in itself all the beauties of creation.

It encircled this land with three enchanting seas and protected it with high mountains. It adorned it with sparkling lakes and irrigated it with limpid and resonant rivers.

It covered this land with olive trees, vineyard, with lemon and orange trees and every other kind of fruit trees.

Later on Nature gave it great minds that enriched it with famous cities, with splendid monuments, with great works of art and with historical achievement.

Such a vast beauty expands from the Alps to Sicily, to Sardinia and from the Tyrrhenian to the Adriatic sea.

Then people came to inhabit it; and these sober workers called this land *Italy.*

Nature took its time and, through earthquakes, seaquakes, hail storms, wind storms, ice ages, eruptions and any other atmospheric phenomenon that

Nature could come up with, achieved what we enjoy now.

Of course it gave this land a beautiful language which is the source of music, songs and romance.

Indeed to learn this language, it takes hard work. You have already realized this. However it will bring as much joy as the work of Nature, when you have completed the entire course.

So far we have gone over the basic parts of speech. Now we have to build on them and refine them.

You know all about the articles: **Il, lo, l', la, l', i, gli, le.** Indeed you have learned how to use them.

We are going to refer back to the noun to find out how we can enrich our vocabulary.

We have dealt with primitive nouns. Now you are going to find out how many nouns can derive from a primitive noun.

First of all I want you to know that every part of speech may become a substantive.

Il bello (adj) viene riconosciuto.

Beautiful is recognized.

Il tu (pron.) non si da a persone rispettate.

You do not address respected people with thou.

Il parlare (verb) poco è molto desiderato.

Talking less is very appreciated.

Il domani (adv.) non è tanto sicuro.

(The) to-morrow is uncertain.

Nomi derivati *Derived nouns*

We call derived those nouns that derive from a primitive noun, even if they have different meaning; although they conserve some relationship.

Giorno (prim.): giornata, giornale, giornalaio, aggiornamento, giornaliero, giornalismo, giornalista, giornalmente, aggiornare.

Day, day, newspaper, newsvendor, bringing up to date, every day, journalism, journalist or reporter, daily, to adjourn.

100

In Italian we can alter primitive nouns through a suffix; in such a case they take a different meaning.

Primitive nouns can be altered by the suffix **ino, etto, ello, uccio, one, accio.**
Ragazzo: ragazz–ino *a young or little or tiny or pretty boy.*
Ragazz-etto: *a small or young boy.*
Ragazz-ello: *a tiny boy.*
Ragazz-uccio: *a nice boy.*
Ragazz-one: *a big boy.*
Ragazz-accio *a bad or ugly boy.*

This is the normal way to alter primitive nouns. However we can achieve the same result by using the adjectives the same way we do in English.

Una casona oppure **una grande casa:** *a large house.*
Un libretto oppure **un piccolo libro:** *a little book*
Un monticello oppure **un piccolo monte:** *a small mountain.*
Una ragazzuccia oppure **una ragazza giovane:** *a young girl.*
Una finestrina oppure **una finestra piccina:** *a tiny window.*
Un cagnaccio oppure **un cane cattivo:** *a nasty dog.*

Sometime nouns change their gender when they pass from the primitive to the altered form.
La via *the street ;* **il viottolo** *the path.*
La scarpa *the shoe;* **lo scarpone** *the boot.*
Il sapone *the soap;* **la saponetta** *the bath soap.*
La stanza *the room*; **lo stanzino** *tiny room.*

False altered are those nouns which seem to be altered; however they have nothing to do with primitive nouns.

Il mulo *the mule;* **il mulino** *the mill.*
La bótte *the barrel;* **il bóttone** *the button.*

Even proper nouns can be altered.

Giuseppe: Giuseppone, Giuseppina, Peppe, Peppina, Beppe, Peppone.
Giulia: Giulietta. Lisa: Lisetta. Maria: Marietta, Mariuccia, Maruzza. Pasquale: Pasqualino, Pasqualone. Marco: Marcello, Marcellino. Francesco: Franceschino. Ciccio, etc.

Special Notes

All nouns derived from sport and gambling are masculine. They are invariable. They do not change in the plural.

**Lo sport, gli sport; il tennis, i tennis; il baseball, i baseball.
Il bar, i bar; il poker, i poker. il pinochle, i pinochle.**

Masculine and feminine nouns ending in **–i– and in stressed vowel are invariable. monosyllables are also invariable.**

Il brindisi, i brindisi *the toast(s).* **La tesi, le tesi** *the thesis.*
La crisi, le crisi *the crisis.* **La parentesi, le parentesi** *parenthesis.*

Il caffè, i caffè *coffee.* **La volontà, le volontà** *the will(s).*
La virtù, le virtù *the virtue(s).* **La bontà, le bontà** *goodness.*

Il re, i re *the king(s).* **La gru, le gru** *the crane(s).*
Il té, i té *tea.* **Il dì, i dì** *the day(s).*

Italian names ending in **–ia–** or **–io–** have a **–y–** ending in English.
Ital-ia *Ital-y;* **Mar-ia** *mar-y;* **territor-io** *territor-y;* **glor-ia** *glor-y.*

Italian nouns ending in **–aggio–** usually correspond to English nouns ending in **–age–** .
Il p-aggio *p-age;* **s-aggio** *s-age;* **cor-aggio** *cour-age;* **person-aggio** *person-age;* **equip-aggio** *equip-age or crew.* **for-aggio** *for-age.*

Italian nouns ending in –**tà**– usually correspond to English nouns ending in –*ty*–. They are feminine and carry the same meaning.

La liber-tà *liber-ty;* **la fraterni-tà** *fraterni-ty;* **la real-tà** *reali-ty;* **la necessi-tà** *necessi-ty;* **la fedel-tà** *fedeli-ty; etc.*

Italian nouns ending in –**udine**– in English they end in –**ude**–. They are feminine nouns, carrying the same meaning.

La gratit-udine *gratit-ude;* **l'altit-udine** *altit-ude;* **la longit-udine** *longit-ude;* **la moltit-udine** *multit-ude.*

Italian nouns ending in –**anza**– correspond to the English –**ance**–. They are feminine nouns, having the same meaning.

La d-anza *d-ance;* **l'arrog-anza** *arrog-ance;* **l'ignor-anza** *ignor-ance;* **la toller-anza** *toler-ance; etc.*

I have already mentioned that double consonant are very much stressed in Italian. Certain consonants in English form double consonants in Italian: *"ct and pt"* become –**tt**– ; **"dm"** –**mm**–; **ammettere** *to admit; etc.* **Atto** *act;* **fatto** *fact;* **patto** *pact;* **dottore** *doctor;* **attore** *actor; etc.*

Exercises to be translated into Italian

My little sister has my nice book. ....
I have seen a young boy to-day. ....
My house has a tiny window. ....
My brother has a big house. ....
That nice little girl is good. ....
My brother is a big boy. ....
My small garden has a tiny door. ....
I saw a nasty dog yesterday. ....
I wash myself with bath soap. ....
We cannot tolerate ignorance. ....

103

Esercizi di lettura *Reading exercises*

Oggi è una bella giornata. Il sole risplende sulla terra. Fa caldo. Ho studiato la seconda lezione molto attentamente. Abbiamo imparato la funzione dell'articolo determinativo e di quello indeterminativo. Abbiamo anche parlato delle altre parti del discorso. Maria è un nome di donna. Bello è un aggettivo qualificativo. Io, tu, egli sono pronomi personali. Amare è un verbo attivo. Domani, bene, avanti sono avverbi. Le preposizioni sono tante. La congiunzione lega tra loro due parole oppure due proposizioni. Ah! quanto lavoro!

Most of the above words are taken from the second lesson.

TWENTY THIRD LESSON

Lezione ventitreesima

Buon giorno, Signora Genovesi. Oggi è l'Epifania. La vedo triste. Non è venuta la Befana? "Si, la Befana mi ha portato tanti regali. Sono triste perché mio figlio è tornato dal Colleggio in vacanza ed ora mi parla con il Lei come te. Sembra di non far più parte della nostra famiglia. Ha scordato che con i genitori, con i fratelli, con i parenti e con gli amici si parla dando il tu. Noi non siamo più i suoi genitori. Noi siamo gente strana per lui.

Good morning, Mrs Genovesi. To-day is the Epiphany. I see you sad. The Old Fairy did not come to you? "Yes, she brought me many presents. I am sad because my son came home from College on vacation and now he speaks to me in the third person. It seems that he does not belong to our family any more. He has forgotten that with parents, with siblings, with relatives and with friends he should speak using the second person. We are no longer his parents. We are strangers to him."

The *Befana* takes the place of *Santa Claus* in Italy. She is an ugly old lady dressed as a witch. She comes down the chimney to bring gifts to good children on the sixth of January. This feast represents the Three Kings who went to Bethlehem to bring gifts to the Baby Jesus. However legend has it that, when Mary and Joseph were looking for lodging in that city, they were denied any type of accommodation by this old fairy. Following the birth of their Child in a manger, she was punished by bringing gifts to every child, so that she could make up for her inconsideration.

In this lesson we continue with the gender and number of various nouns. We are going to explore their full characteristics.

Nomi composti *Compound nouns*

Compound nouns are formed by any two parts of speech joined together. Their plural is usually formed as if they were simple nouns.

Il franco-bollo	*the stamp;*	**i francobolli**	*the stamps.*
Il passa-porto	*the passport;*	**i passaporti**	*the passports.*
Il piano-forte	*the pianoforte;*	**i pianoforti**	*the pianofortes.*
Il sordo-muto	*the deaf-mute;*	**i sordomuti**	*the deaf-mutes.*
Il cavol-fiore	*the cauliflower;*	**i cavolfiori**	*the cauliflowers.*
L'arco-baleno	*the rainbow;*	**gli arcobaleni**	*the rainbows.*
La ferro-via	*the railroad;*	**le ferrovie**	*the railroads.*

Some compound nouns remain invariable.

Il porta-cenere *the ashtray;* **i portacenere** *the ashtrays.*
Il porta-lettere *the postman;* **i portalettere** *the postmen, etc.*

Some compound nouns change both words in the plural.

La terra-cotta *the earthen ware;* **le *terre-cotte*** *earthen wares.*
La cassa-forte *the safe;* **le *casse-forti*** *the safes, etc.*

This is important to know; but to a certain extent. I think that by forming the plural as a simple noun, everybody would understand what you are trying to say.

In compound English words only the second noun changes in the plural, because the first word becomes an adjective which precedes the nouns. In such cases in Italian they are specified by the preposition **di or da.**

A gold watch: **un orologio d'oro.**
Two gold watches: **due orologi d'oro.**
A silk handkerchief: **un fazzoletto di seta.**

A Boston driver: **un autista di Boston**

A summer day: **un giorno d'estate.**

Coffee-mill **macinino da caffé;** *wine-bottle* **bottiglia da (per) vino;**
Watch-chain **catena da orologio;** *watch-chains* **catene da orologio.**
Evening dress **abito da sera; etc.**

Looking at the examples on the formation of the plural, try to form
the plural for the rest of the above exercises on your own.

Nouns ending in **cia** and **gia** are feminine. They form the plural
regularly by changing –a– to –e– when **"i" is stressed or preceded by a
vowel**

La farma-cìa	**le farma-cie**	*pharmacy (ies).*
La bu-gìa	**le bu-gie**	*lie (s) falsehood (s).*
La vali-gìa	**le vali-gie**	*Suit-case (s).*
La cami-cìa	**Le cami-cie**	*Shirt (s).*

However when **cia** and **gia are preceded by a consonant**, such
nouns lose the **"i"**.

La *lan-cia*	**le lance**	*Lance (s).*
La ma*n*-cia	**le mance**	*Tip (s).*
La spiag-gia	**le spiagge**	*Beach (es); etc.*

All the nouns of fruit-trees are masculine. The nouns of the fruit
itself are feminine.

Il melo *the apple tree.* **Il pero** *the pear tree.*
la mela *the apple (fruit).* **La pera** *the pear (fruit).*

All the nouns of cities are feminine.

La Milano; la Napoli; la Roma; la Palermo; la Firenze.

The nouns of rivers are all masculine: **Il Tevere, il Nilo. il Danubio, il Volga, il Tamigi, il Mississipì, l'Amazzone, il San Lorenzo, il Po. etc.**

There are nouns which have a common gender. The article or the vocabulary tell if they are masculine or feminine.

Il nipote   *the nephew.*   **La nipote**   *the niece.*
Il cantante *the singer (he)).* **La cantante** *the singer (she); etc.*

I am going to include a long list of nouns that form the feminine completely irregular.

Masculine		Feminine	
Dio	*God*	**Dea**	*Goddess*
Eroe	*Hero*	**Eroina**	*Heroine*
Re	*King*	**Regina**	*Queen*
Czar	*Czar*	**Czarina**	*Czarina*
Cane	*Dog*	**Cagna**	*Bitch*
Gallo	*Cock*	**Gallina**	*Hen*
Uomo	*Man*	**Donna**	*Woman*
Padre	*Father*	**Madre**	*Mother*
Genero	*Son-in-law*	**Nuora**	*Daughter in law*
Fratello	*Brother*	**Sorella**	*Sister*
Maschio	*Male*	**Femmina**	*Female*
Marito	*Husband*	**Moglie**	*Wife*
Celibe	*Single*	**Nubile**	*Single woman*
Montone	*Ram*	**Pecora**	*Sheep*
Bue	*Bull*	**Vacca**	*Cow*
Porco	*Pig*	**Scrofa**	*Sow*

Many nouns of animals and of birds must be accompanied by **maschio** or **femmina** to indicate if they are male or female.

L'aquila maschio *the male eagle* **l'aquila fem.** *Female eagle*

La rondine m. *the male swallow*   **la rondine fem.** *fem. swallow*
La tigre m.   *the male tiger*   **la tigre fem.** *fem. tiger*
La lepre m.   *the male rabbit*   **la lepre fem.** *fem. rabbit etc.*

Esercizi di lettura *Reading exercises*

Quel ragazzo ha comprato la casa del pittore. È un ragazzo virtouso.

Il padre e la madre di Giorgio abitano vicino al Po. Essi hanno una casa in America e una in Italia. Davanti alla loro casa c'è un pino alto. È difficile determinare la sua altezza.

La donna che abita vicino alla loro casa, è una brava femmina. Lei possiede molti libri e tanti altri articoli di casa.

Most of the above words are taken from the third lesson.

Traduzione degli esercizi proposti nella lezione precedente
Translation of the exercises proposed in the previous lesson

La mia sorellina ha il mio libriccino.
Ho visto un ragazzino oggi.
la mia casa ha una finestrina.
Mio fratello ha una casone.
Quella ragazzuccia è buona.
Mio fratello è un ragazzone.
Il mio giardinetto ha una porticella.
Ho visto un cane cattivo (cagnaccio) ieri.
Io mi lavo con la saponetta.
Non si puó (non possiamo) tollerare l'ignoranza.

If they are all correct, you have accomplished an extraordinary task. Be proud of yourself. If not, continue to review the previous lessons.

TWENTY FOURTH LESSON

Lezione Ventiquattresima

Buon giorno Sig. Rossini, chi aspetti a quest'ora di mattina così presto?

"Aspetto mio fratello Mario. Mi ha promesso di arrivare qui alle ore sei e un quarto. Mancano già dieci minuti alle sei e trenta e lui non si fa ancora vedere. Fa tanto freddo qua fuori! I miei piedi si sono gelati."

Good morning Mr. Rossini, whom are you waiting for so early in the morning?

"I am waiting for my brother Mario. He promised me he would arrive here by six fifteen. It is already six twenty and he has not yet shown up. It is so cold out here. My feet are frozen."

In this lesson we will discover the behavior of time. We are going to have some fun.

Secondo *second;* **minuto** *minute;* **ora** *hour;* **giorno** *day;* **settimana** *week;* **mese** *month;* **anno** *year;* **secolo** *century;* **millennio** *millenium.*

Che ora è? *What time is it?* **Sono le cinque e mezzo; oppure sono le cinque a trenta (minuti).** *It is half past five; or five thirty.* **Sono le due e quaranta; oppure sono le tre meno venti pomeridiane.** *It is two forty* or *forty past two o'clock PM.* **Sono le nove AM. (antemeridiane).** *It is nine o'clock AM.*

I giorni della settimana sono: Lunedì, Martedì, Mercoledì, Giovedì, Venerdì, Sabato, Domenica. *Monday etc.* **Luna, Marte, Mercurio, Giove, Venere.**

As you can see most of the days are named after the planets. Sabato is named for *Sabbath;* Domenica is day of rest and worship, named for Dominus (God).

What follows is a little pleasantry of a tongue-twister.

Lunedì lunedò, Martedì non ce li ho (i soldi), Mercoledì è San Clemente, Giovedì non ho niente, Venerdì son pagato, Sabato alla cantina e Domenica senza quattrini.
Monday, Monday, Tuesday I have no money, Wednesday is S. Clement, (holiday: no work), Thursday I have nothing, Friday I am going to get paid..., Saturday to the bar-room and Sunday without money.

Le stagioni. *The seasons.*

La primavera ci porta i colori, i fiori ed il profumo dell'aria fresca.
Springtime brings colors, flowers and the fragrance of fresh air.
L'estate ci porta il calore e le vacanze.
Summer brings us heat and vacation.
L'autunno ci porta la frutta e ci toglie le foglie.
Autumn brings us fruits and takes away the leaves.
L'inverno ci porta la neve e il freddo d'inferno.
Winter brings snow and is cold like hell.

I mesi dell'anno. *The months of the year.*

Gennaio scossa pagliaio. *January shakes the straw stack (windy).*
Febbraio è corto e maledetto. *February is short and cursed.*
Marzo è pazzo. *March is crazy.*
Aprile piange e ride. *April cries and laughs.*
Maggio ortolano assai paglia e poco grano. *May rain produces a lot of straw and not much wheat.*
Giugno la falce in pugno. *June sickle in hand*
Luglio ci porta il sole leone. *July brings (the) dog days.*

111

Agosto fa l'arrosto. *August roasts everything.*
Settembre è capo d'inverno. *September is the beginning of winter.*
Ottobre mette il vino in bótte. *October puts the wine in the barrel.*
Novembre: per San Martino ogni bótte è vino. *November: for the feast of S. Martin (Nov.11) every barrel is wine.*
Dicembre, davanti ti agghiaccia, dietro ti offende. *December, in the front it freezes you, in the back it offends you.*

Trenta giorni conta Novembre, con Aprile, Giugno e Settembre. Di ventotto ce n'è uno e tutti gli altri hanno trentuno (giorni).
I bet you know this one. I don't have to translate it.

Now take a box of crayons, cut some of them in even length and some of them in uneven length. Keep them handy. You must sort them each one representing a different color.

I anticipate that you know what we are going to do. Yes we are going to learn how to form the **three degrees of the adjectives.**

Let's first name the colors: **Nero** *black;* **marrone** *brown;* **rosso** *red;* **bianco** *white;* **giallo** *yellow;* **verde** *green;* **blu** *blue;* **viola** *violet;* **cenere** *ashes or gray;* **turchino** *cobalt blue.*

Every qualifying adjective is articulated into degrees.

Positive: Veloce *fast;* **bello** *beautiful;* **lungo** *long;* **corto** *short; etc.*

Comparative: divided into three groups:

Uguaglianza, maggioranza, minoranza.
Equality,   Majority,   Minority.

Uguaglianza: It expresses equality between persons or things.

Così... come *so... as;* **tanto... quanto** *as much ... as;* **come** *as...as.*

112

È così intelligente come suo padre. *He is as smart as his father.*
Carlo è alto come Mario. *Charles is as tall as Mario.*

Maggioranza: *In English such a degree of an adj. is formed with* **more...** **than***; or adding* **er.** *In Italian it is always formed with* **più... di** *o* **più...che.**

Small	**piccolo;**	*small-er*	**più piccolo.**
Happy	**felice;**	*happi-er*	**più felice.**
Handsome	**bello;**	*handsom-er*	**più bello.**
Fine	**pregiato;**	*fine-r*	**più pregiato**

La Sicilia è più grande della Sardegna.
Sicily is bigger than Sardinia.
Mia sorella è più bella di mio fratello.
My sister is more beautiful than my brother.

When the comparison is between two qualities or two verbs we must use **più...che.**

Mario è più studioso che sportivo
Mario is more fond of study than he is with sport.
È più semplice lavorare che pensare.
It is easier to work than to think.

Minoranza: it is the reverse of the above examples. Instead of using **più...** **di** or **più... che,** we use **meno... di** or **meno... che** *less... than.*

Dear	**caro;**	*less dear*	**meno caro.**
Faithful	**fedele;**	*less faithful*	**meno fedele.**
Intelligent	**intelligente;**	*less intelligent*	**meno intelligente.**

Vostro figlio è meno bello di vostra figlia.
Your son is less beautiful than your daughter.
La primavera è meno calda che l'estate.
Spring is less warm than summer.

113

Quel ragazzino è meno stanco di <u>me</u>: (not di io) as in English.
That little boy is less tired than I (am).

Superlative: divided into two groups.

Superlative absolute: In English it is formed by placing *–very–* before an adjective or adding *–est–* to it. In Italian it is formed by removing the last vowel and adding **"issimo"** or putting **"molto"** before the positive.

> **Il leone è fort-issimo.**
> *The lion is very strong.*
> **Quello studente è molto intelligente.**
> *That student is very intelligent.*
> **Giovanni è un car-issimo amico.**
> *John is a dear-est friend.*

We can express an absolute superlative by modifying the adjectives with adverbs: **bellissimo oppure assai bello; straordinariamente bello; eccessivamente bello; terribilmente bello; etc.**
Very beautiful; extraordinarily, excessively, terribly beautiful.

Superlative relative: In English it is formed by placing the article before a comparative or by *"the most" or "the least"* before a positive adjective. In Italian we achieve such a form using **"il, la, i, le più"** or **" il, la, i, le, meno"**.

> **Maria è la più felice donna del mondo.**
> *Mary is the happiest woman in the world.*
> **Alessandro è il più intelligente alunno della classe.**
> *Alexander is the most intelligent student of the class.*
> **Anna agì meno gentile di sua sorella; ma Rosa ha agito la meno gentile.**
> *Anna acted less gentle than her sister; but Rosa has acted the least gentle.*
> **Questi due sono i libri più cari che abbia letto (note: i più cari).**
> *These two are the dearest books (that) I have read.*

114

Now let's get back to the colors and have some fun. If you are working on your own, speak aloud. If you are with other students, take turns and say the words aloud.

You have the crayons in front of you cut in different lengths, right?. Pick up the red and the green ones, cut to the same length and say aloud:

"Il colore rosso è lungo come il colore verde."

Then mix them up and continue having fun...

"Il colore nero è più corto del giallo."
"Il colore marrone è meno lungo del bianco."
"Il colore blu è bellissimo."
"I colori viola e turchino sono i più belli di tutti gli altri."
"Dammi il colore più corto che hai... and so on."

This is an exciting exercise for learning the degrees of the adjectives very easily. You can continue doing this if you are having fun.

If you have time available, you should try to translate the above exercises into English.

TWENTY FIFTH LESSON

Lezione Venticinquesima

Ciao Signorina Rossini, che fa qua a quest'ora così presto? Vedo che ha l'ombrello con Lei. Ha paura che venga il cattivo tempo?

"Si, ieri era bellissimo. Oggi non è bello . È già mezz'ora che sto aspettando per l'autobus. Ho fretta. Devo andare a scuola. Farò sicuramente tardi. Il mio professore chiude la porta alle otto precise. Chi è dentro, è dentro. Chi è fuori, è fuori."

Hello Miss Rossini, what are you doing here so early? I can see that you are carrying an umbrella with you. Are you afraid that bad weather will arrive?

"Yes, yesterday it was very beautiful. To-day it is not nice. It has already been a half hour that I have been waiting for the bus. I am in a hurry. I have to go to school. I will certainly be late. My professor shuts the door at exactly eight o'clock. Who is inside, is inside. Who is outside, stays outside."

As you can see, I am using every part of speech. You should feel proud. You have come a long way.

Take a good look at the above sentences. What do you notice? Yes, the sentences are very short. Contrary to English which uses conjunctions a lot (and, and...), the Italian language prefers short, concise and clear sentences. It is much better to pause, than to waist time by using ahm..., uhu and so on. That hesitation takes the fluency away from a good speaker.

You still have more to learn about the adjective; so let's get started.

You already learned that adjectives ending in –co– and –go– in the

116

singular most of the time change to –chi– and –ghi– in the plural.

Sporco changes to **sporchi** *dirty;* **largo** to **larghi** *large; etc.*
However, for euphony sake, **magnifico** fa **magnifici** *magnificent. (masc.)*
Cattolico fa **cattolici** *catholic.*

For the same reason, going back to the nouns **amico** *friend,* **nemico** *enemy,* **greco** *Greek,* fanno **amici, nemici, greci etc.**

Adjectives ending in –ca– and –ga– (fem.) change to –che– and –ghe– in the plural: **magnifica** fa **magnifiche; larga** fa **larghe; etc.**

We can also alter the adjectives: **cattivo** *bad* can be altered to **cattivello** *not bad;* **cattivaccio** *naughty;* **cattivone** *very bad;* **cattivuccio** *little rascal.*

Quella ragazzina è molto carina. *That little girl is very cute.*

Comparatives and superlatives irregular

In addition to their regular form, some adjectives also have an irregular form.

Buono	**migliore** (più buono)	**Ottimo** (buonissimo).
Good	*Better*	Best
Grande	**maggiore**	**Massimo**
Big	*Bigger*	*Biggest*
Piccolo	**minore**	**minimo**
Small	*Smaller*	*Smallest*
Cattivo	**peggiore**	**Pessimo**
Bad	*worse*	*worst*
Molto	**più**	**moltissimo**
Many	*more*	*most*

It is very clear that every language has its irregularities.
Who writes or speaks may choose opportunely one or the other form. In some cases, however, we must use the Latin forms.

Ho ricevuto il massimo rendimento con il minimo studio.
I have received the maximum reward with minimum study.

Old **vecchio** *has two comparatives and two superlatives in English: the first is formed regularly and indicates age. The second indicates age amongst siblings or children.* In Italian *maggiore* is used in such a case.

Charles is the eldest brother.   Carlo è il fratello maggiore.
Mary is the elder sister.   Maria è la sorella maggiore.
Charles is older than Frank. Carlo ha più anni di Franco.
Susan is the oldest woman in the family.
Susanna è la donna più vecchia della famiglia.

Note: In English adjectives which indicate length, width, height, and age are found at the end of a sentence. In Italian they follow the normal pattern.

My room is twelve feet long.
La mia stanza è lunga dodici piedi.
Johnny's cat is three years old.
Il gatto di Giovanni ha tre anni.
My garden is two hundred feet wide.
Il mio giardino è largo duecento piedi.
My sister's table is two feet tall.
Il tavolo di mia sorella è alto due piedi.
Our street is forty feet wide.
La nostra strada è larga quaranta piedi.

Numbers: All *ordinal* numbers are invariable in Italian, except <u>uno</u> *and* <u>una</u> (fem.). On the contrary all the *cardinal* numbers are variable.

Ordinal

1 uno	6 sei	11 undici	16 sedici
2 due	7 sette	12 dodici	17 diciassette
3 tre	8 otto	13 tredici	18 diciotto
4 quattro	9 nov	14 quattordici	19 diciannove
5 cinque	10 dieci	15 quindici	**20 venti**

118

21 vent-uno	31 trent-uno	**80 ottanta**
22 venti-due	32 trenta-due	81 ottant-uno
23 venti-tre	**40 quaranta**	**90 novanta**
24 venti-quattro	43 quaranta-tre	99 novanta-nove
25 venti-cinque	**50 cinquanta**	**100 cento**
26 venti-sei	56 cinquanta-sei	125 centoventicinque
27 venti-sette	**60 sessanta**	**200 duecento**
28 vent-otto	67 sessanta-sette	520 cinquecentoventi
29 venti-nove	**70 settanta**	**1000 mille**
30 trenta	79 settanta-nove	**1000000 un milione**

Cardinal

Starting with number eleven, cardinal numbers in Italian remove the last vowel and add – **esimo** – which in English is equal to *"th" (50th)*.

1st	primo	11th	undic-esimo
2nd	secondo	15th	quindic-esimo
3rd	terzo	20th	vent-esimo
4th	quarto	37th	trentasettesimo
5th	quinto	92th	novantadu-esimo
6th	sesto	125th	centoventicinqu-esimo
7th	settimo	637th	seicentotrentasett-esimo
8th	ottavo	1000000th	milionesimo
9th	nono	1000000000th	miliardesimo
10th	decimo	1200th	milleduecent-esimo

Of course we can make fractions, multipliers and roman numerals out of these numbers.

Un terzo *one third* 1/3; **tre quarti** *three forth 3/4;* **cinque decimi** *five tenths 5/10;* **cinquanta centesimi** *fifty hundredths 50/100; etc.*

Doppio *double;* **duplice** *two fold;* **triplo** *triple;* **triplice** *three fold.*

Il secolo XXI *the XXI century;* **Enrico IV** *Henry IV; etc.*

Mezzo *half* (½) is variable placed before a noun; remains invariable when used after a noun.

Un mezzo litro di latte. *One half liter of milk.*

Dieci litri e mezzo di vino. *Ten and a half liter of wine.*

Dammi una mezza dozzina di uova. *give me half a dozen eggs.*

Dammi una dozzina e *mezzo* di uova. *Give me 1 ½ dozen eggs.*

Numbers can be made collective. In such a case they become nouns and follow the same rules.

Ambo *both,* **decina** *about ten,* **centinaia** *hundreds,* **duello** *duel.* **terzetto** *trio,* **triennio** *triennium, etc.*

Centinaio e migliaio change to the feminine in the plural.

Le centinaia, le migliaia.

Questa mattina ho visto una decina di uccelli.
This morning I have seen (saw) about ten birds.

Gli spettatori vennero a migliaia a guardare la partita.
Spectators came by the thousands to watch the game.

When we indicate dates, we write the days and the years with Arabic numbers. The months are written in figures.

16 gennaio 1975. *January 16, 1975.*

Note: the months are written after the days in Italian.

If the year is omitted we write: **Il 10 di ottobre; il 6 di marzo.** If the year is included, we write: **Il 10 ottobre 1967** without **–di–** .

In English we may write: *In the year nineteen hundred and five; or in the year one thousand nine hundred and five.*

In Italian we use only one form: Nell'anno mille novecento cinque. *In the year one thousand nine hundred and five*

Pratica: esercizi da tradurre in Italiano.

One thousand students went to classes yesterday.

....

I have spent about one hundred dollars.

....

We wish that the XXI century will continue to be good.

....

The bus arrived a half hour late.

....

Our school is ninety three feet wide.

....

How old is your father? He is thirty five years old.

....

My sister is the eldest in the family.

....

Who eats well, will always be healthy.

....

I got home after a two and (one) half hour walk.

....

On October twelfth we celebrate Columbus day.

....

Esercizi di lettura

Il ragazzo ha una barca che si chiama Virtù. Un pittore virtuoso ci ha pitturato il fiume Po ai lati.
Questo libro è molto apprezzato in America. È un articolo molto bello. Mio padre e mia madre vivono in Giorgia. Una donna, loro amica, vive in Florida. Essi hanno due figli maschi e tre figlie femmine. Davanti alla loro casa ci sono tanti pini alti.

Most of the words used in this exercise are taken from the third lesson. Of course you remember them.

TWENTY SIXTH LESSON

Lezione ventiseiesima

Ciao Luigi, l'hai letto il mio libro? Cosa ne pensi? Ti piace?
"Si, ne ho letto la metà. Appena l'avrò finito, te lo restituirò."

*"Hello Luis, have you read my book? What do you think about it?
Do you like it? "Yes, I like it. I have read half of it. As soon as I've finished
it, I shall return it to you."*

As the student may notice, the above sentences use the interrogative
form of the verb. The Italian language has two auxiliary verbs: **to have** and
to be. The English, however, has three: ***to have, to be and to do.***

We have already studied the first two. Now let's learn the function
of **to do.** In Italian the interrogative and negative form of the verbs is done
in the normal way: **Avete scritto?** *Have you written?* **No, io non ho
scritto.** *No, I have not written.* Both languages follow the same function.

English uses **do, did, to emphasize** the importance of the
interrogation. It has no relevance at all in Italian.

> ***Do you know what you are learning? Yes, we do. (Yes, we know).***
> Lo sapete cosa state imparando? Si, lo sappiamo.
> ***Didn't I tell you to stop? Why didn't you do it?***
> Non ti ho detto di fermarti? Perché non l'hai fatto?

In English ***do, does*** is sometime used to substitute another verb. ***Did***
is also used to form the past tenses.

> ***Do you travel often? I do.***
> Viaggiate spesso? Si.

Charles works much harder than his brother does.
Carlo lavora molto di più che suo fratello.
How do you do? I am fine, thank you.
Come stai? Sto bene, grazie.
Did you see my grandmother yesterday? I did.
Avete visto mia nonna ieri? Si, l'ho vista.

Shall, will, should, would, to have and to be follow the same rules as **to do** when used to form the interrogative.

In Italian a simple – **si** – or – **no** – serve the purpose if one does not want to repeat the whole sentence.

Will you go to Naples with me? I will not.
Andrete a Napoli con me? No.
Shouldn't she call her father? She should.
Non dovrebbe chiamare suo padre? Si.
Has your mother received my letter? She has.
Ha tua madre ricevuto la mia lettera? Si. (L'ha ricevuta).
Was John with you on vacation. He was.
C'è stato pure Giovanni a passare le vacanze con te? Si.
Could you repeat what you have said? I could.
Potresti ripetere quello che hai detto? Si.

I have already mentioned that double consonants are very much stressed in Italian. **Q** is reinforced by putting **c** in front of it: **Acqua** *water;* **acquistare** *to acquire;* Only one word doubles the **q: soqquadro** *muddle.* **Q** substitute **c** before the vowels **ua, ue, ui, uo: quale** *which;* **questo** *this;* **aquila** *eagle;* **obliquo** *oblique;* **equatore** *equator;* **equivalente** *equivalent;* **equilibrio** *equilibrium; etc.*

However some words must take – **c** – **and not** – **q** – before those vowels. Here are some examples: **Cospicuo** *conspicuous;* **cuoio** *leather;* **cuore** *heart;* **cuoco** *cook;* **innocuo** *harmless;* **percuotere** *to strike;* **promiscuo** *mixed;* **riscuotere** *to collect;* **scuola** *school;* **scuotere** *to shake; also words derived from these.*

123

There are some words in Italian when **gli (Figlio)** loses its Italian sound and is pronounced like in English: **Glicerina** *glycerine;* **negligente** *negligent;* **geroglifico** *hieroglyfical;* **Anglicano** *Anglican; etc.*

To prevent making a mistake, always use – **m** – in front of **"P" and "B": Compagnia** *company;* **combattere** *to fight;* **campagna** *countryside;* **combinare** *to combine; etc.*

Posing the voice where the accent is indicate, is very important in Italian. There are some words that are written the same way, but have complete different meanings. You must really pay attention to this.

I am going to write down some of the most common:

Àncora *anchor;* **ancóra** *still, yet;* **bàlia** *pediatric nurse;* **balía** *to the mercy of;* **càpitano** *they happen;* **capitàno** *captain;* **compíto** *finished;* **còmpito** *task, duty;* **nèttare** *nectar;* **nettàre** *to clean;* **pèrdono** *they lose;* **perdóno** *forgiveness;* **sùbito** *at once;* **subìto** *undergone; etc.*

When you are not sure of their meaning, please consult the dictionary.

Some words haveone meaning when they carry an accent; and a complete different meaning when they don't:

È *is;* **e** *and;* **dà** *give;* **da** *from;* **dì** *day;* **di** *of;* **sé** *self;* **se** *if;* **né** *neither... nor;* **ne** *about him, her, it, them, about this, that, any, some ;* **là, lì** *there;* **la** *the*; **li** *them;* **ché** *why;* **che** *that;* **sì** *yes;* **si** *self; etc.*

If some of the above words are of interest, you may record them yourself. I wrote them in both languages to make it easier to accede.

Exercises to translate into Italian

Have you written a letter to Peter? I have not.

....

My brother is ten years older than me.

....

124

The weather is very beautiful to day.

....

Did you go to Naples? Not yet.

....

We have learned about the equator in school.

....

The Captain has undergone an operation.

....

Translation of the exercise from the 25th lesson

1) Mille studenti andarono nella classe ieri.
2) Ho speso una centinaia di dollari.
3) Ci auguriamo che il ventunesimo secolo sarà buono.
4) L'autobus è arrivato mezz'ora tardi.
5) La nostra scuola è larga novantatre piedi.
6) Quanti anni ha tuo padre? Ne ha trentacinque.
7) Mia sorella è la maggiore della famiglia.
8) Chi mangia bene, bene sta.
9) Sono arrivato a casa dopo due ore e mezzo di cammino.
10) Il dodici di ottobre noi celebriamo la festa di Cristoforo Colombo.

Esercizi di lettura

Oggi è una bellissima giornata. Non piove. Mi piace stare fuori. Nella classe di Giulio c'insegna un maestro alto. Nella classe di Giulia c'insegna una maestra di Torino. Lei è una signora bella e intelligente. Il professore ha un cavallo e una cavalla. Il dottore e la dottoressa hanno una casa grande. Essi abitano vicino alla casa del poeta e della poetessa. La professoressa abita molto più lontano.
L'attore e l'attrice recitano spesso nel grande palazzo del principe e della principessa. Essi sono ben qualificati nelle loro recite.

I know that you have figured out where most of the words used in this exercise come from. Yes, from the forth lesson.

TWENTY SEVENTH LESSON

Lezione ventisettesima

Che splendido spettacolo ci presenta la campagna oggi! La neve ha dipinto un magnifico quadro. Non possiamo biasimare la Natura per una scena tanto meravigliosa. Che ne dice, Signora Puccini?

"Puó essere; ma non c'è niente di straordinario. Quello che io biasimo è il freddo. Ne sono completamente sicura. Mi sto ghiacciando. Te lo dico sul mio onore.

What a splendid spectacle the countryside presents to us to-day! The snow has painted a magnificent picture. We cannot blame Nature for such an astonishing scene. What do you say, Mrs. Puccini?

"It may be; but there is nothing extraordinary. What I blame is the cold. I am quite sure of it. I am freezing. I tell you this on my honor.

Isn't it astonishing to be so far ahead! We can make up so many meaningful sentences.

Learning a second language is the same as learning a musical instrument. It is very difficult at first; so much as being tempted to throw the instrument through the window. However, after a lot of hard work, that beautiful sound that delights our ears, gives us so much pleasure.

Indeed a musician has to keep practicing, otherwise the flow of harmonious music becomes less virtuous. It is also hard to improvise to make that song magnificent.

Learning a second language takes the same effort. You cannot let go otherwise the time spent learning all those words and rules will slowly fade away. I know it very well. To keep up with the languages that I know, I have to do a lot of reading and listening. Nowadays we are fortunate to have all kinds of resources to practice. We can practice in the stores and at home.

126

Enclitics

Most of the pronominal particles (indirect personal pronouns) will attach themselves to a preceding word and become part of it. In English it is marked with an apostrophe: ***Give'em the work.*** (informal English). **Da loro il da fare.**

In Italian it is a common occurrence: Dici a me: **dimmi** *tell me*; dici lo a me: **dimmelo** *tell it to me;* manda a me: **mandami** *send to me;* manda a me lo: **mandamelo** *send it to me;* date a me ne **dammene** *give me some.*

Ho ordinato dei libri. Vi prego, mandatemeli subito.
I have ordered some books. Please, be kind to send them to me at once.
Dimmi con chi vai e ti dirò chi sei.
Tell me whom you go with and I'll tell you whom you are.

Elision and truncation

You already know that the article **lo, la, una** take the apostrophe before words that begin with vowels. It would sound bad if we should write **lo uomo** (l'uomo) *the man;* **la ape** (l'ape) *the bee;* **la anima** (l'anima) *the soul;* **lo amico** (l'amico) *the friend.*

The same rule applies with the prepositions compounded with such articles: **Dello, alla, dalla etc.** You must apply the above rule.

However the **elision** is facultative with the plural article **gli** when a word begins with "**i**". We can write **gl'ingegneri or gli ingegneri** *the engineers.* We follow the same rule with the pronouns **mi, ti, si, vi, ne, lo**:
Ti aspetto or t'aspetto fuori. *I wait for you outside.*
Il miele si attacca or s'attacca alle dita (il dito sing. le dita plur.).
Honey sticks to the fingers.

Truncation (cutting off the last vowel) occurs for euphonical purpose.
Un amico: *sounds good;* **uno amico:** *sounds bad;*
Quello *that;* ***bello*** *beautiful;* **buono** *good;* **grande** *big;* **santo** *saint,*

lose the last vowel before masculine nouns beginning with consonant. However **Quello** follows the same rule as for the article **lo** before **s impure and z; quel pittore** *that painter;* **quel-lo stupido** *that stupid.*

Io ho regalato un **bel** libro a un **buon** babino.
I have given a nice book to a good boy as a present.

Grande may also be truncated before feminine and plural nouns.

Mi sono tagliato un dito. Che **gran** dolore che sento!
I have cut my finger. What a big pain I feel!
Quella donna ha fatto **gran** carriera. Sono gran cose, sapete?
That woman has had a successful career. Are big things, you know?

Alcuno *some, a few, any;* **nessuno** *no, nobody, anybody;* **ciascuno** *each one,* follow the same rule reserved for the indet. articles **uno** and **una.**

Nessun uomo è venuto a lavorare. *No man has come to work.*
Io non ho fatto alcun errore. *I did not make any mistake*

Tale *such, someone;* **quale** *which, what, who, whom, that, whose,* may be truncated; but they never take the apostrophe: **qual errore** *which error;* **un tal coraggio** *such a courage.*

Lascia la cosa qual è. *Leave the thing the way it is.*
C'è voluto un tal coraggio! *It took such a courage!*

Punctuation marks

In Italian we have the same punctuation marks as in English. They are named differently; but fulfill the same task.

Virgola – , – *comma;* – ; – **punto** e **virgola**; – : – **due punti**; – . – **punto**; – ? – **punto interrogativo**; – ! – **punto esclamativo**; – ... – **punti di sospensione**; – " " – **virgolette**; – ( ) – **parentesi**; – – – **trattino**; (–) **lineetta**.

Capital Letter

Capital letters are used in Italian the same way as in English. However when the names of people and inhabitants are used as adjectives, they do not take capital letters in Italian. The plural is formed regularly.

Gli Italiani sono bravi costruttori. *Italians are brave builders.*
Molti cittadini americani vivono in Italia.
Many American citizens live in Italy.
Un gran numero di Milanesi lavora nell'industria Pirelli.
A large number of Milanese work at the Pirelli factory.
Questa mattina è venuto un Italiano, un Francese e un Inglese.
This morning an Italian, a Frenchman and an Englishman came.
I Francesi, gli Spagnoli, gli Svizzeri, i Portoghesi e i Tedeschi vivono in Europa.
The French, the Spanish, the Swiss, the Portuguese and the Germans live in Europe.
Le contadine lavorano nella campagna.
The countrywomen work on the farm.

Esercizi da tradurre in italiano

To-day is very cold. It is seven degrees below zero.

....

It snowed the whole night. Much snow has fallen.

....

The Alps, the Apennines and the countryside are all white.

....

Have you ever seen so much snow before? I did.

....

You do not have any right to do this to that little boy.

....

Send me ten dozen eggs. Send them to me at once.

....

That's a big building. Whose is it?

....

Which error is worse? Mine or yours.

....

Translation of the exercises from the 26th lesson

1) Avete scritto una lettera a Pietro? No.
2) Mio fratello ha dieci anni più di me.
3) Il tempo è molto bello oggi.
4) Ci sei andato a Napoli? Non ancora.
5) A scuola abbiamo imparato quello che riguarda l'Equatore.
6) Il capitano ha subìto un'operazione.

Esercizi di lettura

È già sera. Fuori si sta facendo buio. Sulla televisione parlano della rivoluzione avvenuta nella stazione della nostra nazione. Che gran disillusione!

Un'amica nostra è andata al parco che sta vicino al lago di Garda. Là ha trovato le sue compagne di scuola.
Suo fratello è rimasto a casa con i suoi genitori. Essi hanno molto lavoro nella campagna. Posseggono una gran proprietà.

Most of the words used for the above exercises are taken from the fifth lesson. It will take you back to recent memories...

TWENTY EIGHTH LESSON

Lezione Ventottèsima

Signore, dove abita Lei? Risiede vicino oppure lontano dal lavoro?
"Abito a Torino. Io lavoro nella FIAT, la fabbrica italiana di automobili di Torino. Risiedo a circa una mezz'oretta di autobus dalla fabbrica. Non è molto dacché lavoro là dentro. Quella fabbrica è conosciuta."

Sir, where do you live? Do you reside near or far from work?
"I live in Turin. I work at FIAT, the Italian automobile factory of Turin. I reside about a half hour bus drive from the factory. I haven't worked there for very long. The factory is a well known place.

I am really proud of you. I can see that your vocabulary is getting rich. You no longer have a deficiency of words. Your thought is no longer foggy and intricate. You are acquiring a major lucidity with your notion and with your words. What was an indifferent matter sometime back, is now acquiring high value which is rewarded with praise. Indeed we should be able to retain what we learn and keep improving ourselves.

The words we learn must be precise, colorful and useful. We must learn as many words as we can, so we will not be in jeopardy of dragging a beautiful sentence.

Pronome intensivo *Intensive pronoun*

Sometime we pretend to insist when we want to say something specifically. We use *himself* **lui;** *herself* **lei;** *themselves* **loro.**
Lui, lei, loro become subjects.

Lui l'ha voluto fare. *He wanted to do it himself.*
Lei ci ha telefonato ripetutamente. *She called repeatedly herself.*
Loro vogliono sempre fare le cose da soli.
They always want to do their things themselves.

It happens more frequently after a verb.

È venuto lui a cercarmi. *He came looking for me himself.*
Me l'ha portato proprio lei. *She brought it to me herself.*
È meglio che ci pensino loro a riportarmelo.
It is better that they worry themselves to bring it back to me.

When we utilize the exclamation mark, we use **lui, lei, loro;** in addition to **me** and **te.**

Beato lui! *Lucky fellow!* **Felice come lei!** *Happy like her!*
Disgraziati loro, poveri figli! *Unlucky them, poor children!*
Infelice me! *Unlucky me!*
Che fregatura hanno fatta a te!
What a swindle they have done to you!
Non c'è nessuno coraggioso come lui.
There is nobody courageous like him.

Partitive article

Partitive indicate a part as distinct from a whole: a certain quantity. In English we use **some, any, no, not any** to accomplish a portion.

In Italian we use **di, del, dello, dei, delle, qialche, alcuno, ne, nessuno, un poco.** When It is used as a preposition plus the determinative article, it is clear that they follow the same rule studied about the article.

If I will have some time left, I'll come to visit you.
Se avrò **del** tempo, verrò a visitarti.
Do you have any idea of what you are doing?
Hai **alcuna** idea di quello che stai facendo?

Mother, do you have any bread? Please give me some.
Mamma, hai **del** pane. Ti prego, dammene **un poco**.
May I give you some apples?
Posso darvi **delle** mele?
Who has some good books to give me. I don't have any.
Chi ha **dei** buoni libri per me? Io non **ne** ho.
Who has some tooth brushes for me? I have some.
Chi ha **dei** spazzolini da denti per me? Io **ne** ho **alcuni**.
May I have some milk for my coffee? Yes, I'll give you some.
Posso avere **del** latte per il mio caffè? Si, te **ne** do un poco.

In English we cannot use a double negation with **no, not, nothing, none.** Nothing changes to *any, anything;* where as in Italian we **must use** a double negation with **nessuno, alcuno, non, nulla, niente.**

I went to the library; but I did not find any books that I wanted.
Sono andato in libreria; ma **non** ho trovato **nessun** libro che volevo.
I have no intention to go to the movies.
Non ho **alcuna** intenzione di andare al cinema.
I cannot find anything I need.
Non posso trovare **nulla** di quello che mi serve.

Calculation signs. Calcoli

Except for the division sign, there is no other difference in either language.
Plus + più: addizione; *minus* - meno; sottrazione, *X or .* moltiplicazione, *(time,* per); : divisione; *% per cent* percentuale; *equal* = uguale; *square root* radice quadrata; *exponent* esponente.

29 + (più)	*9* + 4 make 13; write 3 and carry 1. 2+1 are 3 plu 1
<u>14</u> = (uguale)	*make 4; total 43. Addenda* **addendi.**
43 Totale	**9+4 fanno 13; scrivo 3 e porto 1. 2+1 fanno 3 e 1 fanno 4; totale 43.**

133

38 - (meno)   *Minuend* diminuendo
<u>15</u> = (uguale)   *Subtrahend* sottraendo
23   differenza *Remainder*

4 X 8 = 32;   quattro per otto uguale trentadue.
12 : 3 = 4;   Dodici diviso tre uguale quattro.
Oggi l'interesse è salito al 6% (per cento).
To-day the inerest went up to 6%.

Esercizi da tradurre in Italiano

Yesterday I went to the store and I bought some coffee and some milk.

I paid 3 dollars for milk, plus 5 dollars for coffee: a total of 8 dollars.

The policeman came looking for me himself.

Lucky that woman that does everything for herself!

Not even him would do a thing like that.

Many women are beautiful like her.

Translation of the exercises proposed on the 27th lesson

1) Oggi fa molto freddo. La temperatura è scesa a sette gradi sotto zero.
2) È fioccato la notte intera. È caduta molta neve.
3) Le Alpi, gli Appennini e la campagna sono tutti bianchi.
4) Avete visto tanta neve prima? Si, ne ho vista.
5) Voi non avete alcuna ragione di far questo a quel ragazzino.
6) Mandatemi dieci dozzine di uova. Mandatemele subito.
7) Quello è un gran edificio. Di chi è?
8) Qual errore è peggiore? Il mio o il tuo.

Esercizi di lettura

Gli scienziati studiano gli organi degli animali, quando vanno nel giardino zoologico. Questa è per loro l'arte per dimostrarlo.
Gli studenti intelligenti vanno a scuola e portano i libri nello zaino.
Questo dimostra che cercano una buona educazione.
Gli uomini sono buoni come gli angeli quando essi aiutano gli altri.
L'apostrofo prende il posto dell'ultima vocale della parola precedente.
Questo, quello, quella sono aggettivi oppure pronomi dimostrativi.

The above reading exercise will take you back to the sixth lesson.

Decimal numbers

It is very important to notice that decimal signs in Italian are completely different than in English.

In Italian the comma separates a decimal number from a whole number; and the point indicates groups of whole numbers: 25.342,75.

In English it is the complete opposite: 25,342.75. The point divides the unity from the decimal.

I want to stress this inequity, because I have made many mistakes.

Soon after I arrived in this Country, I was inducted into the United States Army. I didn't know much English; but I was very good with numbers. After I took the exam, the Officer in charge called me over and remarked: "Your calculation is all wrong. The result is right but the decimal is in the wrong place. Don't you know any better?"

He was about to reject me. Before he could put the rejection stamp on my papers, I tried to explain, with my very little English and with hand signals, the cause of the mistakes. Indeed I had the math questions all right.

He, then looked at me, smiled and said: "You'll make a very fine soldier."

TWENTY NINTH LESSON

Lezione Ventinovesima

Buon pomeriggio Signora Ghiberti, vedo che sei stata al super mercato a comprare tutta quella roba. Hai degli invitati questa sera? "Si, oggi è il compleanno di mio marito. Compie quarantatre anni. Questa sera facciamo festa in famiglia. Ho comprato dello spumante, prodotto della provincia d'Asti nel Piemonte. Ho comprato del vino bianco prodotto nel Veneto, nella provinčia di Verona. La frutta fresca e i vegetali vengono dalla Campania, proprio dalla provincia di Napoli. La carne, l'olio d'oliva, gli spaghetti, le uova e i salumi per l'antipasto sono della Toscana: prodotti locali della nostra provincia di Firenze. Solo il prosciutto viene da Parma, una delle otto province dell'Emilia-Romagna."

Good afternoon Mrs. Ghiberti, I can see that you have been at the super market to buy a lot of food. Do you have some guests for this evening?

"I have. To-day is my husband's birthday. He will be forty three years old. To-night we will have a family party for him. I have bought some spumante produced in the province of Asti, in the Piedmont region. I have bought some white wine produced in the Veneto region, in the province of Verona. The fresh fruits and the vegetables come from the Campania region, from the province of Naples. The meat, olive oil, spaghetti, eggs and cold cuts for antipasto are from Tuscany: produced locally in our own province of Florence. Only the prosciutto comes from Parma, one of the eight provinces of Emilia-Romagna."

Translating the use of *one, ones and one's*

In English the word *one*, the plural *ones* and the possessive *one's* are translated in Italian with the partitive **ne** and **dei.** They substitute a noun already expressed in the same sentence or in a preceding question.

I have three pretty birds and you have an ugly one.
Io ho tre graziosi uccelli e tu **ne** hai uno brutto.
Do you know any good places where to go?
Sapete **dei** buoni locali dove andare?
I know some very good ones.
Io **ne** conosco **dei** buonissimi.
Our team is a very strong one. We win all the time.
La nostra squadra è fortissima. Noi vinciamo sempre.

In Italian an adjective can become a substantive. In English it cannot. It must be followed by the noun it specifies. Therefore *one or ones* are used to take their places.

That gentleman bought a new house and sold an old one.
Quel signore comprò una casa nuova e **ne** vendette una vecchia.
My gold watch is more expensive than your silver ones.
Il mio orologio d'oro costa di più dei vostri orologi d'argento.

One and *ones* can also be used to take the place of **bambini, piccini, piccoli, piccolini.**

How many little ones *do you have?*
Quanti bambini avete?
Where do you keep your dog and its young ones?
Dove tieni il tuo cane ed i suoi piccolini?

One's at the end of a sentence indicates possession.

The American woman's husband is younger than the English one's.
Il marito della signora americana è più giovane di quello della signora inglese.

Indefinite pronouns

Indefinite pronouns follow the same rule as **some** and **any**: in Italian they want the double negative, whereas in English they don't.

Qualcuno, alcuno: *someone, somebody.*
Qualcheduno, chiunque: *any one, anybody.*
Nessuno, niuno: *no one, nobody, not anybody, not any one, none.*
Ognuno, ciascuno, tutti: *everybody, every one.*
Qualche cosa, alcuna cosa: *something, anything.*
Nulla, niente: *nothing, not anything.*
Ogni cosa, tutto: *everything.*

Io non ho nulla da dirvi.
I have nothing to tell you; or – I don't have anything to say.–
Non ho visto nessuno dei tuoi amici.
I have seen no one of your friends; or – I have not seen any of them.–
Non c'è nessuna frutta migliore della mia.
There is no fruit better than mine.
Ognuno deve fare il proprio dovere.
Everybody must do his / her own duty.
Non avete scordato niente?
Didn't you forget anything?

Expand your vocabulary

In this lesson you are going to learn the names of some animals and the sound they make.

Animale	**Suono**	*Animal*	*Sound*
La pecora, l'agnello	belare	*The sheep, the lamb*	*to bleat*
La capra	belare	*The goat*	*to bleat*
Il cane	abbaiare	*The dog*	*to bark*
Il gatto	miagolare	*The cat*	*to mew*

Animale	Suono	*Animals*	*Sound*
Il cavallo	nitrire	*The horse*	*to neigh*
La mucca (vacca)	muggire	*The cow*	*to low, to moo*
L'asino, la zebra	ragliare	*The donkey, the zebra*	*to bray*
Il leone, la tigre	ruggire	*The lion, the tiger*	*to roar*
Il maiale (porco)	grugnire	*The pig (pork)*	*to grunt*
Il serpente	sibilare	*The snake*	*to hiss*
L'orso	grugnire	*The bear*	*to growl*
la volpe	ululare	*The fox*	*to howl*
Il lupo	ululare	*The wolf*	*to howl*
Il topo	squittire	*The mouse*	*to yelp*

Esercizi da tradurre in Italiano

Do you know anybody who left the knap-sack here ?

....

I don't know. Nobody has seen anything

....

I have not yet received any of those books that I did order.

....

The dog kept barking all night, hearing the wolf howl.

....

The little lamb kept bleating after his mother.

....

Traduzione degli esercizi proposti nella lezione precedente

1) Ieri andai al supermercato e comprai del caffè e dello zucchero.
2) Pagai 3 dollari per il latte, più 5 dollari per il caffè, per un totale di $ 8.
3) Il poliziotto venne a cercarmi ieri.
4) Beata quella donna che fa tutto per se!
5) Nemmeno lui farebbe una cosa simile.
6) Ci sono tante donne belle come lei.

Esercizi di lettura

È tardi. Ti prego. Devo andare subito. Si sta già facendo buio. Arrivederci. Io abito lontano da qui. Non voglio che mi si faccia notte .

Il marito di mia sorella è un uomo sano. La sua donna lo ama molto. Lei lo dimostra facilmente. Si vede che lui è l'oggetto principale della sua vita. Essi hanno due animali in casa: un cane e un gatto.

Nessuna cosa è difficile, quando si va d'accordo. Si dice che – chi va piano, va sano e va lontano– .

Most of the words used for the above reading exercise are taken from the seventh lesson. It should bring back old memories.

THIRTIETH LESSON

Lezione Trentesima

Alessandro, ciao. Ti vedo vestito in gran tenuta da sciatore. Vai a passare le vacanze in montagna?

"Sì, vado a Fiuggi, a Campo Catino, località di villeggiatura alle pendici dei Monti Èrnici in provincia di Frosinone. In quella zona c'è un magnifico campo di sport invernali, adagiato di attrezzature moderne. Quella zona è molto celebre anche per la salubrità delle sue acque minerali.

Alexander, hello. I see you dressed as a professional skier. Are you going to spend your vacation on the mountain?

"Yes, I am going to Fiuggi, at Campo Catino, a tourist resort at the slopes of the Ernici mountains, province of Frosinone. In that area there is a magnificent sport complex, outfitted with the most modern equipment. That area is very famous for the healthiness of its mineral waters.

Defective verbs

We call defective those verbs that don't have the entire conjugation, but only some persons and some moods.

In English we have already met *shall, should* **dovere** and *will, would* **volere,** which we have used in forming the future and the conditional tenses.

In Italian most of the defective verbs have Latin roots: **ire** *to go,* **lucere** *to shine,* **ùrgere** *to be urgent etc.* They are very seldom used other than in the third person, or in poetry.

The one which is used more often is **solere** *ought to.* However it can be substituted by the auxiliary **essere** with its past participle **sòlito: sono sòlito; era sòlito; fosse sòlito; etc.**

141

For the missing tenses of *shall* and *will,* the English uses *to wish* **desiderare;** *to want* **volere;** *to like* **piacere (aver piacere);** *to intend* **aver l'intenzione.**

Let's see how we are going to translate them into Italian.

You shall write to your father more often.
Voi dovreste scrivere a vostro padre più spesso.
I will do it every week.
Io lo farò ogni settimana.
You should go to Venice on business.
Voi dovreste andare a Venezia per affari.
I would rather go to Milan.
Io andrei piuttosto a Milano.
The doctor would like to see her.
Il dottore avrebbe piacere di vederla.
Mario had intended to come, but the bad weather stopped him.
Mario aveva l'intenzione di venire, ma lo ha fermato il mal tempo.
Will you come to have a cup of coffee with me?
Ti piacerebbe venire con me per una tazza di caffè?
He ought to do it any way he wants it.
Egli suole farlo come piace a lui.

Two other defective verbs which require some attention are *can and could* **potere;** *and may and might; also to be able* **potere.**

As you can see in Italian **potere** takes the place of all of them. It has both the material faculty; and the permissive authority or the doubt to do something.

Potere is an irregular verb, but it has the absolute power.

Can you fix the kitchen faucet?
Puoi accomodare il rubinetto dentro alla cucina?
I cannot do it to-day; but I might come to-morrow.
Non lo posso fare oggi; ma potrei venire domani.
Can you come to-morrow for sure?
Verrai domani di sicuro?

142

I am sorry. I will not be able to come until Sunday.
Mi dispiace. Non potrò venire prima di domenica.

Another defective verb we have to pay attention to is ***must.*** Having only the present tense, ***to be obliged and to be forced*** come to its rescue. In Italian it is translated with **dovere, bisognare, bisogna che... obbligare.**
They are powerful verbs which express obligation, necessity to do something.

I am in Rome. I must at least go to visit the Coliseum.
Sono a Roma. Devo almeno andare a visitare il Colosseo.
Come on now, you should not go. Yes, I must go.
Andiamo ora, voi non dovreste andare. Si, io devo andare.
Nobody forced you to go and commit such a crime.
Nessuno ti ha obbligato di andare a commettere un reato.
I must go and do some work. We must work to eat.
Devo andare a fare del lavoro. Bisogna lavorare per mangiare.

When an action expresses something that should happen without implying an obligation, then ***to have to*** or ***to be to*** is simply translated with **dovere:** literally **essere da... avere da...**

He was supposed to finish his work yesterday.
Doveva finire (era da finire) il suo lavoro ieri.
Now he shall have to finish it to-morrow.
Ora dovrà finirlo (avrà da finirlo) domani.

Expand your vocabulary

In the previous lesson you learned the names of some animals. In this lesson you are going to learn the names and the sounds of some birds.
Each bird has more than a special self sound which they use for different purposes. I am not going to list each special sound for each bird, because it would take too much space. If you are interested, you can listen to them and enjoy their astonishing variations.

143

Uccello	Suono	Bird	Sound
Il corvo	crocitare	*The crow*	*to caw*
Il gallo	cantare	*The rooster*	*to crow*
La gallina	schiamazzare	*The hen*	*to cackle*
La chioccia	chiocciare	*The broody hen*	*to clack*
Il pulcino	pigolare	*The chick*	*to pip*
Il tacchino	gurgugliare	*The turkey*	*to gobble*
la tortora, il piccione	tubare	*The dove, the pigeon*	*to coo*
L'aquila, il falco	zufolare	*The eagle, the falcon*	*to whistle*
Gli insetti	ronzare	*The insects*	*to buzz*

For the sound of most other birds let's categorize them by saying:
– *they sing;* **essi cantano** –

Il **passero** *the sparrow;* il **tordo** *thrush, robin;* il **fringuello** *finch;* la **pernice** *patridge;* la **capinera** *chickadee;* il **picchione** *woodpecker;* la **quaglia** *quail;* la **rondine** *swallow* ; lo **scricciolo** *wren;* il **rigogolo** *oriole;* il **fagiano** *pheasant;* la **cicogna** *stork;* l'**anitra** *duck;* la **beccaccia** *wood cock;* la **pavoncella** *lapwing;* il **merlo** *blackbird;* la **pica** *magpie, blue jay.*

Esercizi da tradurre in Italiano

The hunter goes hunting for pheasants on corn fields.

....

Everybody knows where to go, but nobody goes there.

....

I told my mother to buy me a pair of Italian shoes.

....

"What," she said, "Italian shoes? They are too good for you".

....

Do you know anybody who could tell me where the theater is?

....

Has anybody learned anything?

....

Traduzione degli esercizi assegnati nella lezione precedente

1) Conoscete qualcuno che ha lasciato lo zaino qua?
2) Non lo so. Nessuno non ha visto nulla.
3) Non ho ancora ricevuto nessuno dei libri che ho ordinato.
4) Il cane abbaiava la notte intera, sentendo il lupo ululare.
5) L'agnellino belava appresso alla mamma.

Esercizi di lettura

Ieri fu una bella giornata. Anche oggi il tempo è bello. Spero che domani sarà una giornata che rifletta l'atmosfera mite come oggi, perchè devo ritornare a scuola. Il professore ci ha promesso che verrà fuori con noi se non ci saranno variazioni di tempo.
Lo so che sono cose personali, ma nel passato ha sempre mantenuto la promessa. Quando studiamo il modo, il tempo e il numero dei verbi, riflettendo sulla loro difficoltà, ci manda fuori per un pochino di tempo, a condizione di comportarci bene.

Most of the words used for the reading exercise are taken from the eighth lesson. It will most likely take you back to some nice memories.

THIRTY FIRST LESSON

Lezione Trentunesima

Signora Pisani, la vedo in tenuta da primavera; ma è ancora inverno. Dove va con questo freddo con la sua famiglia?

"Grazie per le vostre gentili parole. Ho ancora una settimana di vacanze. Vogliamo andare a passarle in Sicilia, a Taormina, sotto il picco dell'Etna. Si dice che lungo la costa di Catania c'è sempre primavera."

Mrs. Pisani, I see you dressed in spring clothes; but it is still winter. Where are you going in such a cold weather with your family?

"Thank you for your kind words. I still have one more week of vacation. We want to go and spend it in Sicily, at Taormina, under the peak of Etna. They say that along the coast of Catania it is always springtime."

Indefinite pronoun "si"

As you may have noticed from the above dialogue, in this lesson you are going to learn all about **il pronome indefinito –si– .**

In Italian regardless if it is used in general or restricted, it never changes. In English, however, this pronoun varies; and can be translated with ***one, people, man, we, you, they, it.***

Negli Stati Uniti d'America *si* parla Inglese.
In the United States of America people speak English.
Si deve sempre pensare prima di parlare.
One must always think before speaking.
Si deve sempre fare il proprio dovere.
Man must always do his duty.

146

Scusi signore, si deve aspettare in linea per entrare.
Excuse me Sir, you must wait in line before entering.
Si dice che Carlo è molto intelligente e studia assai.
People say that Charles is very intelligent and he studies a lot.
Si dice in questo giornale che verrà subito la pace.
It is reported in this newspaper that peace will soon come.

Reflexive verbs

Si: in addition to being an affirmative word, *yes,* and an indefinite pronoun *one, people, man, etc.,* "**si**" is also used to form the third person singular and plural of reflexive verbs.

What are reflexive verbs? They express an action exercised by the subject which falls back on the subject itself.

Pietro si è scaldato vicino alla stufa e si è bruciato un dito.
Peter warmed himself near the stove and he burned one finger.
Il gatto si lava con la zampa.
The cat washes himself with his paw.
Essi si rimpròverano per la loro povera responsabilità.
They blame themselves for their poor responsibility.

I have already stressed that reflexive verbs take the auxiliary **essere** in Italian; however I need to warn you again, so you do not make a mistake. Every time a verb ends with **si** in the infinite moods, you must use the auxiliary **essere: lavarsi** *to wash oneself;* **scaldarsi** *to warm oneself;* **pettinarsi** *to comb oneself;* **tagliarsi** *to cut oneself ; etc.* Do not forget...

Of course we also have **mi, ti, ci, vi** that express reflexive action.

Io mi lavo.	*I wash myself.*
Tu ti lavi.	*You wash yourself.*
Egli si lava	*He washes himself*
Noi ci laviamo.	*We wash ourselves.*
Voi vi lavate	*You wash yourselves*
Essi si lavano	*They wash themselves*

Io mi sono lavato.	*I have washed myself.*
Tu ti sei lavato.	*You have washed yourself.*
Egli si è lavato.	*He has washed himself*
Noi ci siamo lavati.	*We have washed ourselves*
Voi vi siete lavati	*You have washed yourselves*
Essi si sono lavati	*They have washed themselves*

State attenti; per piacere non vi bruciate.
Be careful; please do not burn yourself.

When there is reciprocity in the action expressed by the verb amongst two or more persons, *each other* , (if the number is limited) and *one another* (if the number is not limited) are translated with **mi, ti si, etc.**

Voi vi aiutate (l'un l'altro). *You help each other.*
Essi si stanno sempre bisticciando. *They always blame one another.*

Myself, yourself, herself, himself, ourselves, etc. in addition of being translated with **mi, ti, si, ci, vi, si,** they correspond to: **me stesso, te stesso, egli stesso, ella stessa, noi stessi, voi stessi, essi stessi; or da me, da se, da noi, etc.** Used in this way they give more strength to the thought.
Own can be translated into **da me, da se... proprio, propri, etc.**

Posso andare a Torino da me (stesso). *I can go to Turin myself.*
Hai comprato il biglietto tu stesso? *Did you buy the ticket yourself?*
Noi possiamo aprire la porta da noi. *We can open the door ourselves.*
Essi si fanno i loro propri abiti. *They make their own dresses themselves.*
Non si dovrebbe lodare se stesso. *One should not praise oneself.*
Mi sono cavato un dente da me. *I have pulled my own tooth.*

Expand your vocabulary

Let's keep up with Nature. In this lesson you are going to learn the name of some fish.

Trota *trout ;* **anguilla** *eel;* **carpa** *carp;* **luccio** *pike;* **tinca** *tench;* **spinarello** *stickleback;* **acciuga, alice** *anchovy;* **aringa** *herring;* **cefalo** *mullet;* **merluzzo** *cod-fish;* **pescecane** *shark;* **salmone** *salmon;* **sardina** *sardine ;* **seppia** *cattle-fish;* **sgombro** *mackerel;* **sogliola** *sole;* **storione** *sturgeon;* **tonno** *tuna;* **triglia** *red mullet;* **calamaro** *squid, octopus;* **aragosta** *lobster;* **gambero** *shrimp*; **vongola** *clam;* **cozza** *mussel;* **ostrica** *oyster.* **spigola** *bass;* **balena** *whale; etc.*

Traduzione degli esercizi assegnati nella lezione precedente

1) Il cacciatore va a caccia di fagiani nei campi di granturco.
2) Ognuno sa dove andare, ma nessuno ci va.
3) Dissi a mia madre di comprarmi un paio di scarpe italiane.
4) "Che cosa," mi disse, "scarpe italiane? Quelle sono troppo buone per te".
5) Conoscete qualcuno che mi possa dire dove sta il teatro?
6) Ha qualcuno imparato qualche cosa?

Esercizi di lettura

La prima volta che sono andato al negozio, ho speso dieci dollari per comprare tutto quello che mi serve per la scuola. La seconda volta mi sono serviti venti dollari, per comprare quello che ho comprato nel passato. Non so quanto dovrò spendere per comprare la stessa cosa nel futuro.

Mia madre ama servire per fare del bene agli altri. È molto semplice per lei offrirsi a fare del bene, specialmente quando tutti la ringraziano e la salutano.

Most of the words used for the above reading exercise are from the ninth lesson.

THIRTY SECOND LESSON

Lezione Trentaduesima

Signora Rimini, la vedo rattristata questa mattina. C'è qualcosa che non va in famiglia; oppure si sente male?

"No, stiamo tutti bene. Nessuno deve andare in ospedale. E si, una madre fa tanto per essere amata dai figli, e, appena si fa giorno, uno non vuole prendersi il latte, l'altro non vuole lavarsi, il terzo non vuole cambiarsi, il quarto non vuole mettersi il vestito nuovo. Fanno proprio disperare una povera mamma."

Mrs. Rimini, I see you sad and in a bad mood this morning. Is there something wrong with your family?

"No, we are all fine. Nobody has to go to the hospital. Indeed, a mother does so much in order to be loved by her children; yet, as soon as it becomes daylight, one does not want his milk, the other one does not want to wash himself, the third one does not want to change his clothes, the forth does not want to put his new outfit on. They really push a poor mother to despair."

If you read the above conversation again, you may realize that in this lesson you are going to learn about the **passive form of the verb.**

The student will remember that the **passive form** is that in which the subject receives the action.

Una madre fa tanto per essere amata dai figli.
A mother does so much in order to be loved by her children.
Amanda è amata da sua madre.
Amanda is loved by her mother.

As you can see, in Italian the *passive form* is done exactly like in English. Both languages use the auxiliary *to be*: **essere.** With the passive form, the English preposition *by* is translated with the Italian one **da.**

Essere amato	*to be loved*
Essendo amato	*being loved*
Stato amato	*Been loved*

Laura è amata dai suoi genitori.
Laura is loved by her parents.
L'opera Tosca è stata scritta da Puccini.
The opera Tosca was written by Puccini.
Si aspetta il Presidente a Roma domani.
The President is expected in Rome to-morrow.
Si dice che Giulia sia più bella di sua sorella.
Giulia is said to be more beautiful than her sister.

When I was studying Latin, I did not like the frequently used passive form adopted by that language. I always changed it into an active form: **Puccini ha scritto l'opera Tosca.**

Impersonal verbs

Impersonal verbs are only used in the third singular person of the various moods. Their action does not differ from the Italian form. The only difference is that English uses the subject *it* ; the Italian does not use the subject. It is understood.

Impersonal verbs are always intransitive. They require the auxiliary **essere** in Italian. We have already studied these kinds of verbs in previous lessons. We called them atmospheric or celestial actions.

Piove *it rains;* **è piovuto** *it has rained.*
Fiocca *it snows;* **è fioccato** *it has snowed;* **fiocchrà** *it will snow.*

151

Many other verbs are considered impersonal when they are followed by *that:* **che** in italian.

Bisogna che *it is necessary that;* **occorre che** *it occurs that;* **pare che** *it seems that;* **importa che** *it is important that;* **succede che** *it happens that;* **avviene che** *it happens that;* **merita che** *it deserve that; etc.*

Pare che si siano decisi di venire al teatro con me.
It seems that they have decided to come to the theater with me.
Spesso succede che qualcuno si rifiuta di fare il testimone.
Often it happens that someone refuses to become a witness.

In Italian the verb **fare** *to do or to make* and the verb **essere** *to be* form many adverbial phrases: **fa caldo** *it is warm;* **fa giorno** *it is daybreak;* **s'è fatto tardi** *it is getting late;* **si fece buio** *it became dark; etc.*
È necessario *it is necessary;* **è utile** *it is useful;* **è facile** *it is easy;* **è vero** *it is true;* **è giusto** *it is right ;* **è ben fatto** *it is well done; etc.*

Remember: fare is a transitive verb. Therefore if you use it without "si" it takes the auxiliary **avere.**
S'è fatto afoso (si è).   Ha fatto caldo tutta la notte.
It has become sultry.   It has been warm the whole night.

The adverbial phrases *there is* and *there are,* are translated in Italian with **c'è, vi è** and **ci sono, vi sono.** In the past tenses we use **c'era, vi erano.** For the future we use **ci sarà.** We use **ci vi (*there*)** for the third persons of all the other tenses and moods.

Non c'è nessuno per la strada.   *There is nobody on the street.*
Ci sarebbe molto da fare.   *There would be much to do.*
C'erano molte signore al negozio. *There were many ladies at the store.*

"*It is*" when it refers to distance from one place to another or to a space of time, it is translated in Italian with **c'è, vi è, ci sono, vi sono.** For the third persons of the past tenses **c'era, era; c'erano, erano;** and for the third persons of all the other moods, the normal conjugation of the verb

to be can be used.

> **Vi sono otto miglia da Newton a Boston.**
> *It is eight miles from Newton to Boston.*
> **Sono passati tre anni da quando non ci siamo visti.**
> *It is three years since we saw each other.*
> **Saranno due anni il prossimo mese.**
> *It will be two years next month.*
> **Era tanto tempo che lo aspettavo.**
> *It was a long time since I was waiting for it.*

Expand your vocabulary

Throughout the lessons I am giving you many words related to the purpose of our learning. I am not going to list each word, because they are already translated. If you are interested to learn some of them, you could make a list yourself.

If you enjoy geography, you will notice that many words are similar in both language.

Triangolo equilatero *equilateral triangle;* **triangolo rettangolo** *right angle triangle;* **triangolo isoscele** *isosceles triangle;* **triangolo scaleno** *scalene triangle;* **rettangolo** *rectangle;* **rombo** *rhombus;* **trapezio** *trapezoid;* **quadrato** *square;* **pentàgono** *pentagon;* **esàgono** *hexagon;* **ottàgono** *octagon;* **circolo** *circle;* **circonferenza** *circumference;* **arco** *arc;* **secante** *segment;* **diametro** *diameter;* **raggio** *radius;* **corda** *chord;* **tangente** *tangent;* **linea orizzontale** *horizontal line;* **linea verticale** *vertical line;* **linea curva** *curve line;* **linea obliqua** *oblique line;* **linea spezzata** *broken line;* **linee parallele** *parallel lines;* **linee convergenti** *converging lines;* **linee divergenti** *diverging lines;* **piramide** *pyramid;* **sfera** *sphere;* **cono** *cone;* **cubo** *cube; etc.*

I gave you some of the most important words related to geometry. If you need more, you will have to use the dictionary and help yourself.

Do you realize how many words are very similar and easy for you to memorize!

153

Esercizi da tradurre in Italiano

When one works hard, one makes a good life for himself.

....

People said that king Edward the seventh visited Italy.

....

Many famous operas were written by Puccini.

....

It snowed all night; afterwards it rained and melted the snow.

....

It is three months since you came.

....

Esercizi di lettura

Oggi fa cattivo tempo. Piove. È venuto anche un grande temporale poco prima. Maria ha paura dei lampi e dei tuoni. Nel passato anche sua madre aveva paura dei lampi e dei tuoni. Ora lei è più brava. Non ha più paura quando fa cattivo tempo.

Giovanni dice che la forma passiva non gli piace troppo. Per lui è più semplice usare la forma attiva. Nel futuro troverà qualche modo per adattarsi a tali condizioni. Lui ama il bel tempo; ma non esce mai da casa senza ombrello. Dice che il pane e l'ombrello non si lasciano mai a casa.

Most of the words used for the above exercise are taken from the tenth lesson. Some of those not contained in the tenth lesson, have been used along the path of our learning; therefore it should not be hard to understand the meaning and the use of each word.

THIRTY THIRD LESSON

Lezione Trentetreesima

Signore Piemontesi, vi vedo ben vestito, dove andate a quest'ora? I negozi e gli altri commerci stanno ancora chiusi; perchè tanta fretta?

"Vincenzo, mio caro amico, bisogna alzarsi presto quando si gira per affari. C'è qualcosa che mi preme. Ho comprato una casa, ma non ho tutto il denaro per pagarla. Vado in banca per chiedere un prestito a lunga durata. Non c'è nessun altro che possa aiutarmi. Dipende tutto da me."

Mr. Piemontesi, I see you well dressed, where are you going so early? The stores and other commercial places are still closed, why in such a hurry?

"Vincent, my dear friend, one must get up early when one goes looking for business. There is something that pushes me. I have bought a house, but I don't have enough money to pay for it. I am going to the bank to apply for a long term loan. There is nobody else that can help me. It is all up to me."

If you read the above conversation carefully, you will realize that it is a review of what you have learned in the previous lessons. I find this kind of teaching very interesting. It invigorates the student to understand how much he or she has achieved so far. If you can read it fluently without being restrained by falling back on the sounds of the English vowels, you can be proud of yourself. I know that you can read Italian well: yet a little reminder is very helpful.

Only a good friend will tell you that you are coming along very well. It is not an easy task to achieve what you have accomplished already.

If you are able to record your voice, you will hear how much you have progressed.

Useful remarks

A while back we learned about the *possessive* adjectives and pronouns. I want to point out that in English there are two ways of expressing the possession, where as in Italian there is only one way.

Friede is a daughter of the gardener. Friede is the gardener's daughter.
Friede è una delle figlie del giardiniere.
Who is that boy walking with the son of your sister? Who is that boy walking with your sister's son.
Chi è quel ragazzo che va (cammina) insieme con il figlio di vostra sorella?
A friend of mine told me everything. One of my friend told me everything.
Un mio amico mi disse ogni cosa.
Did you go to your mother's? Did you go to see your mother?
Ci sei andato da tua madre?

Progressive form of the verb

The progressive form of the verb in English is accomplished with the tenses of the verb *to be* accompanied by the gerund. In Italian it is translated with the verb **stare.** This form is used most frequently to take the place of the **imperfect** tense. It serves to specify time in which the action takes place.

I am going to the beach. Would you like to go with me?
Io vado alla spiaggia. Vi piacerebbe venire con me?
No, thank you. I am writing my papers to-day.
No, grazie. Sto scrivendo il mio rapporto oggi.
Are you going out to-night? No, to-night I am not going out.
Esci questa sera? No, questa sera non esco.
What were you asking your brother?
Che cosa stavi domandando a tuo fratello?
What are you doing? I don't know what I am going to do with you.
Che stai facendo? Non so cosa dovrò fare con te.

156

John is going to work to-night.
Giovanni va a lavorare questa sera.
What were you going to do with that knife?
Cosa ci volevate fare con quel coltello?
I was going to cut some flowers for my wife.
Ci volevo tagliare dei fiori per mia moglie.
She is going to visit her mother later.
Lei va a visitare sua madre piú tardi.

Portare e condurre

In Italian it is very important to learn the proper action of each one of these two verbs. Many times they are used erroneously.

Portare means carrying a load in one direction or the other.

Condurre means to *lead* someone somewhere; or to *take.*

Frequently people say: **Portami a bere.** It means put me on your shoulder and carry me to where the drink is (wrong). This is a common mistake. The right way is: **portami da bere.** *Bring me something to drink.*

Ti porterò in macchina fino a casa tua.
I will take you home by car.
Portami dieci tonnellate di cemento.
Bring me ten tons of cement.
Il pastore conduce il suo armento al pascolo.
The shepherd leads his flock to the pasture.
Lo sposo condusse la sua sposa all'altare per mano.
The bridegroom took his bride to the alter by hand.

English has the same problem with to bring and to take. I learned the difference the hard way myself. With *to bring* the action moves toward the speaker. With *to take* the action moves away from the speaker. It does not matter if it is a physical action or a spiritual one.

Please buy ten chairs. Bring six to me and take four to my mother.
Per piacere compra dieci sedie. Porta sei a me e porta quattro a mia madre.

157

Expand your vocabulary

La casa	the house, home	il cucchiaio	the spoon
Il tavolo	the table	la forchetta	the fork
La sedia	the chair	il coltello	the knife
Il letto	the bed	l'oliera	the cruet
la fruttiera	the fruit basket	il bicchiere	the glass
La lampada	the lamp	la padella	the frying pan
L'orologio	the watch	la casseruola	the sauce-pan
La cucina	the kitchen	il mestolo	the ladle
La teggia	the pan	la pentola	the pot
Il bacino	the basin	la caffettiera	the coffee-pot
La schiumarola	the skimmer	il frigorifero	the refrigerator
La bottiglia	the bottle	l'elettricità	the electricity
La stufa	the stove	l'olio	the oil
Il gas	the gas	lo zucchero	the sugar
L'aceto	the vinegar	il sale	the salt
Il vino	the wine	l'acqua	the water

Traduzione degli esercizi proposti nella lezione precedente

1) Quando si lavora forte, si raggiunge un buon livello di vita.
2) Si diceva che il re Edoardo Settimo visitò l'Italia.
3) Tante opere famose furono scritte da Puccini.
4) Fioccò tutta la notte; dopo piovve (piovette) e squagliò la neve.
5) Sono tre mesi che non sei venuto.

Esercizi da tradurre in Italiano

My suit is blue, my brother's is black.

....

Who is that lady going to your sister's.

....

A friend of mine asked me to go to the beach with him.

....

Are you going out with your girl friend to-night?

....

Please take this letter to your friend's father.

....

Bring me some fresh fruits and some vegetables.

....

Esercizi di lettura

Signora Tebaldi, le piace parlare Inglese? Si, mi piace; ma preferisco parlare la mia bella lingua italiana. Mi viene più facile cantarla. Grazie a Dio, la nostra lingua è un modello di poesia. È un incanto beato: l'idolo del canto. Quando gli annunziatori parlano dalla radio e dalla televisione: quelli che sanno bene la lingua, intendiamoci, si sente il dolce suono e l'armonia di una risonanza straordinaria. Molti famosi cantanti italiani, classici e popolari, attribuiscono la loro fama al romanzo e all'armonia della nostra lingua.

Impara bene anche tu questa nostra lingua mandataci dal Cielo. Vedrai che ne sarai prode.

Some of the words used to write the above exercise are taken from the eleventh lesson.

THIRTY FOURTH LESSON

Lezione Trentaquattresima

Giorgio, ho sentito che state studiando la geografia a scuola. Quali punti diversi della nostra terra state studiando?

"Benedetto, è vero. Stiamo studiando la geografia fisica. Abbiamo imparato che in Italia ci sono due grandi catene di montagne. A nord ci sono le Alpi. Il Monte Bianco è la cima più alta (4810 m.) nella Valle d'Aosta. Andando verso il sud c'è la catena degli Appennini che attraversa tutta l'Italia fino alla Sicilia. Il picco più alto è il Gran Sasso d'Italia (2914 m.) nell'Abruzzo."

George, I have heard that you are studying geography at school. Which various point of our earth are you studying?

"Benedict, it is true. We are studying physical geography. We have learned that in Italy there are two big mountain chains. In the North there are the Alps. Mount Blanc is the highest peak (4810 m.) in the Valle d'Aosta region. Going toward the South there are the Apennines Mountains that cross the whole of Italy as far down as Sicily. The highest peak is the Gran Sasso d'Italia (2914 m.) in the Abruzzi region."

The present participle

Many verbs in English may become adjectives, using them before nouns in the present participle form. In Italian they are translated with specific nouns.

To write	**scrivere;**	*writing table*	**scrivania.**
To dine	**pranzare;**	*dining room*	**sala da pranzo.**
To read	**leggere;**	*reading stand*	**leggìo**

160

When using a present participle as a noun, in Italian the equivalent noun takes the article.

I like painting very much. Mi piace moltissimo **la** pittura.
Her writing is very beautiful. **La** sua scrittura è molto bella.
The writings of Manzoni are famous. **Gli** scritti del Manzoni sono famosi.

In general cases the present participle is translated with an infinite.

Clear writing is necessary. **Lo scrivere** chiaro è necessario.

Following a preposition (except to) the present participle is translated in Italian also with an infinite verb. There are other cases too.

He went away without informing me. Se ne andò **senza informarmelo.**
You are far from believing him. Vi è impossibile **crederlo.**
She cannot help crying. Non può astenersi **dal piangere.**
Excuse my disturbing you. Scusate se sono venuto a **disturbarvi.**
I am sorry for his behaving so bad. Scusate il suo **comportarsi** male.
Excuse my phoning every day. Perdonate il mio **telefonarvi ogni giorno.**

I know all this is a little hard to learn and to remember; but I think with good will, with time available, with exercises and with practice you are going to overtake the difficulties and master your knowledge.

Useful remarks

Much and *many* are translated with the adjectives **molto, tanto, quanto;** *very much, a great deal of; a good deal of; a great many; a good many* are translated with the superlative **moltissimo.**

He has a great deal of spare time. Ha **moltissimo** tempo libero.
Frank has a great many friends. Franco ha **moltissimi** amici.
It is much warmer than last year. Fa **molto** più caldo dell'anno scorso
How many times do I have to tell you? **Quante** volte te lo devo dire?

O..... o, né.....né, are translated with ***either.....or, neither.....nor.***
However if we deal with the same things **l'uno o l'altro** they are translated
with ***either;*** **né l'uno né** are translated with ***neither.***

O tu o tua sorella venite da noi. *Either you or your sister come to see us.*
Né mia sorella né io possiamo venire. *Neither my sister **nor** I may come.*
Datemi l'uno o l'altro dei due orologi. *Give me **either** of those watches.*
Quale volete l'uno o l'altro? *Which will you have? **Either.***

Expand your vocabulary

La Botanica	*Botany*	**il fiore**	*the flower*
La margherita	*the daisy*	**l'astro**	*the aster*
La rosa	*the rose*	**il giglio**	*the lily*
Lo zafferano	*the saffron*	**il croco**	*the crocus*
Il giacinto	*the hyacinth*	**il narciso**	*the narcissus*
La viola	*the violet*	**la primula**	*the primrose*
Il geranio	*the geranium*	**la bocca di leone**	*the snapdragon*
Il garofano	*the carnation*	**il crisantemo**	*chrysanthemum*
La zinnia	*the zinnia*	**viola colorata**	*the pansy*
Il tulipano	*the tulip*	**il narciso selv.**	*the daffodil*
la dalia	*the dahlia*	**la lilla**	*the lilac*
L'azalea	*the azalea*	**il rododendro**	*rhododendron*
la begonia	*the begonia*	**la camelia**	*the camellia*
Il ciclamino	*the cyclamen*	**il girasole**	*the sunflower*

Traduzione degli esercizi proposti nella lezione precedente

1) Il mio vestito è blu; quello di mio fratello è nero
1) Chi è quella signora che va da tua sorella?
3) Un mio amico mi ha domandato di andare alla spaggia con lui.
4) Uscite con la vostra ragazza questa sera?
5) Per piacere portate questa lettera all'amico di vostro padre.
6) Portami della frutta fresca e dei vegetali.

Esercizi da tradurre in Inglese

Darei ogni cosa per un bicchiere d'acqua.

....

Chi è quella bella ragazza che cammina con il cane?

....

O te o il tuo amico avete scordato di venire da noi ieri.

....

Mia madre non può astenersi dal piangere quando vede suo figlio.

....

La rosa e il garofano sono i miei fiori preferiti.

....

Nessuno dei miei figli ha studiato botanica.

....

Esercizi di lettura

Mamma mia! È il secondo giorno d'impiego e mi hanno caricato con tutto questo lavoro. Ho appena cominciato a lavorare, perciò devo dedicarmi per non farmi giudicare di farlo di cattivo umore. Devo indicare tutta la mia capacità per praticare una buona paga. In tal modo posso recarmi a cavalcare il mio cavallo più spesso.

Il dottore mi ha indicato di masticare il mangiare senza fretta, a fin di restare lontano dal medico.

Molte parole per questo esercizio di lettura sono state prese dalla dodicesima lezione.

THIRTY FIFTH LESSON

Lezione Trentacinquesima

Natalia, chi sono tutte quelle ragazze con le quali stai giocando?
Chi è quella ragazzina che sta più vicino a te?

"Queste ragazze sono le mie amiche di scuola. Stiamo giocando
prima che comincia la classe. Questa ragazzina è Samantha, la quale è la
mia sorellina. Fra poco la devo accompagnare a scuola che sta qua vicino.
Lei frequenta la terza classe elementare. Noi invece frequentiamo le Medie.
Stiamo aspettando l'autobus che viene a prenderci ogni mattina."

*Natalia, who are all those girls with whom you are playing? Who
is that little girl that is nearest to you?*

*"These girls are my school friends. We are playing before class
starts. This little girl is Samantha, who is my little sister. In a short while
I have to take her to school which is close by. She is in the third grade.
Indeed we attend Junior High. We are waiting for the bus which picks us up
every morning."*

If you read the above conversation carefully, you may deduce that
we are going over the ***relative pronouns.***

The pronoun takes the place of a noun. It is called relative because
it puts in relation two sentences by joining them together.

Questa è la casa **(la casa) che** nostro padre comprò.
*This is the house (the house) **that** our father bought.*

You may notice that it sounds harsh repeating *the house* so close
together. It sounds much better substituting it with the relative pron. ***that.***

Let's translate the English relative pronouns into Italian; and seek

164

their function. Their grammatical usage is closely similar.

Who chi; **Which, That:** che, il quale, la quale, i quali, le quali.
Whose, of which il di cui, del quale, della quale etc.
Which quale.
Of whom, of which del quale, della quale, dei quali, delle quali, di cui.
What ciò che, quello che.

Who came to visit you yesterday?
Chi venne a visitarvi ieri?
*You know **which** of these boys goes to school.*
Voi sapete **quale** di questi ragazzi va a scuola.
*I know the lady **whose** child was born this morning.*
Io conosco la signora **il cui** bambino è nato questa mattina.
*Yes, the lady **of whom** I have spoken to you.*
Si, la signora **della quale** ve ne ho parlato.
*I know the gentleman **that** we see very often*
Io conosco il signore **che** vediamo molto spesso.
***Which?** The one **that** you spoke to me of?*
Quale? Quello **del quale** (di cui) mi parlaste?
*Do you understand **what** I am asking for?*
Capisci **quello che (ciò che)** ti sto chiedendo?

Use of the expression "È vero?" — "Non è vero?"

These two expression are found very often at the end of a sentence in Italian. Specially when somebody is insisting on knowing the business of others. Let's find out how they are used in English.

Tu non sei andato a lavorare questa mattina. È vero?
You didn't go to work this morning. Did you?
Voi non avete mai visto il tesoro nascosto. È vero?
You have never seen the hidden treasure. Have you?
Voi siete un pittore famoso. Non è vero?
You are a famous painter. Are you not?

165

Voi siete stato a Venezia molte volte. Non è vero?
You have been to Venice many times. Have you not?
Voi ci tornerete ancora. È vero?
You will go back there again. Will you?

The lazy function of some English verbs

In Italian we have very few verbs that change meaning when accompanied by an adverb, because each one has its specific function.

Venite dentro, (entrate); andate fuori (uscite), vai sopra (salite).
Come in;   Go out;   Come upstairs.
Venite avanti (proseguite); andate via (allontanatevi in fretta).
Come forward;   Get out

In English there are many verbs which change meaning when followed by an adverb. The laziest of them all is the verb ***to get, got, got*** or ***gotten.*** It has various meanings and it is used very frequently.
In Italian it means **avere, prendere, procurare, ottenere, fare, acquistare, ricevere, comprare, guadagnare, procurarsi etc.**

*Can you **get** me another copy of the daily newspaper?*
Potete **procurarmi** un'altra copia del giornale?
*I **got** no reward for all my work.*
Non ho **ottenuto** nessuna ricompensa per tutto il mio lavoro.
*Could you **get** your cousin to come with you?*
Potreste **indurre** vostro cugino a venire con voi?
*We shall **get** there as soon as we can.*
Noi **arriveremo** là appena possiamo.
*You are so rude. You should **get** lessons on good behavior.*
Tu sei cosi scortese. Dovresti **prendere** delle lezioni d'educazione.
***Get** over what you have done. It is too late now.*
Scorda quello che hai fatto. È già troppo tardi.
*I **got** her beautiful red roses for Valentine.*
Ho **comprato** delle belle rose rosse per lei per S. Valentino.

166

Expand your vocabulary

Il corpo umano	*the human body*	**lo scheletro**	*the skeleton*
Il cranio	*the skull*	**frontale**	*frontal bone*
I mascellari	*the jaw bones*	**la clavicola**	*the collar bone*
L'omero	*the humerus*	**la spalla**	*the shoulder*
L'ulna	*the ulna*	**il radio**	*the radius*
Le costole	*the ribs*	**la spina dorsale**	*the spine*
L'osso iliaco	*the coxa*	**l'osso sacro**	*the os sacrum*
L'ischio	*the ischium*	**il femore**	*the femur*
La rotula	*the knee-cap*	**il ginocchio**	*the knee*
La tibia	*the tibia*	**il perone**	*the fibula*
Il carpo	*the carpus*	**il metacarpo**	*the metacarpus*
La falange	*the phalanx*	**il tarso**	*the tarsus*
The metatarso	*the metatarsus*	**la schiena**	*the back*
Il braccio	*the arm*	**il piede**	*the foot*
La gamba	*The leg*	**il dente**	*the tooth*

Traduzione degli esercizi proposti nella lezione precedente

1) I would give anything for a glass of water.
2) Who is that beautiful girl that is walking the dog?
3) Either you or your friend forgot to come and see us yesterday.
4) My mother cannot help crying when she sees her son.
5) The rose and the carnation are my favorite flowers.
6) Neither of my sons has studied botany.

Esercizi da tradurre in Italiano

You will go to Canada in a week. Will you not?

....

Maria said she was going to help you. Did she?

....

The tibia is one of the bones of my leg.

....

You smoke too much. It is not good for your health.

....

My cousin looked everywhere, but he could not find anything.

....

We shall get three dozen red roses for Valentine's day.

....

Esercizi di lettura

Era ora di mangiare. Allora siamo andati al ristorante. Mentre stavamo aspettando, il cameriere ha cominciato a grattare del formaggio per gli spaghetti. Ci ha negato il vino bianco; ma ha accettato di mandare un altro cameriere a controllare se ci fosse del vino rosso. L'altro cameriere ha determinato di aver trovato del vino rosso e ce l'ha comunicato. Lui ha onorato la nostra richiesta e s'è messo a lavorare. Ha adornato un bel tavolo, pertanto abbiamo passato due ore mangiando. Poi ci ha portato delle nespole maturate sulla paglia. Uh!... Erano saporite!
Alla fine ha addizionato quello che abbiamo consumato e ci ha dato il conto. Noi gli abbiamo lasciato una buona mancia e lui ci ha ringraziato immensamente.

La maggior parte delle parole di questo esercizio sono state prese dalla tredicesima lezione.

THIRTY SIXTH LESSON

Lezione Trentaseiesima

Signor Padovani, quali parti dell'Italia vi piace visitare quando portate la vostra famiglia in vacanze?

"Sig. Rimini, Io faccio fare tutto a mia moglie. Lei decide perché conosce l'Italia meglio di me. Usualmente ogni anno visitiamo uno dei grandi laghi che sono nelle regioni del Nord. Finora abbiamo visitato il Lago Maggiore nel Piemonte, il Lago d'Iseo, il Lago di Como e il Lago di Garda nella Lombardia. Quest'anno pensiamo di andare a visitare il Lago di Misurina, sotto le famose cime dell'Avareto nel Veneto."

Mister Padovani, which parts of Italy do you like to visit when you take your family on vacation?

"Mr. Rimini, I get my wife to plan everything as she wishes. She decides because she knows Italy better than me. Usually every year we visit one of the great lakes that are in the northern regions. So far we have visited Lake Maggiore in Piedmont, Lake Iseo, Lake Como and Lake Garda in Lombardy. This year we are thinking to go and visit Lake Misurina, under the famous peaks of Avareto in Venetia."

In the last lesson we talked about the various meanings of the verb **to get, got.** In this lesson you are going to learn how they correspond to the Italian.

Far fare is often used by the common speaker. Therefore let's find out its special functions.

Io mi farò fare un vestito dal sarto.
I'll have a suit made by the tailor; or I got a suit made by the tailor.

Io mi sto facendo fare un vestito.
I am having a suit made; or I am getting a suit made.
Vi avete fatto fare il conto dal cameriere?
Have you got the bill from the waiter?
Non ancora, ma farò fare ogni cosa come voi desiderate.
Not yet, but I will get everything done as you wish.
Perché mi avete fatto fare tanto cammino!
Why have you gotten me to (made me) walk so much!

Let's now see some of the various functions which change the meaning of *to get* when accompanied by an adverb or a preposition. It is really not necessary to use *to get* instead of *to have;* however the use of *to get* is very common.

I have got	avere	*To get down*	scendere
To get back	riavere, ritornare	*To get drunk*	ubriacarsi
To get above	superare, vincere	*To get sick*	ammalarsi
To get across	traversare	*To get home*	arrivare a casa
To get among	trovarsi in mezzo a	*To get in*	entrare
To get away	andar via, allontanarsi	*To get on*	procedere
To get by	passare	*To get out*	uscire
To get by heart	imparare a memoria	*To get made*	far fare
To get clear of	liberarsi di	*To get over*	passare, valicare
To get to sleep	addormentarsi	*To get ready*	prepararsi
To get rid of	sbarazzarsi	*To get up*	alzarsi
To get through	attraversare	*To get well*	ristabilirsi
To get in order	sistemare	*To get fat*	ingrassarsi

There are some more of these combinations. I tried to give the most common ones. Indeed there are verbs which have their proper specific function; yet many times the above set up is more frequently used, as such taking the place of other verbs.

*I am in a hurry to get there: I am in a hurry to **arrive.***
Ho fretta di **arrivare** là.

170

Get in, *quickly, it is cold outside:* ***Enter,*** *quickly, it is cold outside.*
Entrate, presto, fa freddo fuori.
The Police caused me to ***get rid*** *of my nice gun.*
La Polizia mi **fece** sbarazzare del mio bel fucile.

Useful hints

Anch'io, anche noi, anche lei, etc. can be translated with *"so"* in English; or with *"too"* depending on its proper function.

Ho letto l'articolo dal principio alla fine, e voi? **Anch'io.**
I have read the article from beginning to end, and you? ***So have I.***
Noi eravamo completamente disorientati, e voi? **Anche noi.**
We were completely disoriented, and you? ***So were we.***
Ho sentito il cane abbaiare. L'ho sentito **anch'io.**
I heard the dog barking. I have heard it ***too.***

Come, siccome, giacché, mentre, may be translated in English with *as, since, while or like.* Let's find out how they are used.

As I could not lie down any longer, I got up.
Siccome non potevo più giacere per terra, mi alzai.
Since *you told me, I got it done.*
Giacché me lo dicesti, l'ho fatto.
As I looked up, I saw the Sun disappear behind the clouds.
Mentre guardavo in aria, vidi sparire il Sole dietro alle nuvole.
Your brother is ***like*** *your father.*
Vostro fratello è **come** vostro padre.
I like red the same ***as*** *I like green.*
Mi piace il rosso **come** mi piave il verde.
Kurt knew Andrea ***as*** *a young girl* ***since*** *going to High School.*
Kurt conosceva Andrea da ragazza **mentre** andava al Liceo.
My mother likes vegetables ***as much as*** *fruits.*
A mia madre le piacciono i vegetali tanto **come** la frutta.

*Don't go too far, **so** you can **get back** on time.*
Non andate troppo lontano, **giacché** dovete tornare in tempo.

Expanding your vocabulary

La testa	*the head*	**La gola**	*the throat*
I capelli	*the hair*	**Lo stomaco**	*the stomach*
Gli occhi	*the eyes*	**Il cuore**	*the heart*
Gli orecchi	*the ears*	**I polmoni**	*the lungs*
Il naso	*the nose*	**La trachea**	*the trachea*
La bocca	*the mouth*	**Il fegato**	*the liver*
La guancia	*the* cheek	**La milza**	*the spleen*
Le arterie	*the arteries*	**Le vene**	*the veins*
L'aorta	*the aorta*	**La vena cava**	*the vena cava*
L'intestino	*the intestine*	**Il colon**	*the colon*
La vescica	*the bladder*	**I globuli**	*the blood cells*

Traduzione degli esercizi proposti nella lezione precedente

1) Voi andrete in Canada fra una settimana. Non è vero?
2) Maria disse che vi avrebbe aiutato. È vero?
3) La tibia è uno delle ossa della mia gamba.
4) Tu fumi troppo. Questo non è buono per la tua salute.
5) Mio cugino ha guardato dappertutto, ma non ha trovato nulla.
6) Noi compreremo tre dozzine di rose rosse per San Valentino.

Esercizi da tradurre in Inglese

Egli non comprò nè le rose nè i garofani.

....

Abbiamo visto otto tacchini nel bosco (wood), e voi? Anche noi.

....

Perché vi avete fatto fare i capelli così lunghi?

....

Mentre guardavo in aria ho visto dieci corvi attraversare nel cielo (sky).

....

La macchina (car) è arrivata. Entrate subito altrimenti mi farete fare tardi.

....

Mi piace il vino (wine) rosso come mi piace il vino bianco.

....

Reading exercise

Oggi sono molto contento perché ho potuto dedicare più tempo a studiare. Anche perché ho vinto il secondo premio modello. Mi ha fatto molto piacere srtringerlo fra le mie mani.

Mio padre ha venduto la nostra seconda casa perché giaceva in rovina. L'ha venduta a poco prezzo. Mi ha nuociuto vederla vendere perché mi piaceva tanto andare a giocare con i ragazzini che abitavano là vicino. Si dice che non tutti i mali vengono per nuocere. Ogni cosa ha il suo destino.

Some of the words used for the above reading exercise are from the fourteenth lesson.

THIRTY SEVENTH LESSON

Lezione Trentasettesima

Gerardo, so che voi state studiando geografia a scuola. Che cosa avete imparato oggi?

"Signor Melfa, oggi il professore ci ha dato un accenno sui fiumi che bagnano l'Italia. Abbiamo imparato che i fiumi principali sono ventisei. Il fiume più grande e più lungo è il Po. Scende dal Mon Viso, attraversa tutta la Pianura Padana e si butta nell'Adriatico. La sua lunghezza è di 652 Km. L'Adige è secondo con 410 Km. di lunghezza. Segue il Tevere che passa per Roma con 405 Km. di lunghezza. L'Arno che passa per Firenze, sta all'ottavo posto dopo il Ticino. L'Arno è lungo 244 Km. Il fiume più corto è il Simeto che sta in Sicilia: lungo 113 Km. La lunghezza degli altri fiumi la dobbiamo trovare noi."

Gerard, I know that you are studying geography at school. What have you learned to-day?

"Mrs. Melfa, to-day the professor has gone over the principal rivers that flow through Italy. We have learned that there are twenty six important rivers. The biggest and longest river is the Po. It comes down from Mount Viso, crosses the Padana plain and dumps its waters into the Adriatic Sea. It is 652 Km. long. The Adige River takes second place. It is 410 Km. long. The Tiber, which passes through Rome, follows in third place. It is 405 Km. long. The Arno, which flows through Florence, is in the eighth place behind the Ticino River. The Arno River is 244 Km. long. The shortest is the Simeto River in Sicily: 113 Km. long. It is up to us to find the length of the other rivers."

While we were studying the parts of speech, I decided to keep all the various references together for the convenience of the student. Now, as we

174

go along, we'll go over some individual examples to enrich our knowledge.

You learned that the adverbs ending in *"ly"* in English, in Italian end in **"mente"**: *slowly,* **lentamente;** *gently,* **gentilmente;** *monthly,* **mensilmente.**

Let's see how we form adverbs from numbers. The English adds "**ly**" to the ordinal numbers up to ten: *firstly, secondly, etc.* Beginning with eleven, English uses the same format as Italian: *In the first place,* **in primo luogo;** *in the eleventh place,* **nell'undicesimo posto (luogo) etc.**

In English *"too"* is used very frequently. In Italian it is translated with **troppo, molto.**

> *My apple tree is **too** old. I have to cut it down.*
> Il mio melo è **troppo** vecchio. Lo devo tagliare.
> *You walk **too** much. Please walk more **slowly**.*
> Voi camminate **troppo.** Per piacere camminate più **lentamente.**

*Yet, again, still, **more** are translated with* "ancora".

> *Your package did not arrive **yet**?*
> Non è **ancora** arrivato il vostro pacco?
> *That famous young girl will sing **again**.*
> Quella famosa ragazzina canterà **ancora.**
> *My cousin sleeps **too** much. He is **still** in bed.*
> Mio cugino dorme **molto.** Sta **ancora** a letto.
> *Have you **more** time for me?*
> Avete **ancora** tempo per me?

The conj. *"but"* is normally translated with **"ma, però"**. Besides *ma, però,* it can be translated with **fuorché, eccetto, pur, che, nonché, non resta che.**

> *The lion is strong **but** lazy.*
> Il leone è forte **ma** pigro.
> *I had ten books. I found all **but** one.*
> Avevo dieci libri. Li ho trovati tutti **fuorché (eccetto)** uno.

*Rose fell. She broke her leg. Unfortunately it is **but** true.*
Rosa è caduta, Si è rotta la gamba. Peccato, è **pur troppo** vero!
*My cousin does nothing **but** sleep.*
Mio cugino non fa altro **che** dormire.
*You cannot **but** do what you can.*
Non vi **resta che** fare quello che potete.

Expanding your vocabulary

L'orto	*the garden*	**La bietola**	*the beet*
Il pomodoro	*the tomato*	**Il ravanello**	*the radish*
Il peperone	*the pepper*	**La carota**	*the carrot*
Il melone	*the melon*	**Il carciofo**	*the artichoke*
Il cocomero	*the watermelon*	**L'asparago**	*the asparagus*
Il cetriolo	*the cucumber*	**La cipolla**	*the onion*
La zucca	*the pumpkin*	**L'aglio**	*the garlic*
Lo zucchino	*the zucchini*	**Il cappuccio**	*the cabbage*
La patata	*the potato*	**Il cavolfiore**	*the cauliflower*
La rapa	*the turnup*	**Il porro**	*the leek*
Il sedano	*the celery*	**Lo spinacio**	*the spinach*
L'insalata	*the salad*	**Il prezzemolo**	*the parsley*
La fragola	*the strawberry*	**Il basilico**	*the basil*
Il fungo	*the mushroom*	**Il rosmarino**	*the rosemary*
Il fagiolo	*the bean*	**Il pisello**	*the pea*
L'oregano	*the oregano*	**Il finocchio**	*the fennel*
I broccoli	*the broccoli*	**Il cece**	*the chick pea*

Traduzione degli esercizi proposti nella lezione precedente

1) He did not buy neither the roses nor the carnations.
2) We have seen eight turkeys in the wood, and you? So have we.
3) Why did you get your hair to grow so long?
4) You smoke too much. It is not good for your health.
5) The car has arrived. Get in quickly, otherwise I'll be late.
6) I like red wine as much as I like white wine.

Esercizi da tradurre in Inglese

Io coltivo tanti vegetali nel mio orto, fra i quali il pomodoro e i fagioli.

....

Le fragole si maturano a giugno.

....

Mio fratello non fa altro che chiacchierare (to chat).

....

Com'è ch'egli se ne andò così all'improvviso?

....

Alzatevi per piacere, e andate a prendere del prezzemolo nell'orto.

....

Fate attenzione; non cadete nell'acqua.

....

Esercizi di lettura

Il regalo che mi hanno comprato mi ha piaciuto molto. Ho chiesto ai miei genitori con accento piacevole quanto hanno pagato per poter fare un regalo tanto costoso.

"Quello che ho speso non lo devi conoscere." Mi ha detto mio padre mentre rideva. "Io non posso rispondere, perché non posso prendermi tutta la responsabilità. Devo difendere il mio dovere per vincere il mio volere. Tienilo bene in mente per poter vivere una vita accesa di desiderio.

Mentre rimaneva seduto, "quando si nasce" continuò, facendo cadere l'accento sulle parole, "si cresce piangendo e ridendo. Non possiamo assumere, ma dobbiamo rispondere a ciò che ci condividiamo e scriverlo per poterlo leggere nel futuro.

Most of the words used to write the above reading exercise are taken from the fifteenth lesson.

THIRTY EIGHTH LESSON

Lezione Trentottesima

Tommaso, avete finito di studiare geografia a scuola?

"Signor Medici, ancora no. C'è tanto da studiare sulla geografia dell'Italia. Gli aspri fenomeni della Natura hanno creato tanta bellezza affascinante su questa Terra sapiente. Alte montagne, laghi profondi, fiumi lunghissimi, fertili campagne sono il risultato di enormi attività geologiche. Le sue splendide coste sono circondate da tre mari incantevoli."

"Ancora stiamo sui fiumi. Abbiamo imparato che il Volturno e il Garigliano, due fiumi che bagnano il Lazio e la Campania, sono stati di grande importanza storica durante il 1943 e 1944. Le più dure battaglie della Seconda Guerra Mondiale sono state combattute nei loro dintorni per conquistare la famosa Abbazia di Montecassino."

"Thomas, are you done studying geography in school?"

"Mr. Medici, not yet. There is so much to study about the geography of Italy. Nature's bitter phenomena have created so much fascinating beauty on this learned Land. High mountains, deep lakes, long rivers and fertile countryside are the result of enormous geological activities. Its splendid coastline are surrounded by three enchanting seas.

We are still studying the rivers. We have learned that the Volturno and the Garigliano, two rivers that flow through the Lazio and the Campania regions, have been of great historical importance during 1943 and 1944. The hardest fought battles of World War II took place all around them, in order to conquer the famous Monastery of Montecassino."

Beside those conjunctions we studied in the preceding lesson, there are a few more that need our attention.

Until, before are translated with **che, finché, fintanto che, prima di, prima che.**

*Wait **until** she calls you.* Aspettate **finché** lei vi chiami.
*I will not go **before** hearing from her.* Non andrò **prima che** lei mi chiami.

So... as are translated with **così... come, così... da.**

*My friend was **so** good **as** to tell me the whole story.*
Il mio amico fu **così** buono **da** raccontarmi tutta la storia.
*I hope you are not **so** naive **as** to believe everything she says.*
Spero che tu non sia **così** ingenuo **da** credere ogni cosa che lei dice.

Whether or not *are translated with* **che, se, o non.**

Whether *you come **or not**, does not matter to me.*
Se venite **o non** venite, non m'importa.

Both ... and *are translated with* **tanto ... quanto, entrambe.**

Both *mother **and** daughter are very beautiful.*
Tanto la madre **quanto** (che) la figlia sono tutte e due molto belle.
*Edward is **both** an electrician **and** a plumber.*
Edoardo è **entrambe** eletrecista e idraulico.

Out of *is translated with* **fuori di, per.**

*She begged me to help her **out of** kindness.*
Lei mi supplicò di aiutarla **per** gentilezza.
*For heaven sake, get **out of** the house and go **outdoors!***
Santo cielo, esci di casa e vai **fuori!**
*That gentleman curses his neighbor **out of** envy.*
Quel signore maledice il suo vicino **per** invidia.
*My brother-in-law saw a wolf. He is still shaking **out of** fear.*
Mio cognato ha visto un lupo. Ancora trema **per** la paura.

179

Basic emotions

The part of speech that deals with emotion is called *exclamation.* You have already learned the proper function of their characteristics. They deal with *joy,* **gioia;** *grief,* **dolore;** *fear,* **paura;** *exaltation,* **esaltazione;** *exasperation,* **disperazione;** *expression,* **espressione;** *affection,* **affezione;** *passion,* **passione;** *delight,* **piacere;** *nostalgia,* **nostalgìa;** *abandonment,* **abbandono;** *appeal,* **interesse;** *action,* **azione;** *conflict,* **conflitto;** *splendor,* **splendore;** *mood,* **feeling.**

Many exclamation sentences begin with *what. how, how much, how many, what a (an),* **che, come, quanto.**

> *What bad climate!* **Che** clima cattivo!
> *What a good boy!* **Che bravo ragazzo!**
> *How can he be so good!* **Come** può essere tanto buono!
> Good gracious how well she sings! Per bacco **come** canta bene!

There are special expressions which are used to beautify emotions and add splendor to facial feelings in conjunction with words.

What a pity!	Che peccato!	*Indeed!*	Davvero!
Well, well!	Ebbene, ebbene!	*Really!*	Veramente!
O dear! goodness!	Dio mio!	*Strange!*	Strano!
Good gracious!	Per bacco!	*Possible!*	Possibile!
Why!	Come, ma!	*Welcome!*	Benvenuto!
Of course!	Naturalmente!	*Hail!*	Salve, salute!
Hurra!	Evviva!	*Good bye!*	Arrivederci!
Oh, alas!	Ahimé!	*Farewell!*	Addio!
Eh, ah!	Eh, ah!	*Hello!*	Ciao!
Good heaven!	Cielo beato!	*God forbid!*	Dio ne guardi!
Hush!	Zitto, silenzio!	*God grant!*	Volesse Dio!
For God sake!	Per amor di Dio!	*Oh my God!*	Dio aiutami!
For Heaven's sake!	Per amor del cielo!	*What a sin!*	Che peccato!

What a pity seeing those bad boys ruining the park!
Che peccato vedere quei cattivi ragazzi rovinare il parco!
For God sake can't you be more careful!
Per l'amor di Dio non potete metterci più attenzione!
*Please, do it for my **sake!***
Per favore, fatelo per amor mio!
Of course it does not make much sense going out when it pours!
Naturalmente non fa senso di uscire quando piove a diluvio!

Before I forget, I want to mention that **sapere** *(to know)* may also be translated with *to be aware of* in English, depending on its function. Although they can be used indifferently, it is good to know that *to be aware of*, (**essere consapevole**) expresses the knowledge of something and the ability of remembering it.

*What day of the week is this? I don't **know.***
Che giorno della settimana è questo? Non lo **so.**
*Are **you aware** that you owe the bank more money?*
Lo sapete che ancora avete del debito con la banca?

Expanding your vocabulary

Remember that the fruit trees are masculine in Italian, except **la vite e la quercia.** Please add *–tree–* to the English translation: the ***orange-tree,*** etc.

Il frutteto:	*the orchard*	**Il pruno**	*the plum*
L'arancio	*the orange*	**Il noce**	*the walnut*
Il limone	*the lemon*	**Il castagno**	*the chestnut*
Il cedro	*the lime*	**Il nocciolo**	*the hazel nut*
Il pompelmo	*the grapefruit*	**Il fico**	*the fig*
Il banano	*the banana*	**L'ulivo**	*the olive*
Il melo	*the apple*	**La <u>vite</u>**	*the vine*
Il pero	*the pear*	**Il dattero**	*the date-palm*
Il ciliegio	*the cherry*	**Il melograno**	*the pomegranate*
Il pesco	*the peach*	**Il cachì**	*the persimmon*

181

Traduzione degli esercizi proposti nella lezione precedente

1) I grow many vegetables in my garden, among which tomatoes and beans.
2) Strawberries ripen in June.
3) My brother does nothing but chat.
4) Why is it that he left so suddenly?
5) Get up, please, and go to get some parsley in the garden.
6) Be careful, do not fall into the water.

Esercizi da tradurre in Italiano

We cultivate apple trees, cherry trees and pear trees in our orchard.

....

What a sin seeing so much fruit spoiled! (to spoil: guastare)

....

Well, well! What a nice suit you are wearing! (to wear: indossare)

....

Whether you do it or not, it is up to you.

....

Wait until the bus comes, before you start walking.

....

Both Albert and his friend have the same character.

....

Esercizi di lettura

Per piacere porta la frutta guastata fuori di casa. Lo so che fa un freddo infinito; tuttavia devi ubbidire e servirmi. Devi capire che non ho nessuna volontà di ammonirti presentemente. Appena che hai finito di fare il tuo servizio, torna subito dentro, affinché tu non prenda un raffreddore. Nel passato ha fatto molto più freddo durante l'inverno. Quest'anno la neve è caduta solo sulle punte della montagna.

Most of the words used for this reading exercise are taken from the sixteenth lesson.

THIRTY NINTH LESSON

Lezione Trentanovesima

Signor Toscani, che bel tempo fa oggi! Vi vedo occupato. Dove andate? Non ditemi che lasciate dietro le bellezze di Roma per recarvi a qualche altro posto!

"Si, signor Donatello; andiamo in Campania per una gita. Passeremo per Caserta per visitare il famoso Palazzo Reale. Poi proseguiremo per Pompei per visitare gli scavi. Passeremo per Sorrento, continuando lungo la famosa costa amalfitana. Forse passeremo la notte a Positano oppure a Salerno. Tornando, ci fermeremo a Napoli per visitare le famose bellezze della città e anche per goderci un bel piatto di spaghetti con una frittura di pesci, accompagnati da un buon bicchiere di Lacrima Cristi, il pregiato vino del Vesuvio."

Mr. Toscani, what beautiful weather we are having to-day! I see you very busy. Where are you going? Don't tell me that you are leaving behind the beauties of Rome in order to go somewhere else!

"Yes, Mr, Donatello; We are going to the Campania region for a ride. We will pass through Caserta so we can visit the famous Royal Palace. Then we will drive to Pompei to visit the ruins. We will go through Sorrento, continuing along the Amalfi Drive. We might spend the night in Positano or in Salerno. On the way back we will stop in Naples so we can visit the famous beauties of that city and also enjoy a good dish of spaghetti with a fish-fry, accompanied by a good glass of Lacrima Christi, the esteemed wine produced around the Vesuvius.

Collective nouns

Collective nouns are written in the singular, yet they comprise a large number of beings or of things. In English they may take the verb in the singular if they refer to the mass; or the plural form of the verb if they refer to individuals assembled together.

In Italian collective nouns always take the singular form of the verb.

People,	popolo, gente	*Government,*	governo
Crowd,	folla	*Group,*	gruppo
Jury,	giuria	*Formation,*	schiera
Clergy,	clero	*Herd, pack,*	branco
Family,	famiglia	*Flock,*	gregge
Army,	esercito	*Flight,*	stormo
Navy,	marina	*Team*	squadra

*The government **has** many members.*
Il governo **ha** tanti membri.
*People **have** declared victory.*
Il popolo **ha** dichiarato vittoria.
*The army **has** invaded the front line.*
L'esercito ha invaso la prima linea.

Formation of words

We can double, triple, quadruple, etc. our vocabulary by applying prefixes or suffixes to existing words.

Prefixes are attached to the beginning of a word. Suffixes are attached to the end of a word. Both languages use an extensive number of them to form nouns, adjectives, verbs and adverbs.

Some of them can be referenced to Italian. Some of them not. Let's look at some suffixes: *Ship, dom, hood, head, ness, er, ess, ful, less, some, ish, like, able, ible, en, y, ward, fullness, lessness, lessly, wise.*

Friend,	amico	*Friend-ship,*	amicizia
King,	re	*King-dom,*	regno
Free	libero	*Free-dom,*	libertà
Child	bambino	*Child-hood,*	infante

184

God	Dio	**God-head**	divinità
Use	uso	**Use-ful**	utile
Thought	pensiero	**Thought-ful**	Pensieroso
Faith	fede	**Faith-less**	infedele
Care	cura	**Care-less**	trascurato
Polite	cortese	**Polite-ness**	cortesia
Man	uomo	**Man-like**	virile
Lady	signora	**Lady-like**	da signora
Gold	oro	**Gold-en**	di oro
Wood	legno	**Wood-en**	di legno
Sad	triste	**Sadd-en**	attristare
Soft	dolce, soffice	**Soft-en**	addolcire
Fog	nebbia	**Fogg-y**	nebbioso
Red	rosso	**Redd-ish**	rossastro
Faithful	fedele	**Faithful-ness**	fedeltà
Careful	accurato	**Careful-ness**	accuratezza
Home-ward	verso casa	**Down-ward**	all'ingiù
Like	simile	**Like-wise**	parimenti

Let's go over some of the English suffixes that can relate to some of the Italian ones.

Ness can be compared to the Italian suffix **ezza.**

Kind	gentile	**Kind-ness**	gentil-**ezza**
Bitter	amaro	**Bitter-ness**	amar-**ezza**
Sweet	dolce	**Sweet-ness**	dolc-**ezza**

Er can be compared to the Italian **aio and tore** *which indicate possession.*

Hat	cappello	**Hatt-er**	cappell-**aio**
To write	scrivere	**Writ-er**	scrit-**tore**
To love	amare	**Lov-er**	ama-**tore**
To work	lavorare	**Work-er**	lavora-**tore**
To win	vincere	**Winn-er**	vinci-**tore**

Ess is similar to the Italian **essa**. They form feminine words.

Poet	il poeta	*Poet-ess*	la poet-**essa**
Prince	principe	*Princ-ess*	princip-**essa**

ome is translated with the Italian **oso**.

Trouble	fastidio	*Trouble-some*	fastidi-**oso**
To tire	faticare	*Tire-some*	fatic-**oso**
Noise	rumore	*Noi-some*	rumor-**oso**

ih is translated in Italian with **esco**.

Boy	ragazzo	*Boy-ish*	ragazz-**esco**
Knave	briccone	*Knav-ish*	briccon-**esco**

ble, ible are translated in Italian with **abile, ibile**.

To eat	mangiare	*Eat-able*	mangi-**abile**
To drink	bere	*Drink-able*	pot-**abile**
Sense	senso	*Sens-ible*	sens-**ibile**

When learning the above words you should realize that it is possible) double the vocabulary without much effort by referencing words to each ther.

Traduzione degli esercizi proposti nella lezione precedente

) Noi coltiviamo il melo, il ciliegio e il pero nel nostro frutteto
) Che peccato vedere tanta frutta guastata!
) Ebbene, ebbene! Che bel vestito avete indossato!
) Se venite o non venite, dipende da voi.
) Aspetta finché arriva l'autobus, prima di cominciare a camminare.
) Tanto Alberto che il suo amico, entrambi hanno lo stesso carattere.

Exercises to be translated into English

Gino, non piangere. Perché sei così sensibile!

....

L'acqua sporca non è potabile.

....

L'officina di montaggio (assembly shop) è molto rumorosa.

....

Cielo beato! non fate mai una cosa buona!

....

Omero è stato il primo grande poeta. Ada Negri è stata una poetessa.

....

Shakespear è stato un grande scrittore come Alessandro Manzoni.

....

Esercizi di lettura

Il ventuno dicembre esce l'autunno e comincia l'inverno. In quel giorno accade il Solstizio d'Inverno. Il venticinque dello stesso mese viene il Santo Natale. In famiglia si offrono dei regali, i quali si aprono la mattina della festa. Tutti rimangono contenti e soddisfatti. Ogni anno si rifà la stessa cosa per celebrare questo grande evento.
Quelli che possono, escono fuori a mezzanotte per udire le campane suonare a festa.

I generali sogliono rifinire i loro piani se vogliono disfare il nemico, specialmente quando i soldati sono sfiniti.

Most of the words used to write this exercise are taken from the seventeenth lesson.

La maggior parte delle parole usate per scrivere questo esercizio sono state prese dalla diciassettesima lezione.

FORTIETH LESSON

Lezione Quarantesima

Signor Palestrina, perché c'è tanta folla per le strade di Roma oggi? Sono appena le nove e un quarto e già le strade sono piene di gente.

"Signor Belli, oggi è come una bella giornata di primavera. La gente ne approfitta per visitare le famose fontane di Roma ed i suoi illustri capolavori creati da Bernini, da Michelangelo, da Raffaello, da Giulio Romano, da Nicola Salvi, da Bramante e da tanti altri pittori e architetti. I visitatori si possono godere la Roma del periodo dei Re, della Repubblica, dell'Impero, del Cristianesimo; e la Roma dei nostri giorni."

Mr. Palestrina, why are there so many people along the streets of Rome? It is only a quarter past nine and the streets are already crowded.

"Mr. Belli, to-day is like a beautiful spring day. People are taking advantage of it, so they may visit the famous Fountains of Rome and its great masterpieces created by Bernini, Michelangelo, Raffaello, by Giulio Romano, by Nicola Salvi, by Bramante and by many other painters and architects. The visitors can enjoy the Rome of the periods of the Kings, of the Republic, of the Empire, of the Christianity; and Rome of to-day."

Formation of words

In the preceding lesson we looked at the most important suffixes of the English language and the relationship they share with the Italian.

In this lesson we will look at many other Italian suffixes, besides those already mentioned. It is a long list. I think it is my duty to go over the most important ones for the benefit of each student, My suggestion is to learn those you think you may need; and go over the rest of them when the necessity arises.

A particular group is constituted by suffixes which form **altered nouns:** ragazzo, ragazz-**ino,** ragazz-**etto,** ragazz-**uccio,** ragazz-**ello,** ragazz-**one,** ragazz-**accio.** We have already gone over these suffixes, when we were dealing with nouns, as such I am not going to write down the translation.

Aglia – added to a noun gives a collective and pejorative meaning.

Bosco	*wood*	**Bosc-aglia**	*undergrowth*
Gente	*people*	**Gent-aglia**	*louts*
Cane	*dog*	**Can-aglia**	*scoundrel*

Ale – indicate something put together or subjected to do something.

Casa	*House*	**Cas-ale**	*hamlet*
Morte	*death*	**Mort-ale**	*mortal*
Fato	*fate*	**Fat-ale**	*fatal*

Ano – indicates a place of belonging

Isola	*island*	**isol-ano**	*islander*
America	*America*	**Americ-ano**	*American*
Roma	*Rome*	**Rom-ano**	*Roman*

Arlo – indicates real or imaginable things

Visione	*vision*	**vision-ario**	*visionary*
Missione	*mission*	**mission-ario**	*missionary*
Milione	*million*	**milion-ario**	*millionaire*

Ato – may form a past participle or indicate a condition

Celibe	*single*	**celib-ato**	*celibacy*
Gelo	*ice*	**gel-ato**	*ice-cream*
Raffreddore	*cold*	**raffredd-ato**	*nasty cold*

Eria – indicates a place of work

Infermiera	*nurse*	**inferm-eria**	*infirmary*
Macello	*butcher shop*	**macell-eria**	*slaughter house*

Ista – indicates trade

Musica	*music*	**music-ista**	*musician*
Arte	*art*	**art-ista**	*artist*

Mento – indicates happening

Stabile	*stable*	**stabili-mento**	*factory*
Cambio	*change*	**cambia-mento**	*shift*

189

Tura – indicates work in progress

| **Tessere** | *to weave* | **tessi-tura** | *weaving* |

Evole – indicates appreciation

| **Lode** | *praise* | **lod-evole** | *praiseworthy* |

Ico – indicates the form

| **Cono** | *cone* | **con-ico** | *conical* |

Istico – indicates the mood of something

| **Carattere** | *character* | **caratter-istico** | *characteristic* |

Eggiare – forms a verb from a noun

| **Passo** | *pace* | **pass-eggiare** | *to go for a walk* |

There are some more suffixes in Italian. I think this long list is enough for the student to recognize the philosophy of the origin of a word.

Suffixes and prefixes make the spelling of long words much easier.

Let's take the word **use**: we can make use-*ful*, use-*ful-ly*, use- *less*, use-*less-ly*, use-*less-ness*, *us-able*. If we add prefixes, we can make *re-use*, *dis-use*, *re-us-able*.

Traduzione degli esercizi proposti nella lezione precedente

1) Gino, don't cry. Why are you so sensible!

2) Dirty water is not drinkable.

3) The assembly shop is very noisy.

4) Good Heaven! You never do anything right!

5) Homer was the first great poet. Ada Negri was a poetess.

6) Shakespear was a great writer, as was Alessandro Manzoni.

Esercizi da tradurre in Italiano

To-day we are going for a walk along the river.

....

According to Dante, hell had a conical form.

....

My mother was kept in the infirmary for a long time.

....

American missionaries have a mission in Africa.

....

His mortal blow (colpo) was a fatal one.

....

My friend's character is really characteristic.

....

Esercizi di lettura

Ieri abbiamo avuto bel tempo. Verso sera una quantità di nuvole hanno cominciato a imbrunire e addensarsi lentamente e gentilmente. La pallida luna affermava chiaramente che davanti alla sua misera luce si vedeva già un velo di neve.

Il nonno guardò all'insù ed affermò: "Più tardi comincerà a nevicare. Non c'è dubbio. Ce lo dice quel venticello che spira dal Nord. Non c'è modo migliore per annunziarlo."

Quella mattina presto, prima di farsi giorno, sulla terra c'era un manto di neve. Mai era caduta tanta neve. La Natura aveva creato un quadro spettacolare. I bambini gridavano felicemente fuori. Non capita troppo spesso un fenomeno così amabile.

Some of the words used for this reading exercise are taken from the eighteenth lesson.

FORTY FIRST LESSON

Lezione Quarantunesima

Pietro, so che a scuola state studiando storia. Cosa state studiando?
"Cesare, si, stiamo studiando il Risorgimento, il periodo delle Guerre d'Indipendenza. Dopo la caduta di Napoleone, benché ancora divisa in vari stati, il popolo italiano aspirava alla propria unità. In seguito alle Guerre d'Indipendenza, guidate da Garibaldi, Cavour, Vittorio Emanuele Secondo, Mazzini e tanti altri eroi, nel 1861nacque il nuovo Regno d'Italia.
Roma fu proclamata capitale d'Italia il primo Luglio del 1871.

Peter, I know you are studying history in school. What are you studying?

"Caesar, yes, we are studying the "Risorgimento", the period in which the Wars of Independence were fought. After the fall of Napoleon, although still divided into various states, the Italian people aspired to its own unity. Following the Wars of Independence, guided by Garibaldi, Cavour, Victor Emanuel II, Mazzini and many more other heroes, in the year 1861 the new Kingdom of Italy was born.

Rome was proclaimed Capital of Italy on the first of July, 1871.

Prefixes

We have already learned that it is possible to form words from other existing words by adding prefixes and suffixes. Both languages use a various number of them. Some share the same meaning; some do not. Prefixes that preserve the same meaning come from Latin and from Greek.

Let's look at some Greek prefixes: ***Archeo:*** *ancient ;* ***Auto:*** *self;* ***Bio:*** *life;* ***Crono:*** *time;* ***Demo:*** *people;* ***Micro:*** *small;* ***Ortho:*** *bone;* ***Peri:*** *around;* ***Photo:*** *light;* ***Psych:*** *soul;* ***Tele:*** *far;* ***Zoo:*** *animal; etc.*

Let's also find out about some Latin prefixes: **Ante, anti:** before; **Bi:** two; **Inter:** between; **Ex:** past; **Extra:** more; **Post:** after; **Pro:** in favor; **Sub:** under; **Super:** above; **Ultra:** more than; **Vice:** substituting for; **etc.**

Now let's take a look at some of the English prefixes: *a, al, be, by, for, fore, mis, n, out, over, to, un, under, up, wel, with.*

Rise	alzare	*A-rise*	alzarsi
Together	insieme	*Al-together*	tutto insieme
Low	basso	*Be-low*	sotto
Law	legge	*By-law*	regolamento
Get	ottenere	*For-get*	scordare
Tell	dire	*Fore-tell*	pre-dire (shared)
Deed	fatto	*Mis-deed*	mis-fatto (shared)
Ever	mai	*N-ever*	mai più
Live	vivere	*Out-live*	sopravvivere
Time	tempo	*Over-time*	straordinario
Night	notte	*To-night*	questa notte
Happy	felice	*Un-happy*	infelice
Necessary	utile	*Un-necessary*	inutile
Take	prendere	*Under-take*	intraprendere
Come	venire	*Wel-come*	benvenuto
Stand	rizzarsi	*With-stand*	opporsi

Going over the English prefixes we have come across a couple which share the same formation as in Italian.

Now we are going to deal with additional Italian prefixes which are not related at all.

A – denotes the will to do; or not to do.

Spirare	*expire*	**A-spirare**	*inspire*
Politico	*politician*	**A-politico**	*not political*

Arci – denotes superiority.

Prete	*priest*	**Arci-prete**	*dean*
Pelago	*sea*	**Arci-pelago**	*archipelago*

Con – indicates company, sharing. Before *p and b* –n– changes to –m–.

Dividere	*to divide*	**Con-dividere**	*to share*
Portare	*to bring*	**Com-portare**	*to behave*

De, di – indicates renunciation.

Porre	*to place*	**De-porre**	*to put down*
Scendere	*to go down*	**Di-scendere**	*to descend*

Dis – indicates distress, separation.

Perdere	*to lose*	**Dis-perdere**	*to disperse*
Corso	*course*	**Dis-corso**	*speech*

Fra – denotes something in between.

Porre	*to put*	**Fra-pporre**	*interpose*
Cassare	*to cancel*	**Fra-cassare**	*to smash*

In – indicates negation.

Fiamma	*flame*	**In-fiammare**	*to inflame*
Fedele	*faithful*	**In-fedele**	*unfaithful*

Re, ri – indicates an action which repeats itself.

Agire	*to act*	**Re-agire**	*to re-act (shared)*
Fare	*to make*	**Ri-fare**	*to re-make* "

S – Indicates the opposition to an action.

Caricare	*to load*	**S-caricare**	*to unload*
Leale	*loyal*	**S-leale**	*disloyal*

Sopra – indicates over, above.

Fino	*fine*	**Sopra-ffino**	*refined*
Abito	*suit*	**Sopra-bito**	*overcoat*

Sotto – denotes under, below.

Terra	*ground*	**Sotto-terra**	*underground*
Linea	*line*	**Sotto-lineare**	*to underline*

I have listed the most important prefixes in both languages. As I said before, I have done it for the benefit of each student. It is hard to memorize every one; yet it is there if needed.

There are many more prefixes and suffixes that come from Latin and from Greek. A good dictionary will lead you the correct way, if you are willing to enrich your own vocabulary: done with an easy touch.

Traduzione degli esercizi proposti nella lezione precedente

1) Oggi andremo per una passeggiata lungo il fiume.
2) Secondo Dante, l'Inferno aveva una forma conica.
3) Mia madre fu tenuta nell'infermeria per molto tempo.
4) I missionari americani hanno una missione in Africa.
5) Il suo colpo mortale fu un colpo fatale.
6) Il carattere del mio amico è veramente caratteristico.

Esercizi da tradurre in Inglese

Quando gli orsi vanno a letargo (hibernate), essi dormono sottoterra.
....
Non si dovrebbero rifare gli stessi errori.
....
Perchè hai reagito così furiosamente alla cattiva notizia?
....
La mia ferita (wound) s'è infiammata terribilmente.
....
Credevo che i miei amici fossero leali, invece sono stati sleali.
....

Esercizi di lettura

**Buon compleanno, i miei migliori auguri. Indubbiamente niente
è più bello di un giorno come questo. Riceverai certamente generosi
regali. Ti ho visto correre dentro, fuori, lassù, quaggiù, qua, là, sotto,
sopra, costì, costà, davanti, dietro. Sono sicuro che sei molto eccitato.
Nemmeno una lepre corre tanto forte quanto te. È da ieri che ti vedo
molto felice. Probabilmente oggi sarà grande festa in famiglia.
Ora sei un grande ragazzo. Quanti anni hai? Nemmeno tu non me lo
vuoi dire? Allora dimmi se c'indovino. Tu hai dodici anni, vero?
"Si, come hai fatto per indovinarci? Arrivederci a domani".**

Some of the above words are also taken from the eighteenth lesson.

FORTY SECOND LESSON

Lezione Quarantaduesima

Nella classe di storia e geografia il professore chiama Angelo e gli chiede: "Sai dirmi in quante regioni è divisa l'Italia? Ne sai il nome?"

Angelo sorride e risponde: "Sig. professore, l'Italia è divisa in venti regioni. Io so il nome; e anche il nome delle loro capitali."

A Nord c'è la Valle d'Aosta: capitale Aosta; il Piemonte: capitale Torino; la Lombardia: capitale Milano; il Veneto: capitale Venezia; il Trentino Alto Adige: capitale Trento; il Friuli Venezia Giulia: capitale Trieste; la Liguria: capitale Genova.

Al centro c'è l'Emilia Romagna: capitale Bologna; la Toscana: capitale Firenze; le Marche: capitale Ancona; l'Umbria: capitale Perugia; l'Abruzzo: capitale l'Aquila; il Lazio: capitale Roma; il Molise: capitale Campobasso.

A Sud c'è la Campania: capitale Napoli; la Puglia: capitale Bari; la Basilicata: capitale Potenza; la Calabria: capitale Catanzaro.

Poi ci sono le isole: la Sicilia con capitale Palermo; e la Sardegna con Capitale Cagliari."

In the social studies class the professor calls Angelo and asks: "Can you tell me in how many regions is Italy divided? Do you know their names?"

Angelo smiles and answers: "Professor, Italy is divided into twenty regions. I know their names and also the names of each capital.

In the North there is Valle d'Aosta: capital Aosta; Piedmont: capital Turin; Lombardy: capital Milan; Venetia: capital Venice; Trentino Alto Adige: capital Trento; Friuli Venetia Giulia: capital Trieste; Liguria: capital Genoa;

In the center there is Emilia Romagna: capital Bologna; Tuscany:

196

capital Florence; Marche: capital Ancona; Umbria: capital Perugia; Abruzzo: capital l'Aquila; Latium: capital Rome; Molise: capital Campobasso.

In the South there is Campania: capital Naples; Apulia: capital Bari; Basilicata: capital Potenza; Calabria: capital Catanzaro.

Then there are the islands: Sicily: capital Palermo; and Corsica: capital Cagliari.

Fare: *to do or to make*

We have already learned that *to do and to make* are translated in Italian with the verb **fare,** it doesn't matter if they express a general feeling or express a physical, a material or a manual action.

Fare is extensively used in Italian as much as in English. However, sometime *to do or to make* are translated with **commettere; recare; rendere; darsi il piacere; pettinarsi; lavorare; chiedere; allearsi; scusarsi; suicidarsi; deridersi; informarsi; riconciliarsi; scappare; decidersi; diventare.**

Danny has done a good action.	Donato ha fatto una buona azione.
Gino did a favor to me.	Gino mi fece un piacere.
Please do your exercises well.	Per favore fai i tuoi esercizi bene.
Watch out, don't do him harm.	Attenzione, non fargli male.
Why aren't you doing anything?	Perchè non stai facendo niente?
You do wrong like this.	Voi fate male in questo modo.
I do as I please.	Io faccio come mi pare.
I cannot do much business.	Non posso fare troppi affari.
Please, do it out of kindness.	Per piacere, fallo per gentilezza.
Luis did a foolish thing.	Luigi **ha commesso** una sciocchezza.
Bad weather did a lot of damage.	Il cattivo tempo **ha recato** molto danno.
The jury has done justice.	La giuria **ha reso** giustizia.
That girl did her own hair.	Quella ragazza s'è **pettinata.**
My father did a lot of work.	Mio padre **ha lavorato** molto.
It is easier said than done.	Tra il dire e il fare c'è in mezzo il mare.

Lucy made a good bargain.	Lucia ha fatto un buon affare.
Did you make the essay?	Hai fatto il tema?
I know you made a good offer.	Lo so che hai fatto una buona offerta
Angela has made a blunder.	Angela **ha commesso** un errore.
Laura made a long journey.	Laura ha fatto un lungo viaggio.
The Congress made a new law.	Il Congresso ha fatto una legge nuova.
David made a bad mistake.	Davide fece un grande errore.
The senator made a long speech.	Il senatore fece un lungo discorso.
He also made a good proposal.	Fece anche una buona proposta.
My father made a will.	Mio padre ha fatto un testamento.
My parents made an agreement.	I miei genitori **son** a un accordo.
England made alliance with US.	L'Inghilterra **si alleò** con gli Stati Uniti.
Luisa made an apology.	Luisa si **scusò**.
Al made away with himself.	Alberto si **suicidò**.
Mike made fun of me.	Michele si **derise** di me.
Alba made inquiries about me.	Alba **s'informò** su di me.
The dog made it up with the cat.	Il cane **s'è riconciliato** con il gatto.
The prisoner made his escape.	Il prigioniero **scappò** dalla prigione.
The bad news made me unhappy.	La cattiva notizia mi **ha reso** infelice.
Paul couldn't make up his mind.	Paolo non poteva **decidersi.**

Good Leaders should make peace rather than make war.
Buoni Capi di Stato dovrebbero fare la pace piuttosto che fare la guerra.

The list is quite long. Except for those few particular examples I have included in *bold,* every time the students build a sentence using *to do or to make,* it can easily be translated with **fare** all through its conjugation.

Traduzione degli esercizi proposti nella lezione precedente

1) When the bears hibernate, they sleep underground.
2) One should not make the same mistakes twice.
3) Why have you reacted so furiously to the bad news?
4) My wound inflamed itself terribly.
5) I thought that my friends were loyal, yet they have been disloyal.

Esercizi da tradurre in Italiano

Please, do me a big favor; will you go away?

....

Make me a cup of coffee, if you please.

....

Peter will make (diventerà) a good general.

....

Did you make it up with Michael?

....

I teach you the right way; and you always make the same mistakes.

....

It is easier said than done.

....

Esercizi di lettura

Oggi è il venticinque dicembre. È Natale: la grande festa dei Cristiani. Secondo la tradizione i zampognari hanno annunziato il grande Avvenimento suonando le loro zampogne davanti alla porta degli abitanti dei dintorni. È stato un grande piacere sentirli suonare la novena, cominciando nove giorni prima della festa.
A cagione delle vacanze gli alunni hanno messo i libri sopra il tavolo dentro alla loro stanza e sono corsi in mezzo agli altri verso gli zampognari. Alcuni correvano avanti; altri li correvano dietro con la camicia sotto sopra.
La mattina della festa la mamma è rimasta lungo tempo in cucina prima che si riunissero tutti. Ha preparato le nove pietanze per mantenere viva la gloriosa tradizione e le ha servite all'intera famiglia. Dopo il lungo pasto lei ha servito il torrone ed il panettone; e anche il caffè espresso, addolcito con liquore Sambuca.
Il giorno di Natale ogni famiglia celebra insieme questa grande Festa.
Some of the words used to write the above exercise are taken from the nineteenth lesson.

FORTY THIRD LESSON

Lezione Quarantatreesima

Oggi è il diciannove Marzo. In tutta l'Italia si celebra la festa di San Giuseppe. È una bella giornata di sole. Fuori fa già caldo. È un giorno perfetto per andare a far le compre al mercato all'aperto. Ogni regione d'Italia onora questo grande Santo in un unico modo. La sua festa si celebra con le tradizionali zeppole e le famose ciambelle di Sora.

La tradizione vuole che il fidanzato compri delle ciambelle al mercato, per regalarle alla sua fidanzata. Lei, poi, lo ricompenserà con una pizza dolce, fatta con le proprie mani, regalandocela il giorno di Pasqua.

To-day is March nineteenth. All over Italy people celebrate the feast of St. Joseph. It is a beautiful sunny day. It is already warm outside and a perfect day to go shopping at the open market. Every region of Italy honors this great Saint in a unique way. His feast is celebrated with the traditional zeppole (cream filled pastries) and with the famous ciambelle (ring-shaped buns) made in Sora.

Tradition has it that a boyfriend buys some ciambelle at the open market and he gives them as a present to his girlfriend. She, then, will reward him by making a special rum-cake with her own hands and gives it to him on Easter Sunday as a present.

Syntax

So far we have studied words; and we have distinguished them into categories. We have given a name to each category (article, noun, verb, etc.) and we have gone over their form and their usage. Now we have to order them in a sentence which shall express our thoughts.

If we observe how people use the language, speaking among

themselves, we realize that they always make use of entire sentences in which words are joined tidily together to form a speech.

We call syntax that part of grammar which studies the various methods in which the words are connected among themselves; in order to give a sentence a complete and precise meaning.

We have now reached that point of real structure and real logical organization of the language. Who speaks or writes, although having full authority over his or her linguistic liberty, has to conform to the formal logical elements, to the linguistic traditions of one's own Land and to the culture we live in.

Simple syntax: studies the coordination of words in a simple sentence.

Complex syntax: studies compound sentences in a period connected tidily together.

There are many rules regarding the syntax. We have gone over them while studying grammar. We have done this to render a complete and clear usage of the parts of speech.

I have already advised the student to use short sentences. It is a good practice to avoid misunderstandings. Italian does not use the conjunction **"and"** too often to connect sentences together. English speakers, however, are in the habit of repeating *"and"* too many times in a period.

We can express a clear thought by using the subject, the **verbal** or **nominal predicate** and very few complements in a sentence.

By adding many compound sentences in a period, we delude our thoughts. We push the listener away from the complete fluidity of the principal meaning of our simple expression.

I am not going to explain how to form a sentence. I know for certain that you need no help. Both languages build their sentences using the same format. The rules are the same.

Man is at the center of his linguistic activity. Having a rich vocabulary, he can rapidly express his thoughts, his feelings, his will, by skillfully communicating the language which he himself has invented.

201

I will leave the tusk up to the student of always keeping fresh and ready in his mind the rules that he or she has learned. I urge the student to frequently review the lessons which we have studied. I also advise to always read the Italian words we have learned and the reading exercises aloud. Do not read mentally. You'll do a disservice to yourself. If you doubt the pronunciation, go to the vocabulary for help. *A little work goes a long way.*

Instead of talking about subject, predicate and complements, I will give you some sentences which present peculiarities in the translation of their functions in Italian to the particular functions in English.

Verbal predicate: it is constituted by any verbal form, active or passive, which expresses a completed action.

Francesco lavora. *Frank works.* The action is completed. We don't need any other explanation to understand what Frank is doing.

Nominal predicate: it is constituted by the verb *to be* accompanied by a noun or by an adjective.

L'Italia è una penisola. *Italy is a peninsula.*
La strada è pericolosa. *The road is dangerous.*
I miei genitori sono buoni. *My parents are good.*

It may not be important to you, however if *to be* is accompanied by another verb, it is no longer a coupling verb (predicato nominale), it becomes a (predicato verbale).

Mario **è ritornato** a casa. *Mario has **returned** home.*
Luigi **è stato lodato** dal padre. *Louis **was praised** by his father.*

If you observe the above sentences, the construction is the same for both languages.

Let's continue with sentences which do not differ from one language to the other, making sure that we know exactly what we are learning.

202

Credo che sia ora di andare a casa, non è vero?
I think it is time to go home, is it not?
Che peccato, è una giornata così bella!
What a pity, it is such a lovely day!
Lasciami in pace. Che modi son questi?
Leave me alone. What's the matter with you?
Vorrei telefonare, dov'è l'ufficio telefonico?
I would like to make a telephone call. Where is the office?
Sta vicino alla stazione, ma credo che ora non sia aperto.
It is near the station, but I think it is not open now.
Potresti dirmi dov'è un buon ristorante?
Could you tell me where there is a good restaurant?
Si, non troppo lontano da qui. Andate dritto; poi girate a destra.
Yes, no too far from here. Go straight; then turn right.

Expand your vocabulary

Il tavolo	*the table*	Il peso	*the weight*
La sedia	*the chair*	Il grammofono	*gramophone*
Il letto	*the bed*	La borsa	*the bag*
La lampada	*the lamp*	La stanza	*the room*
La stufa	*the stove*	Giovane	*young*
L'orologio	*the watch*	Il cucchiaio	*the spoon*
Lo zio	*the uncle*	La forchetta	*the fork*
La penna	*the pen*	Il coltello	*the knife*
La pipa	*the pipe*	La bottiglia	*the bottle*
Il tamburo	*the drum*	Il bambino	*the child*
Il compasso	*the compasses*	Il sarto	*the tailor*
La giraffa	*the giraffe*	Il tappeto	*the carpet*
La mano	*the hand*	La chiesa	*the church*
Il nido	*the nest*	La bottega	*the shop*
La porta	*the door*	Povero	*poor*
Il cappello	*the hat*	Fresco	*fresh*
L'acqua	*the water*	Stanco	*tired*
La libbra	*the pound*	L'abito	*the dress*

Traduzione degli esercizi proposti nella lezione precedente

1) Fammi il santo piacere. Vai via da qui.
2) Fammi una tazza di caffè, per favore.
3) Pietro diventerà un buon generale.
4) Ti sei riconciliato con Michele?
5) T'insegno la via dritta; e tu fai sempre lo stesso errore.
6) Tra il dire e il fare c'è in mezzo il mare.

Esercizi da tradurre in Inglese

Sono stanco; il viaggio è stato lungo.

....

Le mie sorelle dormono ambedue insieme nella stanza da letto.

....

La bottiglia con il latte caldo del bambino sta sopra al tavolo.

....

Lo zio s'è comprato l'orologio e lo porta messo sul polso (wrist).

....

Domani sera andremo al teatro a goderci l'opera "*Rigoletto*" di Verdi.

....

Esercizi di lettura

Siamo arrivati al ventuno Marzo. Il cielo è chiaro. Il sole ha cominciato a riscaldare non solo la terra, ma anche l'acqua del mare. Infatti in ogni parte della terra il giorno e la notte sono di dodici ore, dunque sono di uguale durata, fuorché i poli. Perciò noi chiamiamo questo fenomeno: *equinozio*. Oggi comincia la primavera, la stagione dei fiori e del rinnovamento, quindi è festa in ogni cuore. È anche la festa di San Benedetto, quando le rondini tornano sul tetto.

A few words used to write the above reading exercise, have been taken from the twentieth lesson.

FORTY FOURTH LESSON

Lezione Quarantaquattresima

Achille, perché non vai a scuola oggi? Ti vedo ben vestito e anche molto eccitato. Che ti è successo?

"Signor Mascagni, oggi cominciano le vacanze di Primavera. Il nostro professore ci porta ad esplorare le bellezze di questa nostra Terra incantante. Lo sai? L'Italia seduce con il suo incomparabile fascino, con la sua storia e con il suo romanticismo. Visiteremo i canali di Venezia, l'arte di Firenze, le rovine di Roma, quelle di Pompei e quelle della Sicilia.

Sarà un viaggio indimenticabile, lungo il quale ci fermeremo a mangiare pranzi squisiti nei famosi ristoranti locali e a bere vino rinomato."

Achilles, why aren't you going to school to-day? I see you are well dressed and also very excited. What has happened to you?

"Mr. Mascagni, spring vacation begins today. Our professor is taking us to explore the beauties of our enchanted Country. Do you know? Italy seduces with its incomparable charms, with its history and with its romance. We shall visit the canals of Venice, the arts of Florence, the ruins of Rome, those of Pompeii and those of Sicily.

It will be an unforgettable trip, along which we'll stop to eat exquisite food in well known local restaurants and to drink famous wines."

In the previous lesson we learned that a sentence is a group of words connected together so as to formulate a clear thought. A subject, a predicate and few complements are enough to declare our intentions.

Il soggetto is usually a noun or a pronoun.

La vacca mangia l'erba. ***The cow*** eats grass.

Voi andate a lavorare.   *You* all go to work.
Nessuno è perfetto.   *Nobody* is perfect.

Often the subject pronoun is omitted in Italian when the verb itself indicates the person to which it refers.

Non mi **avete** ancora mandato quello che **ho** richiesto.
You have not yet sent me what *I* have requested.
Non lo **so** come **sto**. Il dottore non mi ha ancora visitato.
I don't know how I am. The doctor has not visited me yet.

If we, however, want to stress the power of the subject pronoun, then we have to include the pronoun.

Tu sei indisciplinato; lo sai tu?
You are undisciplined; you know it?
Noi, uomini di coraggio, non temiamo il pericolo.
We, men of courage, do not fear danger.

Predicato nominale: as we have already mentioned, it is usually formed by a noun or by an adjective connected to the subject by the verb *to be.*

Noi siamo giovani educati. *We are educated young men.*
Le mie rose sono rosse. *My roses are red.* (every word rimes)

Predicato verbale: it agrees with the subject both in person and number.

Noi cantiamo una canzone popolare. *We sing a popular song.*

Let's look at some English verbs which in their single form may have more than one meaning when translated into Italian.

To cast:	**fóndere, gettàre** (metalli)	*To spread:*	**stèndere, spàrgere**
To hit:	**colpìre, percuòtere**	*To upset:*	**scóncertare, rovésciare**
To hurt:	**far male, nuòcere**	*To wet:*	**bàgnare, inumidìre**

206

To knit:	fare, làvorare a maglia	*To abite:*	abìtare, dìmorare
To let:	perméttere, dare a fitto	*To bent:*	piegàre, curvàre
To put:	méttere, porre, pósare	*To bind:*	legàre, strìngere
To set:	sistémare, méttere, dispórre	*To build:*	fabbrìcare, costrùire
To shed:	versàre lagrime, spàrgere	*To catch:*	piglìare, acchiappàre
To slit:	fèndere, spaccàre	*To creep:*	strìsciare, arrampìcare
To split:	spaccare, fendere	*To deal:*	trafficare, negóziare
To dare:	ardìre, ósare	*To feed:*	nùtrire, pàscere
To fight:	combàttere, bàttersi	*To fling:*	scaglìare, lancìare
To get:	otténere, dìventare	*To lay:*	posàre, mettére
To gild:	dórare, indórare	*To lead:*	guidàre, condùrre
To hang:	appèndere, attaccàre	*To leave:*	làsciare, abbandonàre
To keep:	manténere, conservàre	*To shine:*	splèndere, rilùcere
To mean:	significàre, intèndere	*To shoot:*	spàrare, uccìdere
To meet:	incontràre, imbàttersi	*To smell:*	odórare, aver odore
To spill:	spàrgere, rovescìare	*To stay:*	stàre, rimànere
To strike:	percùotere, cólpìre, suónare le ore, scìoperare		
To string:	infilàre, infilzàre	*To sweep:*	scopàre, spazzàre
To understand:	capìre, intèndere	*To wring:*	tòrcere, svellàre
To win:	vìncere, guadagnàre	*To wax:*	incérare, divenìre

I know exactly what you are going to ask me: "How can we decide which verb to use between the two or more of them?"

Except for a few, one or the other verb will fulfill approximately the same action.

Please, put the table-cloth on the table.
Per favore, metta, *ponga, posi,* la tovaglia sul tavolo.

However, often we have only one choice. We cannot use **porre, posare,** if we go to buy some gasoline. We can only use **mettere.**

Attendant, please put 10 liters of gas in my tank.
Servitore, per piacere mi metta 10 litri di benzina nel serbatoio.

Using the first of the two verbs is a close choice; not the best. A good dictionary will help, as you become familiar with the true meaning of each verb.

207

Traduzione degli esercizi proposti nella lezione precedente

1) I am tired; the trip has been long.
2) My sisters sleep together in the same bed room.
3) The bottle with the baby's warm milk is on the table.
4) The uncle bought himself a watch and wears it on his wrist.
5) To-morrow evening we'll go to the theater to enjoy Verdi's opera *"Rigoletto"*.

Esercizi da tradurre in Italiano

Everybody blamed me, but I did not say one word.
....
Leave him alone; stay away from him.
....
What does this mean? I cannot understand it.
....
Savoy Construction has built two houses next to the road.
....
I met my friend on the street. He was wet from head to toes
....

Esercizi di lettura

    Dicembre è stato un mese freddo ma gioioso. A mezzanotte del trentuno le bótte, i fuochi artificiali, il suono delle campane, il pop dello spumante si son sparsi tutto intorno.

    È entrato l'Anno Nuovo fra gli abbracci e l'allegria. Tutti esclamano urrà! ahimé! Evviva l'anno passato! Peccato che se n'è andato! É stato un anno indimenticabile.

    Ogni anno a mezzanotte la gente comincia a scagliare fuori vecchi utensili attraverso le finestre e i balconi. Si fa questo per mantenere viva la tradizione a fin di rinnovare prosperità e felicità.

Some of the above words are taken from the twenty first lesson.

FORTY FIFTH LESSON

Lezione Quarantacinquesima

Ehi Gerardo! Lo sai che porti pittato dietro alle spalle della giacca? C'è un pesce bianco. Pare che non abbi usato la testa.

"Grazie, signor Ariosto; ah, che sciocco sono io! Oggi è il primo Aprile... Avevo dimenticato che oggi sono *i Pesci d'Aprile.* I miei compagni di scuola mi hanno fatto questo scherzino... Bravi! Che stupido sono stato! Ecco perché hanno rubato del gesso dalla lavagna!... Lo hanno fatto per spargerlo sul pesce di suola che avevano tagliato dalle scarpe vecchie di Filippo. Che diavoli! E dove lo tenevano nascosto...

Ora dovrò pensare anch'io come potrò vendicarmi. Bene! Il giorno non è ancora finito...

Hey Jerry! Do you know what you carry painted behind the shoulders of you jacket? Looks like you have not used your head.

*"Thank you Mr Ariosto; ah! what a fool am I! Today is the first day of April... I had forgotten that it is **All Fool's Day.** My school friends have played a little joke on me. Clever! How stupid I was! That's why they stole some chalk from the blackboard!... They did it so they could spread it on the leather fish they cut out of Philip's old shoes. Good devils! Where could they have kept it hidden...*

Now it is my turn to think how I may take revenge. Well! The day is not yet over!...

Complemento oggetto: *Direct object*

Often we use more words or groups of words to complete a sentence besides the subject and the predicate. We call these words **complements.**

There are many types of complements. Usually we recognize them by the preposition which precedes them.

The most important is the direct object which is made up by a noun or an adjective held without a preposition by a transitive verb.

> Ernesto ha scopato **la sua stanza e l'ha** spolverata.
> *Ernest swept **his room** and he dusted **it** off.*
> Te **lo** chiedo ancora: per piacere dici **la verità.**
> *I am asking **it** again: please tell the truth.*
> I pastori vivono una **vita felice.**
> *Shepherds live **a happy life.***
> Ho dato a fitto **il mio appartamento** a mio cugino.
> *I have sublet **my** apartment **to my** cousin.*
> Quella bella ragazza ha **gli occhi azzurri.**
> *That beautiful girl has **blue eyes.***

I know you have studied grammar in school; therefore I am not going to list the function of each complement. The formation of a sentence in Italian is not different than the same sentence in English.

> La porta **della nostra chiesa** è stata decorata **da un fomoso artista.**
> *The door **of our church** was decorated **by a famous artist.***
> Il Presidente **degli Stati Uniti ha** parlato **per un'ora intera.**
> *The President **of the United States** spoke **for a full hour**.*
> **L'anno scorso** regalai **un orologio d'oro a mio fratello.**
> *Last year I presented **a gold watch to my brother.***

The above sentences are formed by different complements. One of which specifies the door; one indicates the agent in a passive form; one specifies the Country; one indicates the time; one indicates the material; one indicates the person that received the material: where it terminates to.

Let's continue with more English verbs which, in their single form, may have more than one meaning when translated into Italian.

By the way the verbs we are dealing with are all irregular in English.

210

To arise	alzarsi, levarsi	To mow	mietere, falciare
To bear	sopportare, reggere	To rise	alzarsi,elevarsi
To become	divenire, diventare	To rive	fendere, spaccare
To beget	generare, produrre	To shave	radersi, farsi la barba
To begin	cominciare, iniziare	To shrink	rifuggire, raggrinzarsi
To break	rompere, spezzare	To slay	trucidare, uccidere
To draw	disegnare, tirare, trarre	To smite	colpire, percuotere
To drive	guidare, menare	To spring	saltare, scaturire
To forbear	evitare, astenersi	To steal	rubare, involare
To forget	dimenticare, scordare	To strive	sforzarsi, lottare
To grow	crescere, divenire	To swear	giurare, bestemmare
To heave	alzare, sollevare	To take	prendere, pigliare
To know	conoscere, sapere	To tear	stracciare, lacerare
To lie	giacere, riposare	To thrive	prosperare, profittare
To mistake	sbagliare, sbagliarsi	To wring	torcere, attorcigliare,

Here are Italian verbs translated with more than one English verb.

Abbandonare	to forsake, abandon	Mettere	to put, to place
Abitare	to live, to dwell	Notare	to note, to write down
Alzarsi	to rise, to get up	Piangere	to cry, to weep
Cercare	to seek, to look for	Portare	to bring, to take
Chiudere	to shut, to close	Posare	to put down, to place
Cominciare	to begin, to start	Prendere	to take, to catch
Dire	to say, to tell	Prosperare	to thrive, to prosper
Fare	to make, to do	Saltare	to jump, to leap
Far male	to hurt, to injure	Spaccare	to split, to cleave
Fermare	to stop, to halt	Sudare	to sweat, to perspire

Traduzione degli esercizi proposti nella lezione precedente

1) Tutti mi hanno accusato, ma io non ho detto una parola.
2) Lascialo stare; vai via da lui.
3) Che significa questo? Non posso capirlo.
4) La ditta di costruzione Savoia ha costruito due case vicino la strada.
5) Ho incontrato il mio amico sulla strada. Era bagnato da capo a piedi.

Esercizi da tradurre in Italiano

Darius was hit on the head. He spilt (lost) a lot of blood.

....

It hurts to hear that your father has to work so hard to send you to school

....

You must get up early to prosper.

....

That bad boy jumped the fence and tore his trousers (pantaloni).

....

Please, bring me half of the books and take the rest to the library.

....

Esercizi di lettura

Ho riconosciuto che sei di famiglia rispettata. Tanti auguri di buona salute, di prosperità e di felicità.

So che da ragazzino parlanvi spesso di farti giornalista; hai sempre desederato il giornalismo. Devo ammettere che ci hai messo tutta le volontà. È stato un atto saggio, eseguito con realtà e fedeltà.

Ora sei diventato Dottore in Lettere. Il coraggio e la virtù sono la gloria del tuo personaggio.

So che scrivi molto sullo sport; e soprattutto sul Baseball. Hai una casone; eppure ti vedo spesso affacciato al finestrino dello stanzino che guarda sul viottolo.

Marcello, sono molto felice per il progresso che hai fatto. Dove c'è volontà, c'è libertà. I miei cordiali auguri.

Most of the words used to write this reading exercise, are taken from lesson twenty two.

FORTY SIXTH LESSON

Lezione Quarantaseesima

Signor Tasso, vi vedo tutto attillato oggi; non solo voi ma anche il resto della vostra famiglia. Dove andate tutti insieme?

"Signora Veronese, oggi è Pasqua. È il giorno più sacro e più festivo dell'anno fra noi Cristiani. Andiamo tutti alla Santa Messa per celebrare questa grande festa di Resurrezione.

Si, indosso un vestito nuovo. La tradizione vuole che ogni membro della famiglia deve mettersi almeno un indumento nuovo il giorno di Pasqua. In chiesa si rinnova l'Acquasanta; in famiglia si rinnova la felicità e la prosperità.

Mia moglie ha cominciato già da Giovedì Santo a fare dei dolci tradizionali. Ha fatto la Colomba, la pizza dolce, la pizza rustica, dolci ripieni con ricotta o con formaggio grattato e altri dolci tradizionali.

Ha colorato anche delle uova per i bambini. Oltre ai vestiti nuovi, abbiamo comprato delle uova di cioccolato per loro, adornate con carta elaborata, le quali contengono piccoli regali . I dolci e le uova di cioccolato sono la loro gioia. Buona Pasqua, Signora: felici auguri a tutta la vostra famiglia."

Mr. Tasso, I see you all spruced up to-day; not only you but also your entire family. Where are you all going?

"Mrs. Veronesi, to day is Easter Sunday. It is the holiest and the greatest of all Christian Feast. We are all going to church to hear the Mass, in order to celebrate this great feast of Resurrection.

Yes, I am wearing a new suit. Tradition wants that every member of the family should wear new clothes on Easter Day. In the church Holy Water is renewed; in the family happiness and prosperity is renewed.

My wife began making traditional sweets since Holy Thursday. She

213

made the "Colomba" (Italian Easter cake), the rum cake, the rustic pizza, sweets filled with ricotta or grated cheese and other traditional pastries.

She also colored eggs for the children. Besides the new clothes, we have bought chocolate eggs adorned with elaborate wrapping. They contain special gifts inside. Sweets and Easter eggs are their joy.

Happy Easter, Mrs. Veronese: Many pleasant wishes to you and to your family."

Lexicon

We may define lexicon a complex of words which belong to a language: a treasure of words. A good dictionary will help us to explain the precise meaning of words and their proper function.

Each one of us, the most modest scholar, the greatest writer, the highest poet, the learned scientist, uses his own vocabulary. Knowing an abundance of words, they can express themselves with a colorful accuracy.

When learning a new language, it is the duty of the student to learn a certain amount of words and also their precise meaning.

We can make ourselves understood as best as we can, even not knowing the right terms. However if we have a deficiency of words, our thoughts remain entangled in a fog.

As we expand our vocabulary, we can express ourselves with a greater accuracy. We must acquire as many words as possible, so we may become fluent and proud of ourselves. Such a difficult task cannot be accomplished in a short time. Yet we must try very hard. Even if we memorize one word a day, we will reach our intentions. *"Never say never"*.

I am saying this because I do not want to discourage you. I am bombarding you with long lists of verbs and other words. I realize that this might be exhausting. You do not have to memorize them in one day. I am trying to list them together for your convenience. You'll see: in no time you will master them. I'll bet you anything... I have gone through such tough experiences myself. Yet I continued on, slowly and resolutely.

I am trying to make it as easy and fun as possible. You'll see; in time you will be proud of yourself

Reflexive verbs

We have already learned the function of reflexive verbs. The action gets back to the person that accomplishes it. In English it is indicated with myself, yourselves. In Italian the pronouns **mi, ti, si, ci, vi, si** are used.

Io **mi** sono pettinato.   *I have combed **myself.***
Rosetta **s'è** tagliata   *Rosetta has cut **herself.***

As you may remember, Italian must use the auxiliary **essere** to form reflexive compound tenses.

For the convenience of the student, I will include a list of the most common reflexive Italian verbs,

Accendèrsi	*to get on fire*	**Meravigliàrsi**	*to wonder*
Accorgèrsi	*to perceive*	**Maritàrsi**	*to marry*
Addormentàrsi	*to fall asleep*	**Muovérsi**	*to move*
Adiràrsi	*to get angry*	**Offendèrsi**	*to get offended*
Adunàrsi	*to assemble*	**Pentìrsi**	*to repent*
Affrettàrsi	*to rush*	**Precipitàrsi**	*to precipitate*
Ammalàrsi	*to fall sick*	**Propórsi**	*to propose*
Ammogliàrsi	*to get married*	**Radunàrsi**	*to assemble*
Appoggiàrsi	*to lean*	**Raffreddàrsi**	*to catch a cold*
Arrendèrsi	*to surrender*	**Rallegràrsi**	*to rejoice*
Arricchìrsi	*to get rich*	**Rammentàrsi**	*to remember*
Astenérsi	*to abstain*	**Risolvèrsi**	*to resolve*
Battérsi	*to fight*	**Ritiràrsi**	*to retire*
Chinàrsi	*to stoop down*	**Sedérsi**	*to sit down*
Fidàrsi	*to trust*	**Sentìrsi**	*to feel*
Guastàrsi	*to spoil*	**Separàrsi**	*to split*
Imbarcàrsi	*to embark*	**Sposàrsi**	*to get married*
Immaginàrsi	*to imagine*	**Stabilìrsi**	*to settle*
Ingannàrsi	*to be mistaken*	**Stancàrsi**	*to get tired*
Inginocchiàrsi	*to kneel*	**Svegliàrsi**	*to awake*
Innamoràrsi	*to fall in love*	**Ubriacàrsi**	*to get drunk*
Lagnàrsi	*to complain*	**Vantàrsi**	*to boast*

215

As you may have noticed, the accent falls on the vowel before the last, for each one of the Italian reflexive verb.

Expand your vocabulary

La sala da bagno	*bath-room*	La vasca	*bath-tub*
L'accappatoio	*bath-robe*	La tazza	*bowl*
L'asciugamano	*bath-towel*	Lo specchio	*mirror*
Il pettine	*comb*	La spazzola	*brush*
Lo spazzolino da denti	*tooth brush*	La brocca	*pitcher*
Il lavabo	*wash-basin*	Il rubinetto	*faucet*
La doccia	*shower*	La tendina	*shower curtain*
L'asciuga-capelli	*hair-drier*	Gabinetto	*closet*

Traduzione degli esercizi proposti nella lezione precedente

1) Dario fu colpito alla testa. Ha sparso molto sangue.
2) Fa male sentire che tuo padre deve lavorare così forte per farti studiare.
3) Ti devi alzare presto se desideri prosperare.
4) Quel ragazzaccio saltò il recinto e si strappò i pantaloni.
5) Per piacere portami la metà dei libri; e porta il resto in libreria.

Esercizi da tradurre in Inglese

La mia sala da bagno ha una grande vasca e una doccia moderna.

....

Dopo avermi fatto la doccia, mi sono asciugato con l'asciugamano.

....

Mi sono asciugato i capelli con l'asciuga-capelli elettrico e mi son pettinato.

....

Mi sento molto bene, quando mi siedo per riposare un pochettino.

....

Mi sono affrettato, anzi mi sono precipitato per meritarmi il primo posto.

....

Mi sono battuto per stabilirmi. Ora mi posso vantare.

....

Esercizi di lettura

Il cielo ci ha regalato un fenomeno strano. Il sole splende attraverso una foschìa, formando un vivido arcobaleno. Sembra un fazzoletto di seta, colorito da un grande artista.

Mio genero e mia nuora hanno ottenuto i passaporti. Ce li ha portato il portalettere. Ora si hanno comprato due valigie per potersi portare le camicie e gli abiti da sera. Lui ha messo il suo orologio d'oro nella cassaforte. Essi desiderano visitare Roma bagnata dal Tevere; e Londra bagnata dal Tamigi.

Mia nipote è una cantante famosa. Lei ha cantato per il Re e per la Regina di Spagna. Anche mio nipote è un buon cantante. Lui si accompagna con il pianoforte.

Some of the words used to write this exercise are taken from the twenty third lesson.

FORTY SEVENTH LESSON

Lezione Quarantasettesima

Signor Petrarca, sono appena le sei e un quarto. Tu sei già qui. Ancora fa tanto freddo. Dove vai così presto questa mattina?

"Signor Vivaldi, son dieci minuti che aspetto per l'autobus. È Aprile, ma il tempo non promette. Fa tanto freddo. Ho i piedi gelati. Mi sembra un secolo dacché sto aspettando. Stiamo in piena Primavera; eppure pare di soffrire le pene d'Inverno. Si dice che in Aprile è –*dolce dormire, gli uccelli a cantare e gli alberi a fiorire,–* purtroppo Aprile piange e non ride. Invece di portare l'aria fresca e il profumo dei fiori, quest'anno Aprile ci agghiaccia. Le foglie dovrebbero essere verdi, purtroppo sono ricoperte di gelo primaverile. Ebbene, l'Estate non sta troppo lontano!"

Mr. Petrarca, it is hardly a quarter after six o'clock. You are here already. It is still so cold. Where are you going so early this morning?

*"Mr. Vivaldi, it has been ten minutes that I am waiting for the bus. It is April, but the weather is not promising. It is so cold. My feet are frozen. It seems an eternity that I am waiting. We are in the heart of Spring; yet it feels like suffering Winter pains. They say that in April it is –*sweet sleeping, birds singing and trees blooming– *however this year April cries and does not laugh. Instead of bringing fresh air and the fragrance of flowers, April keeps freezing us. The leaves should be green; yet they are covered with spring frost. Well, Summer is not too far away!"*

Useful syntax notes

Let's look at the characteristics of some sentences which may be formed the same or with some difference from English to Italian.

If you consider it a repetition, it may still be a valuable review.

Half, quite, such, require the indefinite article ***"a, an"*** before a fractionate object. Italian does not require it.

*The half of **a** melon is mine.*
La metà di melone è mio.
*My friend is quite **a** swimmer. He won the quarter of **a** mile race.*
Il mio amico è un buon nuotatore. Ha vinto la gara di 1/4 di miglio.

In English ***as*** come; ***so*** così; ***too*** troppo; ***however*** pur quanto; ***no*** non; and ***how*** quale, che; when they are part of special expressions, they also require the indefinite article ***a (an).*** Italian does not require it.

*That gentleman is **as** good **a** husband **as a** lady can wish for.*
Quel signore è un marito buono quanto si possa desiderare.
***However** smart **a** man may be, he ought to be humble.*
Per quanto intelligente un uomo possa essere, deve rimanere umile.
*Rosina was **too great a** girl to do such **a** thing.*
Rosina era una ragazza **troppo** brava per fare una cosa simile.
*I have never seen **so gentle a** boy **as** that.*
Non ho mai visto un ragazzo **così** gentile.
*Alexander is **as** good **a** swimmer **as** one can find anywhere.*
Alessandro è un buon nuotatore **quanto** si possa trovare altrove.

Sometimes we find special expressions in English with the indefinite article ***a (an)*** which cannot be literally translated into Italian.

*I am in **a** hurry.* Ho fretta.
*I am at **a** loss.*   Mi sento perduto.
*The cat has **a** mind of its own.* Il gatto ha il cervello a modo suo.
*Rosa goes to work three times **a** week. She gets paid once **a** month.*
Rosa va a lavorare tre volte la settimana. La paga è una volta al mese.

English nouns which indicate an entire species, do not take the article in the plural. **Man and woman** do not take the article neither in the

219

singular. In Italian they do.

> *Young **children** must go to school.*
> **I bambini** devono andare a scuola.
> *I prefer eating **turkeys** to **chickens**.*
> Preferisco mangiare i tacchini che le galline.
> ***Man** must go to work to support his family.*
> **L'uomo** deve andare a lavorare per sopportare la sua famiglia.

Titles take the article in Italian; except when these titles are in apposition to the name.

> **Il Colonnello Giusti** sconfisse il **Re Carlo IV** di Sardegna
> ***Colonel Giusti** defeated **King Charles IV** of Sardinia.*
> **Il Principe di Orleans** è un buon amico del **Duca di Siviglia**.
> ***The Prince of Orleans** is a good friend of the **Duke of Seville**.*
> **Umberto, Re d'Italia**, era della famiglia **Savoia**.
> ***Humbert, King of Italy**, belonged to the **Savoy** family.*
> **L'Inferno, il Purgatorio e il Paradiso** sono la trama della **Divina Commedia di Dante Alighieri**.
> ***Hell, Purgatory and Paradise** are the plot of **The Devine Comedy**, written by **Dante Alighieri**.*
> Che **il buon Dio** vi benedica.
> *May **the good God** bless you.*
> **L'inverno** è una stagione fredda.
> ***Winter** is a cold season.*
> **L'immortale Shakespear** fu un drammaturgo e un poeta inglese.
> ***The immortal Shakespear** was an English dramatist and poet.*

Gender: Most abstract nouns are feminine in Italian. They take the article **la, le, una**.

> L'amore *love;* la morte ***death;*** la guerra ***war;*** la terra ***earth;*** la luna ***moon;*** la natura ***nature;*** la notte ***night;*** la bellezza ***beauty;*** la speranza ***hope;*** la pace ***peace;*** la virtù ***virtue;*** la religione ***religion;*** la chiesa ***church;***

220

la providenza *providence;* la fortuna *fortune;* la poesia *poetry;* la fama *fame;* la pietà *piety;* la gloria *glory;* l'ora *hour;* la libertà *liberty;* l'aria *air;* la necessità *necessity;* l'ansietà *anxiety;* l'ambizione *ambition;* la follia *folly;* la ricchezza *wealth;* la povertà *poverty;* l'evidenza *evidence;* la distanza *distance;* la memoria *memory;* la lode *praise;* la saggezza *wisdom;* l'intelligenza *intelligence;* la rabbia *rage, anger;* la furia *fury; etc.*

I listed so many words because most of them are similar both in pronunciation and in meaning. You can add some more, if they could be useful to your studies.

Expand your vocabulary

La pesca:	*fishing*	La caccia:	*hunting*
Il pescatore	*fisher-man*	Il cacciatore	*hunter*
La rete	*fishing net*	Il porto d'armi	*hunting licence*
La canna	*fishing-rod*	Il fucile	*hunting gun*
La lenza	*fishing-line*	La cartuccia	*cartridge*
L'amo	*hook*	La cartucciera	*cartridge-belt*
La fiocina	*harpoon*	La carniera	*game-bag*
L'esca	*bait*	Il cane da caccia	*hunting-dog*
Il verme	*worm*	La caccia	*game*
Il cestino	*basket*	Il bosco	*wood*
La barca	*boat*	La montagna	*mountain*
Gli stivali	*boots*	Gli scarponi	*hunting-boots*
La licenza	*licence*	Il compasso	*compass*
Pescare	*to fish, catch fish*	Sparare	*to shoot*
Il lago	*lake*	Fermo	*standing*
L'oceano	*ocean*	A volo	*flying*

Traduzione degli esercizi proposti nella lezione precedente

1) My bathroom has a large bathtub and a modern shower.
2) After I took a shower, I dried myself with a bath towel.
3) I dried my hair with an electric hair-drier and I combed myself.

4) I feel very well when I sit to rest a bit.
5) I rushed, indeed I dashed in order to deserve first place.
6) I fought to settle myself. Now I can boast.

Esercizi da tradurre in Italiano

The Rocky's, a majestic chain of mountains, run across the United States.

....

The fisherman caught half a dozen trouts.

....

The partridge is a tasty game bird.

....

Hunting dogs help the hunters to find the game.

....

Washington, capital of the United States, is situated on the East Cost.

....

Reading exercise

Il cielo è tutto un blu-turchino. Un cupo rossore va accendendo l'orizzonte a Ponente. Gli uccelli cantano le loro ultime note gioiose e vanno a dormire. È Aprile. È dolce dormire. La Primavera si fa sentire. I fiori emanano un profumo gradevole attraverso l'aria fresca. Le foglie nuove degli alberi frushiano (rustle) lentamente.

Le stelle brillano accese. Venere scintilla più delle altre a Ovest. La luna già inonda la terra con la sua chiara luce. Saturno le sta vicino e le fa compagnia. Questo è un periodo felice e pregiato, offertoci dalla straordinaria intelligenza della Natura.

La maggior parte delle parole usate per scrivere questo esercizio di lettura, sono state prese dalla ventiquattresima lezione.

FORTY EIGHTH LESSON

Lezione Quarantottesima

Signorina Carducci, la vedo venire con l'ombrello in mano. Dove va così in fretta. Ha forse paura che venga sorpresa dal cattivo tempo?

"Signor Pascoli, devo trovarmi a scuola per le otto in punto, altrimenti troverò sicuramente la porta chiusa. Il nostro professore di storia e geografia è preciso. Con lui non si scherza. Mi porto l'ombrello perchè oggi predicono la pioggia.

Nella classe di geografia stiamo studiando la Liguria. Questa regione ha quattro province: Genova, (capitale) Imperia, La Spezia e Savona. Essa è fatta di mare e di montagne. È povera di risorse; eppure è la regione più ricca d'Italia. È Terra di marinai e di commercianti. La sua incantevole Riviera è sempre affollata di turisti. Uno dei suoi famosi marinai è Cristoforo Colombo, quello che ha scoperto l'America."

Miss Carducci, I see you walking with umbrella in hand. Where are you going in such a hurry? Are you perhaps afraid that you will be caught in bad weather?

"Mr. Pascoli, I have to be at school at exactly eight o'clock, otherwise I will certainly find the door shut. Our Social Studies professor is precise. He is not a man to trifle with. I take the umbrella because they are predicting rain today.

In our geography class we are studying Liguria. This Region has four provinces: Genoa (Capital), Imperia, La Spezia and Savona. It is made of sea and mountains. It is poor in resources; yet it is the richest region of Italy. It is the Land of sailors and businessmen. Its charming Riviera is always swarmed with tourists. One of its famous sailors is Christopher Columbus, who discovered America.

223

Useful syntax notes

When I began speaking English, I was often corrected, as I tried to translate a reciprocal preposition directly from Italian into English, especially when using *in, on, to, at, from, by.*

Example: Ci facciamo il bagno **con** l'acqua fredda.
We take a bath in cold water.
Io lavoro **nella** campagna.
I work on the farm.
Ti aspetterò **alle** tre e un quarto esatte.
I'll wait for you at exactly a quarter past three.
Io vado **a** Nuova York **col** treno.
I go to New York by train.
Erina tornò **da** San Francisco con una cassa di vino.
Erin returned from San Francisco with a case of wine.
Da ora in poi andrai **da** tua sorella **da** sola.
From now on you will go to your sister's by yourself.
Noi andiamo a scuola prestissimo **la** mattina.
We go to school very early in the morning.
Mio zio Michele è stato come un padre **per** me.
My uncle Michael has been like a father to me.
La mia sorella maggiore è gentile **con** la mia sorella minore.
My elder sister is kind to my younger sister.

We have gone through a long list of verbs, which we have used for the purpose of learning and for doing many exercises. Of course I cannot write down every verb contained in the vocabulary; however I am going to list a few more that are very common for every day usage.

You already know how to expand your vocabulary by deriving words from other words.

Let's take the verb **to strike.** We derive from it: *stroke* colpo di paralisi; *strike* sciopero; *striker* scioperante, battitore, tiratore; *striking* sorprendente, impressionante; *strikingly* sorprendentemente; *strikingness* carattere sorprendente.

List of common verbs

To bake	cuocere	*To hide*	nascondere
To beat	bastonare	*To ride*	cavalcare
To behold	osservare	*To run*	correre
To bite	mordere	*To saw*	*segare*
To blow	soffiare	*To sew*	*cucire*
To burn	bruciare	*To shake*	scuotere
To buy	comprare	*To shear*	tosare
To choose	scegliere	*To show*	mostrare
To cling	arrampicarsi	*To sink*	affondare
To dare	ardire, osare	*To sit*	sedersi
To dig	scavare	*To speak*	parlare
To dream	sognare	*To spin*	filare
To drink	bere	*To spit*	sputare
To drive	guidare	*To sting*	pungere
To eat	mangiare	*To swell*	gonfiare
To engrave	incidere	*To swim*	nuotare
To fall	cadere	*To swing*	dondolare
To fight	combattere	*To undertake*	intraprendere
To find	trovare	*To wake*	svegliare
To fly	volare	*To wear*	vestire
To forbid	proibire	*To weave*	tessere
To forgive	perdonare	*To withdraw*	ritirarsi
To freeze	gelare	*To write*	scrivere
To give	dare	*To wrong*	far torto

Expand your vocabulary: commercial words

Bakery panetteria; *barber-shop* barberia; *beauty-salon* salone di bellezza; *building industry* edilizia; *butcher-shop* macelleria; *carpentry* falegnameria; *cement factory* cementificio; *dairy products* latticini; *delicatessen* salumeria; *dyes* tinture; *electronics* elettronica; *factories* fabbriche; *fashion house* sartoria; *florist* fioraio; *furrier's shop* pellicceria; *glass-ware* vetrami; *goods* merceria; *grocery-store* drogheria;

hardware ferrame; *jewellery* gioielleria; *lathe* turno; *library* libreria; *linen* telerie; *mechanics* meccanica; *merchandise* mercanzia; *mill* mulino; *open market* mrcato all'aperto; *pastry-shop* pasticceria; *perfumery* profumeria; *pharmacy* farmacia; *photography* fotografo; *printer-shop* tipografia; *seeds* sementi; *shop* bottega; *spices* spezieria; *silk-factory* seteria; *supermarket* supermercato; *warehouse* magazzino.

Traduzione degli esercizi proposti nella lezione precedente

1) Le Montagne Rocciose, grandiosa catena, attraversano tutto gli Stati Uniti.
2) Il pescatore ha pescato una mezza dozzina di trote.
3) La pernice è una selvaggina deliziosa.
4) I cani da caccia aiutano il cacciatore a trovare la caccia.
5) Washington, capitale degli Stati Uniti, è situata sulla costa orientale.

Esercizi da tradurre in Inglese

Mia sorella lavora in un salone di bellezza.
....
Ogni lunedì la gente va a far la spesa (shopping) al mercato all'aperto.
....
Noi andiamo a comprare i nostri dolci nella pasticceria vicino casa.
....
Molti gelano la carne che comprano nella macelleria.
....
Il fioraio vende fiori freschi e profumati.
....

Reading exercise

Nella sala del barbiere ognuno vanta il suo mestiere, mentre aspettano il turno per farsi tagliare i capelli. La barberia è il luogo dove si raccolgono notizie sugli affari degli altri. Quando, poi, si parla di sport, ognuno si fa forte, costringendo il barbiere a chiudere le porte.

FORTY NINTH LESSON

Lezione Quarantanovesima

Rita, dove vai con questo brutto tempo. Guarda; il cielo sta coperto di nuvoloni neri temporaleschi. Sulle montagne pare ci stia fioccando. Il vento soffia così forte da far mettere paura ai lupi. I lampi stanno accendendo il cielo, seguiti da rumori spaventosi. La grandine che sta cadendo sulle montagne farà sicuramente anche da noi. Poveri contadini! Il loro lavoro verrà totalmente distrutto: specialmente ora a Primavera avanzata, quando i fiori biancheggiano tra il verde delicato.

"Signor Ariosto, quando si deve andare a lavorare, si deve uscire col cattivo o con il bel tempo. Un buon impermeabile salverà la situazione."

Rita, where are you going with such ugly weather! Look up: the sky is covered with dark stormy clouds. It seem that it is snowing on the mountains. The wind is blowing with such an impetus as to scare wolves. Lightning bolts are lighting up the sky, followed by dreadful thunder. Hail which is falling on the mountains, will certainly strike us down here also. Poor farmers! Their work will be totally destroyed, specially now at Springtime, when the trees are white with flowers and a delicate green.

"Mr. Ariosto, when one must go to work, one must go out rain or shine. A good rain-coat will save the situation."

Language and style

A language always presents two complementary aspects: one individual and one social.

Speaking as individuals, the expression acquires more value when it is personal and clear. We should not go overboard to exalt ourselves.

Socially, the best qualification is the unity of a language.

The Italian language is relatively not very united. Besides the strong dialects, there are regional differences of pronunciation.

For example, a northern Italian will say: Luciano parla béne, a central Italian will say: Luciano parla bène; a southern Italian will say: Luciano parla bbène. (*Pay attention to the accent over the e*)

Regardless, through the media, the Italian language has acquired a united tone throughout the Country. The young generation speaks the national language well. This great effort has been achieved through education. When people know a language well, they can create unmistakable expressions, using suited words. It is very important to enrich our vocabulary, so we can build our sentences effortlessly. In this way, although respecting grammar and lexical propriety, we can regulate our thinking, our taste and our aim which we desire to embellish.

If our inspiration is deeply felt, the words that we use to make ourselves clearly understood, will express the warmth and the vibration which will distinguish our individual achievement.

"*A tongue can make or break a bone*". –La lingua puó fare oppure rompere l'osso– "*The pen is sharper than the sword*" –Ferisce più la lingua che la spada– "*Leaders can build or destroy a nation*" –Un Capo di Stato puó arricchire oppure distruggere la sua Nazione– Therefore we have to choose words which will give a healthy sensation to the listeners or to the readers. Related words can express different meanings for different situations. It is up to us to put them in the right place in a sentence. Let's take the word ***prominent.*** *Webster's Thesaurus* gives us: *distinguished, illustrious, outstanding, renowned, influential, famous, well-known, noted, notable, important, conspicuous, eminent, leading, celebrated.*

Every language has its own characteristics. To have reached this point, you must know your language well. To express yourself in the same way in a second language, takes a tremendous effort. It is hard work that will reward you and make you proud. Using the perfect words and the right tone of voice, will make your sentences brilliant.

Let's consider the reaction that certain news will bring to a number of persons: "*Our team has won.*" –La nostra squadra ha vinto.– It is just a simple announcement. –won?– the surprise; –won?!– the disbelief or delusion; –won!– confirmation or exultation. We can express all this, using

228

the same word.

An artist that wants to paint the sky, will use different shades of blue to show the time of day in which the action is taking place; however he has to stay within the limits of the color blue. So it is for an architect who wants to construct a building. If he is a true artist, he will obey to the idea of what is prominent; thus designing a beautiful building. He can choose the best and richest materials; yet he has to consider the practical necessities. The walls have to be strong enough to sustain the weight, regardless if it is an enormous building or a modest little house.

What I am trying to say, is that we have to respect the rules. We must remain in touch with grammar, in order to build powerful sentences.

Italian is the language of romance, of songs, of music. A lot of rhetoric is used when speaking and writing. Everybody likes to adorn their style, using rich words and imitative sounds.

Gli occhi di quella ragazza sono blu come l'acqua del mare di Sorrento; e brillano come le stelle sotto un cielo chiaro e senza luna.
The eyes of that girl are blue like the sea which surrounds Sorrento; and spark like the stars under a clear and moonless sky.

Many great Italian poets and novelists have forged the Italian language, giving a refined touch to it.

English has many great poets and novelists. They have also embellished the English language by the expressive value of their artistic style. Indeed you have learned a great deal about how you want to express your thoughts and your feelings. There is not much difference amongst languages. The greater our vocabulary, the better we can excel.

What is important, is not to fill the gaps with *hum*... A good speaker will not surrender to such a low motivation. If you are looking for specific words, stop dry... then start again.

E quell'asino di Leonardo è passato... al Liceo?
And that donkey of Leonard has been promoted... to High School?
Ma che dici?... Guglielmo vuol fare il...professore? Tu sei pazzo!
What do you mean?... William wants to be a...professor? Crazy!

List of common verbs

To address	indirizzàre	*To delay*	ritardare
To allow	permettere	*To discover*	scoprire
To ally	allearsi	*To die*	morire
To admire	ammirare	*To employ*	impiegare
To advise	avvisare	*To enjoy*	gioire
To agree	accordarsi	*To enter*	entrare
To amuse	divertire	*To escape*	sfuggire
To arrest	arrestare	*To excite*	eccitare
To assign	assegnare	*To expire*	spirare
To astonish	meravigliare	*To fail*	mancare
To attempt	attentare	*To finish*	finire
To avoid	evitare, schivare	*To foresee*	prevedere
To beg	implorare	*To foretell*	predire
To beautify	abbellire	*To frequent*	frequentare
To become	divenire	*To gather*	riunire
To bet	scommettere	*To grant*	accordare
To blow	soffiare	*To grow*	crescere
To boil	bollire	*To insist*	insistere
To breathe	respirare	*To instruct*	istruire
To cease	cessare	*To interrupt*	interrompere
To chatter	chiacchierare	*To invoke*	invocare
To collect	raccogliere	*To judge*	giudicare
To compel	obbligare	*To jump*	saltare
To concern	riguardare	*To leave*	tralasciare
To confer	conferire	*To lament*	lamentarsi
To continue	continuare	*To let*	permettere
To cook	cucinare, cuocere	*To mean*	intendere
To create	creare	*To milk*	mungere
To cross	attraversre	*To miss*	mancare
To crush	schiacciare	*To nail*	inchiodare
To deceit	ingannare	*To name*	nominare
To delight	dilettare	*To need*	occorrere
To deck	decorare	*To neglect*	trascurare
To decline	rifiutare	*To note*	notare

Look at the above verbs: the accent falls on the vowel before the last for every one of them, as indicated with **indirizzàre.**

Expand your vocabulary: commercial words

Acorn ghianda; *asphalt* asfalto; *ashes* cenere;

Balls palle;.*barley* orzo; *bars* verghe; *beans* fagioli; *berries* bacche; *blades* lame; *brackets* mensole; *bran* crusca; *bread* pane; *bricks* mattoni; *boxes* scatole; *brass* ottone; *brooms* scope; *brushes* spazzole; *butter* burro.

Candle candela; *cast-iron* ghisa; *chalk* gesso; *charcoal* carbone; *cheese* formaggio; *chemical produce* prodotti chimici; *chestnuts* castagne; *chisels* scalpelli; *cinnamon* cannella; *clogs* zoccoli; *cloth* panno; *cocoa* cacao; *coffee* caffè; *coral* corallo; *cotton* cottone;

Dates datteri; *diamonds* diamanti; *drinks* bibite; *drugs* droghe.

Ebony ebano; *egg:* l'uovo, *eggs* le uova; *elder* sambuco.

Fans ventagli; *felt* feltro; *fir* legno di pino; *fire engine* pompieri; *flour* farina; *furniture* fornitura, mobili; *fringe* frangia; *funnels* imputi; *furs* pellicce.

Gall fiele; *gasoline* benzina; *gems* pietre preziose; *glass* vetro; *glycerine* glicerina; *granite* granito; *grease* grasso.

Ham prosciutto; *hair* pelo, capelli; *hairpins* forcelle; *herbs* erbe; *hides* pelli; *honey* miele; *hooks* ganci.

Ice ghiaccio; *ice-cream* gelato; *iodine* jodio; *iron* ferro.

Jar brocca; *jelly* gelatina; *jewels* gioielli.

Kennel canile; *key* chiave; *knives* coltelli.

Laces merletti; *lard* lardo; *lavender* lavanda; *lead* piombo; *lettuce* lattuga; *licorice* liquirizia; *lime* calce; *linings* fodere.

Traduzione degli esercizi proposti nella lezione precedente

1) My sister works in a beauty salon.
2) Every Monday people go shopping at the open market.
3) We go to buy our pastries at the nearby pastry-shop..
4) Many people freeze the meat they buy in the butcher store.
5) The florist sells fresh, fragrant flowers.

Esercizi da tradurre in Inglese

Noi comprimo la medicina in una farmacia che appartiene al nostro amico.

....

Carlo si fa cùcire i suoi vestiti nella sartoria di suo fratello.

....

I diamanti costano più delle pietre preziose; ma sono la gioia delle donne.

....

L'Imperatore Nerone fu l'inventore del gelato.

....

La ruota (wheel) è meschina (mean), senza grasso non cammina.

....

Esercizi di lettura

La signorina Boiardi cammina a piedi veloci lungo il suo giardino. Viene verso di noi con l'ombrello in mano. Forse ha paura che farà cattivo tempo. Lei ha sicuramente molta fretta per arrivare a scuola alle otto precise, perché non si è accorta nemmeno che ha le scarpe sporche. Quel cattivuccio di suo fratello minore doveva pulirle, ma l'ha fatto col minimo impegno.

Lei ha dei magnifici professori i quali riconoscono la profonda volontà che dedica verso lo studio. Riceve sempre ottimi voti. Lei é la prodezza della sua famiglia e dei suoi amici. È la prima della sua classe.

Prima di chiudere le porte, il professore fa leggere ogni studente ad alta voce, a fin di migliorare il suono della pronunzia.

Il sei di Marzo i professori conducono l'intera scuola a guardare la partita di calcio nello Stadio Olimpico, dove si riuniscono migliaia e migliaia di spettatori.

Some of the words used to write this reading exercise, are taken from the twenty fifth lesson.

FIFTIETH LESSON

Lezione Cinquantesima

Ma guarda come si combinano le cose! Tiberio, che fai qua a Roma? Ci siamo incontrati per caso. Perché non me l'hai fatto sapere? Potevamo fare un giro per la città insieme. Siamo amici, no...?

"Ciao Cincinnato, sono molto contento di averti incontrato. Il mio viaggio è stato di sorpresa. Senti, potresti indicarmi dov'è la fermata dell'autobus?"

"Sì, certo: all'uscita della stazione del treno, gira a destra. Cammina per circa un mezzo chilometro. A sinistra c'è un fiorista; c'è una gelateria; c'è un salone di bellezza e una gioielleria. Proprio difronte c'è la fermata. Il traffico è terribile. Fai attenzione quando attraversi la strada. Ciao!"

Can you figure out how things happen! Tiberius, what are you doing here in Rome? We met by chance. Why didn't you let me know? We could have toured the city together. What are friends for...!

"Hello Cincinnati, I am very happy to have met you. My trip has come up in a blink of an eye. Listen, could you tell me where the bus stop is?"

"Sure: at the exit of the train station, turn to the right. Walk for about half a kilometer. At your left you'll see a florist, an ice cream parlor, a beauty salon and a jewelry store . Right across from there is the bus stop. The traffic is terrible. Be careful when you cross the street. So long!"

Lingua e stile

Often we like to render the expression of our thoughts lively and evident. As such we use mottos or proverbs. They are part of the wealth of a language. In Italian we use many of them.

A bird in hand is worth two in the bush.
È meglio un uovo oggi che una gallina domani.
To kill two birds with one stone.
Prendere due piccioni ad una fava.
There is no love lost between them.
Vanno d'accordo come il diavolo e l'acqua santa.
To put a spoke in someone's wheel.
Mettere bastoni fra le ruote.

Many times we like to stress our feelings accurately; so if we want to sell something quickly we say: ***It is of the very best quality.*** **È di primissima qualità.**

We may hear: ***breaking news; or the latest news.*** **Le ultime notizie; oppure le ultimissime notizie.**

Dead tired –stanco morto– is more expressive than ***very tired*** **stanchissimo.** So is ***madly in love*** –**innamorato cotto–.**

Sometimes we exchange words mentioning a characteristic part of an object to indicate the whole of it.

The Sails of the United States cover every Ocean; and its Wings guard the sky. (Sails is exchanged for Navy; and Wings for Air Force.)
Le Vele degli Stati Uniti coprono tutti gli Oceani; e le sue Ali proteggono il cielo.

Emotion expresses an effective formula of courtesy, depending on the length of time people know each other. In public places one should be very courteous when asking for something.

Lei, signor Vivaldi, dove abita?
Mr. Vivaldi, where do you live?
Signora mia, è la verità! la verità! i tempi sono cambiati!
My dear Lady, it is the truth! yes, the truth! time has changed!
Cameriere, mi potrebbe portare un po' di pane, per favore.
Waiter, could you bring me some bread, if you please!

234

Grazie mille, mi parta anche il conto a suo piacere.
Thanks, can you also bring me the bill, please.
Andiamo, su; fammi un grande piacere. Fai qualcosa di buono.
Come on; do me a great favor. Make something good out of you.
A suo comando: ecco il listino dei prezzi.
As you wish: here is the price-list.

List of common verbs

To obey	ubbidìre	*To refund*	rimborsare
To observe	osservàre	*To refuse*	rifiutare
To offer	offrìre	*To regret*	spiacere
To oppose	resistere	*To remain*	rimanere
To order	ordinare	*To remind*	ricordare
To outlive	sopravvivere	*To repeat*	ripetere
To owe	dovere	*To resist*	resistere
To pardon	perdonare	*To return*	restituire
To pay	pagare	*To reward*	ricompensare
To plant	piantare	*To rise*	salire
To poison	avvelenare	*To risk*	rischiare
To profit	far profitto	*To roast*	arrostire
To pour	versare	*To roll*	rotolare
To present	presentare	*To row*	remare
To procure	procurare	*To rule*	governare
To promise	promettere	*To run*	correre
To propose	proporre	*To scold*	sgridare
To pull	tirare	*To scream*	strillare
To pump	pompare	*To seal*	sigillare
to punish	punire	*To search*	cercare
To push	spingere	*To secure*	proteggere
To qualify	qualificare	*To send*	mandare
To quarrel	litigare	*To ship*	spedire
To quit	lasciare	*To shiver*	rabbrividire
To quiver	tremare	*To shock*	colpire, scuotere
To reach	raggiungere	*To shovel*	spalare

As noted in the previous lesson, the accent falls on the vowel before the last, for every one of them.

Expand your vocabulary: commercial words

Manufacturing goods manifatture; *manure* concime; *marble* marmo; *metals* metalli; *mint* menta; *molasses* melassa; *music* musica; *musk* muschio; *must* mosto.

Neon lights luci di neon; *nets* reti; *note book* quaderno; *note paper* carta da lettera; *notary* notaio; *novel* romanzo; *nuclear* nucleare; *nutmegs* noci moscate; *nuts* noci.

Oak legno di quercia; *ochre* ocra; *office* ufficio; *olive oil* olio d'oliva; *olives* olive; *opium* oppio; *oro* gold; *oxygen* ossigeno.

Pearls perle; *paintings* dipinti; *paper* carta; *pegs* piuolo; *pens* penne; *pepper* pepe; *perfumes* profumi; *plate* argenteria; *plumb levels* piombo livelli; *poultry* pollame; *powder* polvere; *produce* prodotti naturali.

Rags cenci; *raw materials* materie gregge; *rice* riso; *rifle* fucile; *revolver* rivoltella; *ring* anello cerchio; *rink* pista di pattinaggio; *rod* canna da pesca; *rope* fune; *rubber* gomma; *rubbish* immondizie.

Saffron zafferano; *salted meat* carne salata; *seeds* semi, sementi; *silks* seterie; *silver* argento; *soda* soda; *spices* spezie; *sponges* spugne; *salted fish* baccalà; *stones* pietre; *sulphur* zolfo; *swords* spade.

Traduzione degli esercizi proposti nella lezione precedente

1) We buy medicine at a pharmacy that our friend owes.
2) Charles has his suits made at the designer house his brother owes.
3) Diamonds cost more than gems; but they are the joy of women.
4) Emperor Nero was the inventor of ice cream...
5) The wheel is mean, it does not turn without grease.

Esercizi da tradurre in Italiano

Italian farmers use a lot of manure to grow their produce.

....

Why have you quit your job? What are you going to do now!

....

Italy does not have much raw material, but it has a lot of marble.

....

Leonardo's paintings are famous the world over.

....

La Spezia is a city in Liguria named after the spices trade (commercio).

....

Sicily is famous for its sulphur and its Marsala wine.

....

Reading exercise: Civiltà Romana
Taken from Epopea e Mito by C.A. Sambugar

I Romani, popolo pratico, ci lasciarono la sapienza delle loro leggi che servirono di base al vivere civile del mondo. In tutti i paesi del vastissimo Impero resta l'impronta della loro civiltà: archi di trionfo, templi, anfiteatri, teatri, acquedotti, monumenti, ponti. Essi costruirono anche strade (via Aurelia, Cassia, Emilia, Appia, Flaminia), che si irragiavano da Roma in ogni direzione. Dalla civiltà romana fiorirono quella dell'Italia e quella delle altre terre su cui passarono vittoriose le legioni di Roma.

FIFTY FIRST LESSON

Lezione Cinquantunesima

Cesare, fra una settimana finirà la scuola. Cosa intendi fare durante le vacanze estive? Naturalmente tutto sta se saremo promossi.

"Augusto, se riusciremo a superare gli esami di Maturità, vorrei sùbito prendermi due settimane di vacanza. Massimo, Claudio, Valerio, Enrico, Giulio, Angelo, Franco, Beniamino, Cesidio, Loreto, Nazzareno, Corrado, Umberto, Tullio, Vincenzo, Emilio, Ennio, Bruno, Raffaele, Luciano, Giacinto, Alberico, Arturo, Donato, Giacomo, Elio e altri della nostra classe andranno alla spiaggia. Vogliono che vada anch'io con loro. Purtroppo non posso. Ho deciso di andare in montagna e tornare sùbito a casa perché devo lavorare durante l'estate. Devo finire di pagare le tasse e i miei debiti. Oltre al resto non ho denaro per pagare l'ammissione all'Università. Non desidero affatto cominciare l'Università col peso dei debiti. –Chi ben comincia, è a metà dell'opera.–"

Caesar, school will be over in a week. What are you planning to do during summer vacation? Of course it depends if we will be promoted.

"August, If we will be successful with the High School exams, I would like to take two weeks of vacation soon after. Maximus, Claudius, Valerius, Henry, Julius, Angelo, Frank, Benjamin, Cesidio, Larry, Ned, Konrad, Humbert, Tully, Vincent, Emil, Ennio, Bruno, Rafael, Lucian, Hyacinth, Alberico, Arthur, Danny, Jack, Elio and others from our class are going to the beach. They have asked me to go with them. However I cannot go. I have decided to go to the mountains for two weeks and come back home right away, because I have to work during the summer. I still have to pay my taxes and my debts. Besides I have no money to pay for the admission to the University. I do not wish to enter the University with the heavy burden of debts. –Well begun, is half done.–"

Style

Exhortations and commands have forms and tone of various kind.

Ma che dici: non vuoi venire? Via, andiamo.
You mean you do not want to come? Come on, let's go.
Non farti pregare. Su, andiamo!
Please, don't let me beg you. Let's go!
Ma fammi il piacere: vai, vai. Ti sei mostrato poco gentile.
Do me a favor: please go; go away. You have not acted very kind.
Senti un po' a questo che mi racconta! È proprio roba da pazzi.
Listen a little to what he wants to tell me! It is really foolishness.

One word that offers many different meanings according to the tone in Italian, is **sistemare:** *to arrange, to settle, to fix.*

Dopo un lungo fidanzamento, quel giuovane s'è finalmente sistemato.
Following a long engagement, that young man has finally gotten married.
Se lo prenderò, lo sistemerò io!
If I catch him, I'll fix him!
Il padre l'ha sistemato ai pressi della città.
His father bought him a house close to the city line.
Sua madre lo ha sistemato nella sua casa nuova.
His mother settled him down in his new home.
L'hanno sistemato bene in corte!
He got a well deserved sentence in court!
Ho ben sistemato mio figlio nella ditta di un mio amico.
I have found a very good job for my son in the firm of a friend of mine.

Affirmation and negation: have a large quantity of shades of tone and meaning in Italian. **Si** and **no** are frequently used in conversations; especially when someone is looking for the right words.

Sì, Davide, sì, andiamo. – Sì, sì, verrò presto – .
Yes, David, come on, let's go. – Ok., I'll be there right away– .

No! no! non lo fate più quello che avete fatto!
Please, don't do any more what you have just done!
Hai sbagliato, sì? – Oh no! ho fatto bene – .
You have made a mistake, right? – Not at all! I did ok. – .
Viene anche lei? – Ma sì, ti ho detto di sì – .
Are you coming too? – Of course, I told you so – .
Sei stato tu a dirglielo, sì? – Ma no, non sono stato io! –
You have told him, right? – Of course not! Not me. –
Puoi confermare quello che hai detto? – Sì, te lo giuro – .
Can you confirm what you've said?–Yes, I can swear on the Bible–.

Figurative expressions

We have already seen the many forms and the many ways to render the expression of our thoughts lively and evident; especially when we exceed the limit of a sentence.

I would like to add a few more phrases which give color and harmony to our thoughts.

Molto raramente. *Once in a blue moon.*
Tipo spiaggia. *Show off.*
Chi tocca il miele, si lecca le dita.
Who touches honey, licks his fingers.
Radice profonda non teme il vento.
Deep roots do not fear wind.
Solo un vero amico ti dirà che hai la faccia sporca.
Only a good friend will tell you that you have a dirty face.
Non c'è spazio per girarsi.
There is no room to swing a cat.
Il gatto furioso fa il gattino cieco.
Haste makes waste.
L'esperienza fa maturare il giudizio.
Experience ripens judgement.
Chi ha tempo, non aspetti tempo.
A stitch in time, saves nine.

Ad ogni uccello il suo nido è bello.
There is no place like home.
Chi va piano, va sano e va lontano.
Who goes slow, goes safe and goes far.
Non tutti i mali vengono per nuocere.
Every cloud has a silver lining.
Una rondine non fa primavera.
One swallow does not make a summer.
Chi dorme non piglia pesci.
The early bird catches its worms.
Chi di speranza campa, disperato muore.
Who lives in hope, dies desperate.
Chi cerca trova. *If you seek, you'll find.*
La goccia scava la pietra.
Little strokes fell great oaks.
Fai bene e scorda; fai male e pensa.
Do good and forget; do bad and think.
Non fare il passo più lungo della gamba.
Cut one's coat according to one's cloth.
Chiari termini fanno eterna amicizia.
Clear terms make long friends.
Promettete poco, fate molto.
Promise little, do much.
Non è tutt'oro quel che luce.
All that glitters is not gold.

There are many other figurative expressions which enrich our thoughts: **dormire fra due guanciali,** to have no worries; **dar la polvere negli occhi,** *to deceive, to fool;* **ha speso l'osso del collo,** *he spent too much;* **tanto va la gatta al lardo che ci lascia lo zampino,** *the pitcher went to the well once too often;* **gatta ci cova,** *there is something in the wind;* **Chi si loda, s'imbroda,** *pride goes before a fall;* **non lodar il bel giorno innanzi sera**; *praise day at night, and life at the end...*

There is nothing to blame, when we squeeze such coloring mottos in our conversation; however we should not exaggerate.

List of common verbs

To shove	spingere	To test	esaminare
To smile	sorridere	To thank	ringraziare
To smash	scontrare	To throw	lanciare, gettare
To sound	risuonare	To tie	legare
To starve	morir di fame	To touch	toccare
To stoop	piegarsi	To trim	potare
To stop	fermarsi	To trust	confidare
To stretch	stendere	To try	provare
To strike	colpire	To wait	aspettare
To stroke	lisciare	To water	innaffiare
To succeed	riuscire	To welcome	accogliere
To suggest	suggerire	To withdraw	ritirarsi
To suit	soddisfare	To undergo	sottoporsi
To tackle	affrontare	To undertake	intraprendere
To tame	domare	To unlock	aprire con chiave
To taste	gustare	To value	valutare
To tax	tassare	To wonder	meravigliarsi
To tear	strappare	To zip	chiudere a lampo

As noted in the previous lesson, the accent falls on the vowel before the last, for each one of them.

Expand your vocabulary: commercial words

Tar catrame; *thread* filo; *thyme* timo; *timber* legname; *tin* stagno; *tissues* tessuti; *toys* giocattoli; *twist* filati; *uranium* uranio; *utensils* utensili; *utilities* utilità; *valuables* oggetti preziosi; *varnish* vernice; *vehicle* veicolo; *veil* velo; *velvet* velluto; *victuals* vettovaglie; *visa* visto consolare; *wafers* ostie; *ware* articoli, merce; *waste* scarto; *web* ragnatela; *weight* peso; *wheels* ruote; *wine* vino; *wire* corda; *woolen* lanerie; *wooden ware* legnami;

242

wrench chiave; *yard* iarda; *yarn* filo, filato; *yogurt* yougurt; *zinc* zinco.

Traduzione degli esercizi proposti nella lezione precedente

1) I contadini italiani usano assai concime per coltivare i loro prodotti.
2) Perché hai lasciato il tuo lavoro? Che cosa farai ora?
3) L'Italia non ha molte materie gregge, ma ha molto marmo.
4) I dipinti di Leonardo sono famosi in tutto il mondo.
5) La spezia è una città della Liguria nominata per il suo commercio di spezie.
6) La Sicilia è famosa per il suo zolfo e per il suo vino Marsala.

Esercizi da tradurre in Inglese

I ragazzini sono contentissimi quando ricevono dei dolci.

....

Il riso italiano viene coltivato nella Pianura Padana.

....

L'olio d'oliva non possiede colesterolo. È molto buono per la salute.

....

Gli Italiani amano la musica tanto quanto la pasta fatta con le uova.

....

Bisogna ricordare che si deve rimanere fedele agli studi.

....

Mi sono proposto di presentare un lavoro ben fatto. Spero ci sia riuscito.

....

Esercizio di lettura, preso dalle favole di Esopo
Il lupo e l'agnello

Un lupo vide un agnello presso un torrente che beveva. Vedendolo, gli venne voglia di mangiarselo. Il lupo, stando più sopra dell'agnello, cominciò quindi ad accusarlo di insudiciare l'acqua, così che egli non poteva bere. L'agnello gli fece notare che sfiorava appena l'acqua con il muso, e, stando a valle, non gli era possibile intorbidare

243

la corrente a monte. Venutogli meno il protesto, il lupo allora gli disse: "Ma tu sei quello che l'anno scorso hai insultato mio padre". E l'agnello cercava di spiegargli che a quella data egli non era ancora venuto al mondo. "Bene", concluse il lupo, "se tu sei così bravo a trovar delle scuse, io non posso mica rinunziare a mangiarti".

La favola mostra che contro chi ha deciso di fare un torto, non c'è giusta difesa che valga.

"Il lupo perde il pelo ma non il vizio. *Old habits die hard.*"

As you read this Aesop's fable, you are reading Italian to its outmost achievement. You have accomplished a super task. I know you are proud of all your hard work.

When you began studying Italian, you were a young child...; now you can call yourself a well accomplished individual.

FIFTY SECOND LESSON

Lezione Cinquantaduesima

Marco, ti vedo molto contento oggi, cosa ti rende così fragrante? Ti ho visto spesso con il volto cereo, anzi bianco come la neve durante l'anno scolastico; invece ora ti vedo camminare veloce come una freccia con occhi trasparenti come il cristallo e col viso rosso come il sangue. Cosa c'è di nuovo nella tua vita?

"Guido, altro che buone notizie! È meglio che te lo dica. Come è vero Iddio, sono estrememente contento! Chi comincia bene, finisce meglio! Ho finalmente completato gli studi e ci sono riuscito a gonfie vele. Mi sono laureato in lingue. Dopo tante richieste, ho deciso di cominciare a lavorare nell'ufficio turistico della nostra città. Purtroppo sogno, anzi ardo di desiderio di farmi Console nel futuro, perché mi piace la vita sociale."

Mark, I can see you are very happy today, What makes you so fragrant? I have often seen your face extremely pale, indeed white like snow during your school days; yet, now I see you walking as quick as an arrow with eyes transparent like crystal and with face red as blood. What has changed in your life?

" Guido, anything but good news! It is better I'll tell you. As true as God is, I am extremely happy! Who begins well, ends better! I have finally completed my studies and I came out smelling like roses. I graduated in languages. Following many requests, I decided to begin working for the tourist office of our city. However I dream, indeed I burn with desire, to become a Consul in the future, because I like to work for social relations. "

Commercial terms

Auction incanto; *arbitration* giudizio d'arbitri; *average price* prezzo medio; *bail* garanzia; *bankruptcy* fallimento; *bill of sale* ipoteca su merci; *bond* buono del tesoro; *broker* mediatore; *bulk* massa; *cash* danaro contante; *claims* reclami; *consignment* merci in consegna; *custom house* dogana; *dealings* operazioni; *dividend* dividendo; *firm* ditta; *goods for sale* merci in vendita; *gross* lordo; *import duty* diritto d'entrata; *invoice* fattura; *liabilities* impegni, debito; *liquidation* liquidazione; *market* mercato; *mortgage* ipoteca; *net* netto; *packing* imballaggio; *parcel post* pacco postale; *power of attorney* procura; *retail dealer* mercante al dettaglio; *sender* mittente; *storage* magazzinaggio; *stocks* fondi pubblici; *trustee* fiduciario; *warehouse* magazzino; *wholesale dealer* mercante all'ingrosso.

I have prepared a list putting together the most common commercial words and terms for the benefit of the student. Of course each one of us chooses a trade or a profession suitable for one's own interest. Then it is up to the individual to expand his or her vocabulary according to the need that such profession requires. A good dictionary will be a very helpful friend.

I am fluent in many languages; yet many times I have to consult my dictionaries. As I said before, it is very important to know the right meaning of a word for building a correct sentence; especially when speaking a second language. Sometimes I have to alter my style by using more words in place of the one I am not sure of, or I cannot pronounce correctly.

Indeed, don't be afraid to speak. People who listen to you, will be proud of your achievement. Very few people know more than one language. You have put so much effort learning another language. Show your elegant fluency. By achieving so much, you are certainly equal or superior to any common native speaker.

I made a fool of myself many times; especially while learning the German language. However, while people were laughing at my mistakes, I was learning with a smile on my face.

When I began this work, I intended to prepare a helpful summary of my native language, for the purpose of benefitting my grandchildren who are studying Italian in school.

I wanted to present a short work, simple, but well done. Indeed, my daughter, the editor, suggested that, if I was going to put the effort to develop such a good idea, I should elaborate in formalizing a complete text.

"Use the experience you have with languages," she insinuated with her face suggesting encouragement. "Moreover you have been teaching in the Bilingual Program for many years. You taught English to students coming to America from many countries of the world. They could not speak one word of English; yet within a short time, through your language experience, they became fluent such to be able to function in regular classrooms as well as students born with the English language. They felt so comfortable in your classroom. The smile on their faces said everything. Most of them are either professionals or they have a good trade. Indeed many people could benefit from your knowledge besides your grandchildren."

As a result I felt a deep inspiration. I made an effort to create a gem of unmistakable expressions: a complete course with such warmth and vibration which would be recognized as a work of art. I tried to realize a personal language using the subject matter, the form and style of a common elocution; and conform to it even when trying to come up with personal inventive. The knowledge of a language is not complete if we limit ourselves to the rules of grammar and words as they are presented by the lexicon. We must learn the various processes in order to build clear sentences which will express what we really want to manifest.

I have tried to build a complete and clear course, using determinate and necessary material in every respect equally comprehensive to everybody. Indeed, it is up to every student to master the language he or she chooses to learn... and retain it with the best possible accuracy, in order to choose words which reveal our feelings; and the fondness that breathes through our works.

I planned to prepare a full year course; as such I divided the text into fifty two lessons. However the student should not rush anything: *poco e bene.*

I have put a lot of effort to lead the student up to this point. Now it is up to him or her to continue on the right path. I hope that my advice, acquired through my experience, will be rewarding and appreciated.

Alexander, my grandchild, acknowledges that it is a super achievement. "It is a remarkable work which will benefit us students".

247

Traduzione degli esercizi proposti nella lezione precedente

1) Little children are very happy when they receive some sweets.
2) Italian rice is cultivated on the Padana Plain.
3) Olive oil does not contain cholesterol. It is very good for our health.
4) Italians love music as much as home made egg noodles.
5) It is important to remember that we must remain faithful to studying.
6) I intended to present a work well done. I hope I have been successful.

Esercizio di lettura, preso dal *Libro Garzanti della geografia*
La lingua Italiana

L'Italiano, erede del Latino, si è consolidato come lingua letteraria sin dal XIII secolo; e da allora è la lingua di tutti gli abitanti dell'Italia. Accanto ad esso restano nell'uso vivo di buona parte della popolazione i dialetti, assai diversi da una regione all'altra; e spesso fra località non lontane di una stessa regione: ciò si deve alla storia complessa del Paese, alle diverse invasioni subìte, al perdurare della divisione in molti staterelli fino all'unità raggiunta soltanto nel XIX secolo.

Solo ai margini del territorio nazionale vi sono piccole zone in cui si parlano altre lingue, perché le popolazioni che vi abitano non sono di origine italiana. Nell'Alto Adige circa 200 mila persone hanno come lingua madre il Tedesco; nella Valle d'Aosta si parla un dialetto simile alla lingua francese sudoccidentale; nel Friuli-Venezia Giulia una minoranza della popolazione è di lingua Slovena.

In Calabria e in Sicilia vi sono piccoli centri abitati in cui la popolazione parla Graco e Albanese. Infine, in alcune valli dolomitiche si parla ancora la lingua di origine Latina.

Complessivamente gli Italiani che parlano una lingua diversa dalla lingua madre sono circa 250 mila.

Acknowledgment

I enjoyed preparing this work. It took me back to the elementary school years, during which I always had the same teacher. She came from Florence where the Italian Language was born. She spoke it with a floral fluency and with a harmonious sense of pride.
She made us farmers learn Italian well. She was all grammar. We had to learn the declination of the verbs like the *Our Father.*

Going into the secondary grades, it did not get much better. Our professor of Italian was also infatuated with grammar. He knew that we needed to know it well when we began learning Latin. Of course it was also very helpful when I was studying French.

I learned English on my own, using the *Poliglotta Moderno* by Ernesto Da-Nova, written to learn a language without a teacher.

While stationed in Germany with the U. S. Army, I took advantage of the situation. I sent for the *Poliglotta Moderno* by Da-Nova, also written to learn German without a teacher; and I began learning German.

By playing my accordion in some German events, I made many German friends; as a result I was forced to speak as good as I could. *Believe me, there is no better way to learn a language than through necessity.*

I learned Spanish by the *Cortina Method.* I became quite fluent while teaching Spanish speaking students. This method also helped me with the Portuguese language.

Preparing this work I referred to all my experiences. In addition I referred to the *Grammatica Italiana* by R. Sirri and E. Di Ronza; and *Lingua e Stile* by B. Migliorini and F. Chiappelli.

My best friend, however, has been ***Il Dizionario Hazon Garzanti*** **English Italian / Italiano Inglese.**

There is no time wasted when you study to better yourself!